DO

TAMING
YOUR
MONEY
MONSTER

NINE PATHS TO
MONEY MASTERY WITH
THE ENNEAGRAM

W PUBLISHING GROUP

AN IMPRINT OF THOMAS NELSON

Taming Your Money Monster

Copyright © 2025 Doug Lynam

Published in Nashville, Tennessee, by W Publishing, an imprint of Thomas Nelson.

Thomas Nelson titles may be purchased in bulk for educational, business, fundraising, or sales promotional use. For information, please email SpecialMarkets@ThomasNelson.com.

This book is written as a source of information only. The information contained in this book should by no means be considered a substitute for the advice, decisions, or judgment of the reader's professional or financial advisors. All efforts have been made to ensure the accuracy of the information contained in this book as of the date published. The author and the publisher expressly disclaim responsibility for any adverse effects arising from the use or application of the information contained herein.

Scripture quotations are taken from The Holy Bible, New International Version®, NIV®. Copyright © 1973, 1978, 1984, 2011 by Biblica, Inc.® Used by permission of Zondervan. All rights reserved worldwide. www.Zondervan.com. The "NIV" and "New International Version" are trademarks registered in the United States Patent and Trademark Office by Biblica, Inc.®

Any internet addresses, phone numbers, or company or product information printed in this book are offered as a resource and are not intended in any way to be or to imply an endorsement by Thomas Nelson, nor does Thomas Nelson vouch for the existence, content, or services of these sites, phone numbers, companies, or products beyond the life of this book.

ISBN 978-0-7852-2391-7 (ePub)
ISBN 978-0-7852-2392-4 (Audio)
ISBN 978-0-7852-2390-0 (TP)

Library of Congress Control Number: 2025930782

Printed in the United States of America
25 26 27 28 29 LBC 5 4 3 2 1

DEDICATION

To Richard Rohr: This is my love letter to you.
And to my mother, Lois Pollard: Thank you
for showing me unconditional love.

CONTENTS

CONTENTS

FOREWORD

DOES MONEY NEED REDEEMING?

People who present us with profound answers are the same people who first hear the profundity and the necessity of good questions! Doug Lynam is such a man and such a writer. Get ready to be thrilled by the kind of wisdom that transcends easy categories or agendas.

If you think this book is only about money, prepare to be surprised. If you think it is about personality typologies, look forward to having your imagination stretched. Of course, it is about both, but overlapping and mutually informing, interwoven with spiritual insight! That is the way wise souls write.

For most of my adult life, I tried to define *mystery* in a way that I hoped others could value. In childhood, I was taught that you could not understand mystery, so you should not even try—just trust and believe. I know my Irish nuns meant well and were fully half right, but that attitude set many of us on an anti-intellectual path that has not served us well. We got educated in a secular Western culture, and without knowing it, we became dualistic thinkers.

Over time, I learned that mystery is not unintelligible but something that never stops unfolding and revealing itself. Mystery offers us endless understanding of things like God, the universe, love, the soul—and now even the Enneagram. These have all shown themselves to be true mysteries unfolding before our eyes.

Mystery always invites us into something greater. It does not leave us smug and certain, as far too much religion has done, but it leaves us constantly searching for more. Thus, it also keeps us humble. Life shows us that there is always more on the horizon. Knowing always contains the search for more knowing.

A surrender to mystery probably marks the line between mere utilitarian knowledge and transformative wisdom. It is what Albert Einstein was referring to when he said, "Problems we face cannot be solved at the same level of thinking that was used when we created them."[1] We must leap into a new arena where truth is allowed to unfold over time and slowly show itself to any sincere searcher. This is non-dualistic thinking, which resists creating false opposites.

If you will allow me to quote Albert a second time, he said of himself, "It's not that I'm so smart, it's just that I stay with problems longer."[2] The wisdom tradition of all great world religions called this deeper mind *contemplation*, something beyond and better than just information. Doug Lynam is a contemplative knower, and you are about to enjoy the fruits of his labor.

I have been with Doug in his studio many times, a space in his home dedicated to contemplation, with a massive whiteboard installed from wall to wall. I have watched him race back and forth with endless enthusiasm as he developed an idea he was sharing with me. Further, he was continually open to anything I might question or add to his analysis. Or is it synthesis? At any rate, I have given him the happy nickname "Greyhound," in homage to my father, who raised and raced greyhounds in Kansas, and also because I cannot keep up with Doug's speed and agility!

This brilliant opus now in your hands was generated during a time of great personal trial for Doug, and the book is better, perhaps, because of it. While writing, he allowed at least three things to *remain* mysteries for him: money, spirituality, and the ever-unfolding schema called the Enneagram.

I was first taught the Enneagram in 1972–73 by some Cincinnati Jesuits who had just brought it back from the Arica Institute in Chile. They rightly saw it as a very helpful tool in their Ignatian work of the "discernment of spirits" (1 Corinthians 12:10). Thank God I followed their cautionary advice not to write it down until I had lengthy and living knowledge of its use in practical settings—which I could not claim until the late 1980s. Since this wisdom first hit the scene, it has continued to unfold more and more in every decade, moving beyond the early spiritual direction and retreat world to psychology, education, business, and even athletic and executive coaching. It is very generative.

You cannot limit or put artificial boundaries on true wisdom. *Wisdom* is a word that points to the common domain, where knowledge flourishes in, through, and with the collective unconscious. No one owns or copyrights wisdom. It is too big, and is always self-revealing and self-unfolding. Here, you will see it even includes what some, myself included, foolishly called "filthy lucre." You will discover that even money and its uses are multifaceted and redeemable. Money better be redeemable, or we are all in serious trouble!

True mystery just keeps growing, showing, and connecting. This is the sign that something is a mystery in the truest sense and not just another passing thought or trend. As you are about to see, a truly holy idea will keep coming around for another orbit and further enlightenment. Here it comes again!

Richard Rohr, O.F.M.

WELCOME TO THE FINANCIAL CIRCUS

Taming Your Money Monster is a wild journey that combines the ancient wisdom of the Enneagram with modern financial savvy. Whether you're an Enneagram enthusiast, a financial advisor, someone struggling with money, or just curious about how your personality affects your wallet, this book is for you.

For those already familiar with the Enneagram, and for those discovering it for the first time, a brief introduction is necessary to avoid confusion and set the stage for the journey ahead. For those new to the concept, the Enneagram is a powerful system of personality typing that identifies nine distinct ego archetypes, each with its own core motivations, fears, and behavior patterns. It's like a GPS for your psyche, helping you navigate the twists and turns of your inner landscape.

Now, I know combining personality theory with financial advice might raise some eyebrows. It's not exactly conventional wisdom in the world of finance. But after years of working with clients, I've found that understanding your Enneagram type can be as valuable as knowing your credit score when it comes to improving your financial health.

As a former monk turned investment advisor (yes, you read that right), I've spent years exploring the intersection of spirituality, psychology, and finance. What I've discovered is that our relationship with money is deeply intertwined with our personality type. Our financial behaviors—from splurging to hoarding, from generosity to greed—are often direct expressions of our deepest fears, desires, and unconscious patterns.

The Enneagram isn't just some hot trend or cosmic horoscope. It's the hidden blueprint for the human psyche. Think of it as the spiritual equivalent of the Human Genome Project,[1] but instead of mapping DNA, we're mapping our soul's journey.

It's not an overstatement to say that the Enneagram represents the universal laws of the spiritual adventure within us—it's the bedrock upon which all our spiritual traditions are built. Like physics, our understanding of it will never be complete, but we can make steady progress. It doesn't matter if you're into praying the Rosary, burning sage, or just trying not to lose your mind in rush hour traffic—the Enneagram is working its magic behind the scenes.

It's as if all our world religions and spiritual practices are different apps running on the same cosmic smartphone. The Enneagram? That's the operating system. It doesn't care if you're swiping right on Christianity or scrolling through Buddhism—it is the underlying code that makes it all function. It's why we can agree that there are virtues like honesty, courage, and humility, even if we disagree on how best to practice them.

So, whether you're a devout believer, a skeptical agnostic, or someone who occasionally yells at the universe when you stub your toe, the Enneagram has something for you. Just remember—knowing the code doesn't mean you've beaten the game. (I certainly haven't, as my friends can attest.) We're all still playing this crazy game called life.

The Enneagram helps us understand why we keep making the same silly mistakes over and over and offers a healthier way forward.

Throughout this book, I've made significant changes to classical Enneagram concepts and terminology, and I'd like to explain why. If you're an Enneagram purist, you might want to grab a stress ball before reading further.

The Enneagram has a logical structure that claims to explain much of our past behavior, predict future patterns, and show us healthier ways forward. Such a remarkable claim requires an equally remarkable justification for how and why the system works. While most authors and teachers of the Enneagram explain how it works, none satisfactorily explain why the system operates as it does.

Nonetheless, after an in-depth review of the existing research, *The American Journal of Psychiatry, Residents' Journal* concluded:

- The Enneagram is a comprehensive system of personality that can be applied to clinical psychiatry.
- The Enneagram has been widely used and is validated in literature.
- Psychiatry residents can become familiar with the basics of the Enneagram model and use it as a tool to aid in patient formulation and psychotherapy.[2]

In addition, neurobiologists and researchers such as Dan Siegel, David Daniels, Jack Killen, Denise Daniels, Laura Baker, and Saleh Vallander have found strong correlations between the Enneagram and brain patterns, with practical application to clinical psychology.[3]

So the research shows us that it works. As a former mathematics and science teacher, however (and yes, I can hear your groans), I've always rebelled against accepting any system without understanding its underlying mechanics. Without grasping the "why" behind a system and exposing it to critical inquiry, it remains in the esoteric realm for me. And without a clear "why it works," I struggle to fully comprehend any system, let alone write a book about it. Call it the curse of a chronic overthinker, if you will.

The Enneagram is a work in progress and wasn't discovered overnight by someone having a "eureka!" moment in the bathtub. Instead, it's the result of generations of research into the nature of the human mind, with contributions from countless individuals across various cultures and religions.

As a result, the modern Enneagram synthesizes ideas from numerous sources and schools of thought. While each contributes valuable insights, combining them can create logical inconsistencies. It's like trying to bake one cake with recipes from five different grandmothers—interesting but chaotic. To address this and expose the "why" behind the Enneagram, I've refined and restructured key aspects of it to create a more streamlined and comprehensible framework.

The Enneagram as we know it today was primarily developed by Oscar Ichazo, a Bolivian philosopher, and Claudio Naranjo, a Chilean psychiatrist, in the latter half of the twentieth century. Their pioneering work into the structure of human personality was akin to the breakthroughs of Galileo and Newton in physics. Just as Galileo's and Newton's combined efforts gave us a powerful model for understanding the universe's physical laws, Ichazo and Naranjo provided us with a road map to the human psyche.[4]

But the story continues to evolve. I've attempted to clearly map the spiritual dimension of the Enneagram, which opens up new and exciting possibilities in our understanding of human consciousness. It's like upgrading from a flip phone to a smartphone—there's a learning curve, but the results are worth it.

Here are the key modifications I've made to the classical Enneagram model. Don't worry if this goes over your head right now. It will make more sense later, I promise.

1. Representing the Enneagram as a 3-D double cone: This radical new model incorporates the vertical or spiritual dimension more fully into the Enneagram.
2. A deeper explanation of the Childhood Wound with an attempt to ground it in childhood developmental psychology.
3. Introduction of the concept of the Sacred Wound.
4. Incorporating a Jungian understanding of the Shadow and detailing the Shadow Structure for each type.
5. Describing the Enlightenment Structure or path to Awakening for each type.
6. Recasting the traditional lines of stress and relaxation as secondary ego addictions and secondary recovery virtues (making my recommendations more like AA for your personality type).
7. Introducing a formulaic pattern for moving from our greatest vice to our greatest virtue (math nerds, rejoice!).
8. Presenting a new concept I call the faux virtues (because sometimes our supposed virtues are just vices in disguise).
9. Transforming the Holy Ideas into Sacred Gifts.
10. Pairing the Enneagram with the Attachment Theory of Money, which is based on the Attachment Theory of Relationships, to create a path to spiritual and financial mastery.

To fully accept the Enneagram as a practical tool, I needed to develop a coherent model based on clearly defined axiomatic assumptions and a linear argument following deductive logic. (I know that sentence had more big words than a spelling bee, but stick with me.) Without these elements, it's impossible to stress-test the model, leaving any explanation in the realm of the unverifiable. However, I've endeavored to present these concepts in an accessible manner for a broad audience while reserving some of the more technical aspects for future works.[5]

In the process, I adjusted traditional Enneagram terminology to make the linear logic more transparent. The goal is to present the Enneagram in a way that's easier to understand and apply, particularly for those new to the system. Most importantly, these changes allow the terminology in the Shadow and Enlightenment Structures I've developed to mirror each other.

For those familiar with traditional Enneagram language, I've retained the original terms in parentheses alongside the new terminology. This allows experienced practitioners to connect familiar concepts within the updated framework.

One key axiom in this book is the existence of what we might call the "Ground of All Being" or an "Ultimate Reality That Includes All." For simplicity, I use the term *God* but assign no specific theology or religion to it, leaving the interpretation of that term up to you, the reader. However, I occasionally use my Christian background to illustrate a few concepts, as it's the only tradition I can speak from with authenticity. I want to clarify that any use of biblical quotes or themes is intended to demonstrate psychological wisdom only, not to contradict or support any doctrinal interpretations of this sacred text. In other words, we're here for the psychological insights, not a theological debate.

So, as we embark on this journey, I invite you to approach these ideas with an open mind. Whether you're drowning in debt, building your empire, or just trying to make sense of your love-hate relationship with your wallet, this book offers a fresh perspective. We'll explore how each Enneagram type approaches money, from the perfectionistic One to the conflict-avoidant Nine. You'll learn to identify your money monster—that pesky internal saboteur that keeps you from achieving financial peace—and, more importantly, how to tame it.

In the chapters ahead, we'll explore each Enneagram type in depth, examining their unique financial strengths and challenges. We'll look at how childhood experiences shape your money attitudes and discover how to leverage your personality traits for financial success.

By the end of this book, you'll have a deeper understanding of not just the Enneagram but of yourself and your relationship with money. You'll have tools to break free from destructive financial patterns, capitalize on your strengths, and create a healthier, wealthier future.

So, whether you're a financial guru or someone who thinks a diversified portfolio means having multiple flavors of ramen in your pantry, this book has something for you. Grab your favorite beverage and get comfortable. It's time to meet your money monster—and learn how to tame it once and for all.

Let's get started!

CHAPTER ONE

MONEY MAKES THE WORLD GO AROUND

HOW YOUR WALLET BECAME A PSYCH WARD

Meet the Johnsons: Sarah, a high-powered attorney with a corner office and a penchant for power suits that cost more than some people's monthly rent; and Mike, a talented artist whose abstract paintings are as unpredictable as his income. On paper, they were living the American dream with a sprawling Victorian house, two kids attending private school, and vacations to exotic locales that made their Instagram followers green with envy.

But beneath this glossy veneer lurked a financial nightmare that would make any financial advisor break out in a cold sweat.

Sarah, an Enneagram Type Three, was bringing in six figures, but it was vanishing faster than snow in the Sahara. Her "Blinger" money monster had her firmly in its grasp, whispering seductively about the need for the right car, the right clothes, the right everything to maintain her image of success. She'd rather eat glass than admit she couldn't afford something, so the credit card debt kept piling up as she "blinged out" her life.

Mike, an Enneagram Type Four, was the yang to Sarah's yin. His "Flinger" money monster had him on a financial roller coaster. One month, he'd sell a piece of art and almost immediately "fling" all the money away on some state-of-the-art equipment for his studio, artisanal paints made from crushed gemstones, or something equally absurd. The next month, he'd be too deep in an artistic funk to even pick up a brush, morosely comparing himself to Van Gogh while neglecting his responsibilities around the house, driving Sarah crazy.

One fateful evening, as Sarah sat at their dining table staring at a stack of overdue bills, reality finally broke through her carefully cultivated image. Their financial house of cards was one Amex swipe away from collapsing.

"Mike," she called out, her voice shaking, "I think we need help."

Mike emerged from his studio, looking like he'd lost a paintball war with a rainbow. "Financial help or psychological help?" he quipped, only half joking.

"Probably both," Sarah admitted, "but let's start with the money."

Enter yours truly—the monk turned money manager they never knew they needed.

Peering into their bank statements was like opening Pandora's box, if Pandora had been really into retail therapy. Sarah's childhood in a hyper-competitive family had left her with a burning need to prove her worth through external success. Every designer purchase, every lavish dinner, every first-class upgrade was a desperate attempt to fill a void that no amount of money could satisfy. Sarah's spending habits screamed, "Validate me! I'm successful!"

Mike, on the other hand, had grown up in a family that valued practicality over passion and stifled his individuality. His periodic splurges were as much an act of rebellion against his past as they were expressions of his artistic temperament. Each time he spent recklessly, he was really saying, "See? I can do everything my way. I am special!"

Their money monsters were hosting a full-blown Mardi Gras parade through the family's finances, with Sarah's Blinger and Mike's Flinger dancing their way through every last dollar in their savings account. But here's the kicker: Their financial chaos wasn't just about dollars and cents. It was a symphony of unresolved childhood issues, deep-seated fears, and ego-driven decisions that would make Freud reach for the aspirin. Each transaction in their bank statement was a breadcrumb leading back to their deepest insecurities and unfulfilled needs.

As we embarked on the journey to tame their money monsters, I could see the mixture of hope and skepticism in their eyes. Sarah, ever the achiever, was already mentally drafting a to-do list, while Mike's artistic soul was bracing for what he feared would be a stifling budget.

Little did they know they were about to get a crash course in financial mindfulness, personality deep dives, and spiritual growth.

When we first sat down together, I clapped my hands and said, "Okay! Who's ready to make friends with their inner financial saboteurs?"

Sarah and Mike exchanged looks that were equal parts confusion and concern. This was going to be interesting.

I'll get back to the Johnsons shortly. In the meantime, get ready to meet your own money monster—and learn how to turn it from fiscal fiend into financial friend.

But first, you might be wondering what qualifies me to guide you through this financial jungle gym. Well, to be honest, my career path has been wilder than a roller coaster designed by Salvador Dali on a sugar high. I've gone from being a marine to a monk to a money manager. Now I'm an author, speaker, and coach, helping others build a healthy relationship with money. I've experienced both sides of the financial coin and even spent time on the edge spinning like a top.

I've lived in a monastery under a vow of poverty, and I've navigated the high-stakes world of Wall Street. I've been broke, I've been comfortable, and I've helped others build real wealth. I've also made every money mistake in the book (and probably invented a few new ones). Bankruptcy? Been there. Divorce? Done that. Recovery? Working on it daily, just like my budget. But I've also learned how to turn those stumbles into stepping stones. So when I talk about taming money monsters, it's not just theory—it's battle-tested, real-world experience.

And here's the good news: If a financial train wreck like me can turn things around, you've got this. I've helped clients go from money messes to financial freedom, and it's not about becoming a miser. It's about building your wealth to spread a little more love around and do some good in this crazy world.

The trick is to integrate contemplation, compassion, and action to align your money habits with your highest self. This holistic approach is about thinking deeply, feeling deeply, and then getting off your butt and doing something. The Enneagram is what helps us figure out our unique strengths and challenges in all three areas.

But before we go full-on Enneagram, let's take a quick detour and discuss what money really is and why we struggle so much with it.

Money and Trauma

Sadly, most of our money issues are not about money at all. They're about trauma. We've all got emotional baggage, some heavier than others. And when we don't deal with that baggage, it seeps into everything we do, especially how we handle our finances.

The simple truth is that money is just a tool for action. Money is stored work energy and the most powerful tool we've got for getting stuff done in this world. Money, when used right, is an incredible tool for good. It's not just about buying stuff. It's about creating connections, showing compassion, and being of service to a suffering world. Turning your back on money is like a carpenter refusing to use a hammer. It's crazy, and it leaves you powerless.

As Enneagram expert Richard Rohr said, "If we do not transform our pain, we will most assuredly transmit it."[1] Since money is the tool for most actions, when used without proper discernment, it transmits our trauma.

Our money monsters are how we act out our trauma in unhealthy and unproductive ways through our money habits. This book is your road map to healing that trauma. I'll teach you to use money like the tool it is—to help yourself and make the world around you a little better while you're at it.

Whether we realize it or not, we're all walking around with financial mindsets and beliefs in our heads, courtesy of our families, cultures, and difficult life experiences. Even those of us who've sworn to do the opposite of what our parents did. We're still dancing to the tune of those same old money beliefs, just backward and in high heels.

We all got our financial education from somewhere, even if that somewhere is the University of Hard Knocks and Bounced Checks. Maybe it was from watching Mom clip coupons, seeing Dad stress over bills, or just absorbing the money vibes floating around in our culture. Unfortunately, a lot of what we picked up isn't exactly helpful, including the emotional scars.

This is not a how-to guide on building wealth. For a detailed how-to resource for managing your finances, please refer to my first book, *From Monk to Money Manager: A Former Monk's Financial Guide to Becoming a Little Bit Wealthy—And Why That's Okay.*[2] *Taming Your Money Monster* is a "why do" book of psychological and spiritual insights that will reveal why you make unproductive decisions with your money, and show you how to heal the wounds that drive those decisions and grow into spiritual wholeness.

Implementing the how-to tips for building wealth or using wealth effectively is difficult until you understand why you repeatedly make the same self-destructive financial mistakes. It's like trying to fix a car without understanding how the engine works—you might get lucky, but you're just as likely to make things worse.

Do you know that quote attributed to Albert Einstein about insanity? "Insanity is doing the same thing over and over while expecting different results." This book is designed to help you finally stop being insane about money. Exploring and healing our inner wounds is never easy, but the alternative is unnecessary suffering, especially the pain we unconsciously transmit to those we love. With humor, humility, and compassion, your money monster can be tamed to become the greatest ally on your financial journey and help make your money a force for good. It's like turning your financial Frankenstein's monster into a friendly neighborhood Spider-Man.

This isn't about white-knuckling change or forcing yourself to act and behave like someone you are not. It's about exploring the unconscious pain behind your conscious pain and learning how, when healed, those wounds can become your greatest strength and source of purpose. What awaits is your transformation into a money master, one who uses the energy of money in harmony with your unique personality to help love flow with abundance. But first, you need to understand what money is all about.

The Power of Money

Money is power. Plain and simple. With enough cash, you can snap your fingers and make stuff happen. Want that new gadget? Click, ordered. Need your house painted? Boom, hired. It's like having a magic wand, except it's real and it's in your bank account.

However, without some wisdom to govern your wallet, you'll end up letting your money monster call the shots. And that beast doesn't give a darn about your best interests. It's all about instant gratification and short-term thinking to soothe your inner wounds. Sarah and Mike Johnson had plenty of cash coming in, but they were using it to feed their demons. Sarah couldn't stop chasing status, and Mike was using money to avoid real responsibility and to make himself feel special and unique.

Being truly poor, on the other hand, is not just inconvenient; it's downright dangerous. It's like a neon sign flashing Early Death This Way. The best predictor of mortality is your socioeconomic status, because the poor get hit with a laundry list of horrible things that you don't want.[3] They have much higher rates of domestic abuse, alcoholism, addiction, violence, obesity, injury, physical illness, and mental illness.[4] Ever lived paycheck to paycheck? Then you know it's like walking a tightrope over a pit of alligators. Every. Single. Day. And if you haven't experienced it, count your blessings and keep it that way. Or as Mark Twain humorously said, "The lack of money is the root of all evil."[5]

Even garden-variety financial stress can turn a rock-solid relationship into a dumpster fire. Money problems are like termites in the foundation of your relationship; ignore them long enough, and the whole thing comes crashing down. It is why money stress is a leading cause of marital conflict and divorce.[6]

So money matters—a lot. Anyone who tells you otherwise is either lying or not paying attention.

Whatever your money monster is, whether it's trapping you in poverty or trapping you in your wealth, this book can help. Like it or not, money absolutely makes the world go around. The big question is: Go around what? Rich, poor, or somewhere in between, how do we put our time, talent, and treasure to work so that we might live in material, emotional, and spiritual abundance?

The bottom line is that the energy of money is morally neutral and will flow wherever we, or our culture, direct it. It can build schools or bombs, bandages or bullets. And too often, our individual money monsters are the axis around which the world of money revolves. They cause us to hoard cash or divert it to gratify our worst impulses, creating unnecessary suffering for ourselves and those around us. Our money monsters can also derail our financial lives, pushing us into debt and financial despair, a bleak reality I've experienced firsthand.

Here's the truth: Refusing to think deeply about money is about as effective as trying to outrun your shadow. Money doesn't magically disappear from our lives just because we close our eyes to it. In fact, it tends to misbehave even more when we're not looking.

Money Masters

I've met and worked with a lot of folks who've really got their financial act together. I call them the money masters. And they're not the stressed-out, money-obsessed people you might imagine. Not at all; these folks have a kind of peaceful confidence about money and know how to use it as a tool for right action.

They're not afraid of hard work, that's for sure. They roll up their sleeves and earn a good living. But here's the key: They're smart about saving and investing. They're building a future not just for themselves, but for the people they care about. And when they do well? They don't let it go to their heads. They stay grounded, generous even.

Here's the beautiful side—money, when wielded with wisdom, is the lifeblood of compassion in action. You can't feed the poor or tend the sick without money, unless you've mastered the art of multiplying loaves and fishes. One of the greatest joys of being financially secure is an increased capacity for acts of selfless service. We must decide whether to use our money for good or ill, because money is simply a tool and an extension of our free will. It's the financial equivalent of choosing whether to be Batman or the Joker.

The point is that when we approach money with wisdom and compassion, it can be a force for good in our lives and in the world. It's about finding a balance between meeting our own needs and caring for others. And you know what? I think it's okay to enjoy life a little too. We're not monks (well, I was, but that's another story). Life's tough enough without denying ourselves every pleasure. A little comfort, a few adventures now and then—these things make life richer and fuller. Real wealth is not about having a lot of money, it's about having options to live a life that makes your soul sing.

In time, I was able to help Sarah and Mike tame their money monsters and get their lives back on track by showing them the hidden traumas that created their monsters and how to heal those wounds. Sarah learned to be less anxious about status and how to use her wealth and talents to serve others, including her family, not just her public image. At the same time, Mike learned how to stop trying so hard to be so authentic and unique that he neglected his financial and familial responsibilities while moping around the house in artistic funks.

The great irony is that they were perfectly matched for each other. Each complemented the other's weaknesses and brought more balance and harmony to each other's lives. Working together, they built a strong financial future through prudent earning, saving, and investing, got their financial life back on track, and healed their family.

As you dive into this book, be prepared for some emotional turbulence. Seeing ourselves clearly can be a humbling experience, like catching an unflattering glimpse of yourself in a store window. Many difficult memories and emotions may surface as you explore your deepest pains. Be patient and kind to yourself—this isn't a race. Go at your own pace. And if you need support, don't hesitate to reach out for professional help. Trust me, I've been there (like, last week).

This isn't your typical finance book. We're going to dive into the kind of stuff that, back when I was in the monastery, we called *mystical thinking*. Now, don't roll your eyes just yet—it's not as woo-woo as it sounds. Mystical thinking is about seeing the bigger picture and embracing the fact that life isn't always black-and-white. It's about being comfortable with the gray areas, the in-betweens. Most of us like to put things in neat little boxes. But mystics? They understand that real life is messier and much grander than that. They're okay with things being a little fuzzy around the edges at times.

This approach will help us steer clear of oversimplified ideas. You know, those knee-jerk prejudices such as "rich people are evil and poor people are purehearted" or "poor people are just lazy losers and rich people poop gold." It turns out that kindness and decency aren't correlated to your tax bracket. Shocking, I know. It's not like there's a Be a Decent Human switch that flips on or off depending on your bank balance. If only it were that simple, right?

As we dive into this journey together, I'm going to ask you to embrace a little of that mystical thinking. Be open to new perspectives, to challenging your assumptions. It might feel a bit uncomfortable at first, but trust me, it's worth it. Because when it comes to mastering your finances, sometimes the most valuable insights come from the most unexpected places.

CHAPTER TWO

THE ATTACHMENT THEORY OF MONEY

WHY YOUR RELATIONSHIP WITH CASH NEEDS A TUNE-UP

Experiences of financial trauma or prolonged periods of financial stress, particularly in childhood, can profoundly impact our relationship with money. Our brains aren't exactly wired for prolonged stress or the complexities of modern finance. When faced with money trauma, they do what any self-respecting chunk of gray matter would do—they freak out. They instinctively choose between fight, fawn, flight, freeze . . . or refinance.

For many of us, our past money trauma leaves us stuck in a constant state of financial "freak out." This becomes our default mode, leading to either an anxious attachment to money (fight or fawn) or a fearful avoidance of it (flight or freeze). This dynamic is remarkably similar to how we develop unhealthy attachment styles in romantic relationships.

Unfortunately, financial trauma is more common than we might think. According to a 2016 report in *Forbes*, one in four Americans has PTSD-like symptoms from financial stress, with this figure rising to one in three among millennials.[1]

That number is probably much higher now, following the economic upheaval of the Covid pandemic.

Those with money anxiety often find themselves in a perpetual state of fight-or-fawn, desperately seeking safety, status, or power through wealth. They become hypervigilant about their finances, driven by fear and insecurity. Ebenezer Scrooge from *A Christmas Carol* exemplifies this money-anxious archetype, obsessively hoarding wealth to his own detriment and creating suffering for those around him.

The core issue for money-anxious individuals like Scrooge is their attempt to solve internal, spiritual problems with external solutions. They're trying to soothe emotional pain and fear with material wealth, which is ultimately ineffective. No amount of money can truly heal our inner anxieties or bolster our self-esteem; it can only temporarily distract us from these deeper issues.

Now, don't get me wrong—money *can* solve a lot of problems. It's pretty darn effective at paying bills, buying groceries, and funding the occasional much-needed vacation. But it's not a cure-all for our deepest insecurities or emotional wounds. No amount of money can heal that nagging feeling that you're not good enough or that the world is out to get you.

The money-anxious individual lives in a state of constant financial fear. They dread abandonment, punishment, catastrophe, or humiliation concerning their finances, which leads them to cling desperately to money. Wealth then provides them with a sense of control, security, or validation, allowing them to temporarily alleviate their existential terrors. It's their attempt to control the uncontrollable, buy security in an uncertain world, or bolster their self-esteem.

For those with severe money anxiety, the fear of financial ruin can be as intense as the fear of death itself. They tend to equate money directly with sustenance and live in constant fear of their resources run-ning out. It's as if their bank balance is directly linked to their heartbeat.

This anxiety helps explain certain behaviors that might otherwise seem puzzling. For instance, it sheds light on why some millionaires and billionaires struggle to donate to charity, or why certain friends always run to the bathroom right before the dinner tab arrives. Behind what may appear as stinginess often lies a deep-seated anxiety.

On the flip side of money anxiety is money avoidance. As someone who's in this camp, I can attest to the challenges it presents. Those of us who are money-avoidant often struggle to engage with our finances because we've unconsciously labeled money as shameful, selfish, or scary. We are trapped in a flight-or-freeze response when it comes to money. We tend to recoil from anything finance-related due to the fear, anger, or sadness it triggers.

This avoidance often leads to self-sabotage in our efforts to build wealth, creating a vicious cycle. The resulting financial struggles gen-erate more negative emotions, dragging us further down the financial drain. By running away from or ignoring money out of fear and inse-curity, we risk ending up broke, in financial disarray, or dependent on others for our care.

Interestingly, many money-avoidant folks actually desire wealth. However, their apprehension or insecurity prevents them from becom-ing financially literate. Finance remains a foreign language to them, and without understanding the basics of how to read or write in the language of money, everything in the world of finance remains an enduring mystery or source of chronic stress.

This avoidance manifests in various ways. We might underearn relative to our potential, struggle to save, accumulate debt, or rarely invest. When we do invest, it's often in bizarre or inappropriate assets that rarely perform well, reinforcing our fears about money.

It's important to note that few of us fall neatly into one category of anxious or avoidant across all aspects of our financial lives. We might be anxious in one area, avoidant in another, and reasonably healthy in a third. For instance, we might anxiously earn a lot but then act avoidant by overspending or neglecting to invest for our future. I call this the "MC Hammer Maneuver," after the pop star who went bankrupt despite earning over $70 million in the 1980s and '90s.[2]

This anxiety or avoidance often leads to dualistic thinking about money—viewing it as either all good or all bad. We end up either glorifying or demonizing finance. We're either Gordon Gekko or St. Francis of Assisi, with no room for a balanced perspective. We can't glorify greed, but we also can't glorify poverty, as some spiritual traditions might suggest. Both extremes represent the dualistic, black-and-white thinking our contemplative wisdom traditions aim to transcend.

As already noted, I once took a vow of poverty, believing it would lead to spiritual growth. Instead, it led to chaos and hardship. The lesson? Money isn't inherently good or evil—it's a tool, and its impact depends on how we use it. And like any tool, it can be used to build something beautiful or to whack yourself on the thumb.

While in the monastery, I lived with a monk who staunchly refused to handle money. Let's call him Br. Pious. He went years without touching cash, credit cards, or debit cards, convinced that this extreme renunciation would propel him along the spiritual path. Unfortunately, the results were quite the opposite of what he intended.

As time went on, Br. Pious became increasingly judgmental, self-righteous, and critical of everyone and everything around him. He developed a superiority complex, believing himself more virtuous than the other monks who worked diligently to keep the community fed, clothed, and sheltered. His money-avoidance issues strengthened

THE ATTACHMENT THEORY OF MONEY

his sense of separation from the world, inflating his ego rather than diminishing it.

If we were to entertain Br. Pious's somewhat misguided hypothesis that touching money creates impurity, we'd have to acknowledge that his extreme renunciation forced the rest of us to handle money even more frequently to maintain his perceived purity. His hands may have stayed "clean," but at the expense of his brothers—hardly a loving or compassionate approach. What Br. Pious believed to be a spiritual practice was, in reality, just another manifestation of an unchecked money monster.

This experience taught me an important lesson: Rejecting money for the wrong reasons doesn't reduce one's ego—it often strengthens it. It's a form of cheap grace, both literally and metaphorically. Br. Pious's renunciation of money gave him an unassailable perch from which to judge the world, fostering anger and resentment rather than compassion and understanding. It turns out that worshiping money and completely rejecting it are two sides of the same dysfunctional coin.

It's crucial to note that there are indeed money masters who live in poverty, choosing austerity as a form of solidarity with the oppressed. The key difference is that they have mindfully chosen this path rather than falling into it due to unresolved money issues.

Attaching our identity to poverty can be just as problematic as attaching it to wealth. Instead of allowing either extreme to inflate our ego, we should strive for a middle way. The goal should be to fully enjoy life without creating problems for our neighbors or the planet through an unsustainable lifestyle. Balance, as in most things, is key.

To help you tame your money monsters, I've layered on top of the Enneagram what I call the Attachment Theory of Money, which describes why and how we relate to money in three predictable yet unhealthy ways.[3] I've spent a lot of time talking with people about their money, and I have seen that most of my clients are either:

- Anxiously attached to money (money-anxious): These individuals constantly worry about money, leaving them scrambling for more, even when they might have enough. They might compulsively check their bank accounts or struggle to make even small purchases without guilt.
- Fearfully avoidant of it (money-avoidant): These people tend to ignore their finances, or aspects of them, altogether. They might not know their bank balance, avoid opening bills, or refuse to engage in financial planning.
- A combination of both anxious and avoidant in different parts of their financial lives: Many people fluctuate between anxiety and avoidance depending on the situation, their stress levels, or the time of day.

The Attachment Theory of Money helps explain why we seek wealth out of anxiety or unconsciously push money away out of fear. Taming your money monster requires a healthy, secure emotional relationship with money, which I'll show you how to build. The exciting news is that this theory pairs really well with the Enneagram, like peanut butter with jelly.

Your Enneagram type describes the unique and quirky ways your money anxiety or avoidance manifests in your day-to-day life. There are nine archetypal personality types in the Enneagram, and when we layer the two primary options of being either money-anxious or money-avoidant atop each of the nine types, we can identify eighteen distinct money monsters that can derail your financial life. It's like a zoo of financial dysfunction, but the good news is that *you* have only one or two money monsters to tame. The trick is to accurately identify the one(s) you struggle with, understand their origin, and work toward healing the wounds that created your money attachment style and your Enneagram personality type. Fortunately, there is a high probability that the same wounds caused both issues, which makes the project less complicated. If you're lucky, it's a "fix one problem, solve one for free" sale. Who doesn't love a bargain?

Building a Healthy Relationship with Money Using the Enneagram

The key to a healthy relationship with money starts with having a healthy relationship with yourself. Otherwise, our unconscious emotional wounds distort our thoughts, feelings, and actions in ways so predictable that you'd think they were following a script written by a sadistic playwright. Regardless of whether your tax bracket puts you in the ramen noodle club or among the caviar connoisseurs, we all need to roll up our sleeves and do some inner work. We need to heal those traumas that lead to a distorted relationship with ourselves so that love can flow through us and into our financial decisions.

Perhaps the most valuable lesson I've learned from the Enneagram is this: Every time I've seriously hurt someone (including myself), it was because I was acting out an unhealthy aspect of my type. And when someone wounded me deeply, they were acting out an unhealthy trait of theirs. As the saying goes, "hurt people hurt people," and one of the most effective ways to hurt someone is with misspent money.

For example, my father's journey up the corporate ladder to CEO, while impressive on paper, came at a high cost to those he loved. Growing up in a poor immigrant family with an alcoholic father shed light on his behaviors. These traumatic experiences left deep scars, leading him to seek solace and validation in wealth and status as an Enneagram Type Three. Understanding this offered me an easier path to forgiveness and compassion.

It's a poignant reminder that financial success, no matter how grand, cannot heal our deepest emotional wounds or bring true happiness. Had my father been equipped with the tools for emotional healing and self-reflection, his life's trajectory—and mine—might have been markedly different.

I'd love to say I learned from his mistakes, but I swung to the opposite extreme. Reacting against my dad's example, I took a vow of poverty as a monk and avoided money like it was radioactive. My approach was just as destructive as his, just on the other end of the spectrum.

The truth is, we all have to wrestle with inner demons. Our personalities form around Childhood Wounds that shape our relationships with money and everything else. These early traumas often drive our self-sabotaging behaviors and create much of our adult suffering, especially in our financial lives. It's as if we're all carrying invisible backpacks filled with emotional weights, wondering why life feels so heavy sometimes.

Simply put, if we don't learn to master our money, we will be mastered by our money.

But here's the good news: There's a better way forward, and I'm here to share it with you. It's time to unpack those emotional backpacks and learn how to navigate our financial lives with more wisdom and compassion. And the even better news: You don't need to be perfect or solve all your issues to be a money master. Making steady progress is enough because healing on any level positively impacts our lives.

First, we must bring those unconscious Childhood Wounds into conscious awareness. Next, we must offer self-compassion and forgiveness for those traumas and learn to have a healthy relationship with ourselves. The scars from those wounds may always linger, but we can stop transmitting the pain of that trauma. It's like surfing—you can't control the waves, but you can learn to ride them and not get pulled under. (You might still wipe out occasionally, but you'll look cooler doing it.)

Since everyone has a unique life situation and childhood traumas, there is no one-size-fits-all formula for emotional and spiritual health. There are, however, nine trauma response patterns around which our egos form and create the lens through which we see the world. Understanding these patterns is the first step to a healthy relationship with yourself and money.

The decoder ring for this inner journey is the Enneagram, a robust and well-researched tool for understanding our personality structure. The Enneagram guides us into the dark corners where our money monsters lurk, feeding on our fears and Childhood Wounds like they're at an all-you-can-eat buffet of neuroses. Confronting our inner darkness is necessary to tame our money monster and become a money master—a person with a healthy relationship with money who ethically builds wealth and uses their abundance as a tool for connection, love, and service.

At its core, the Enneagram helps explain who we are, why we are the way we are, and what our unique core fear is that drives our unhealthy behavior. Once we know the answers to those questions, right action becomes easier to discern, and better money habits are likely to follow. Most importantly, we all have a unique, Sacred Gift to manifest and offer in love and service to a suffering world. I'll teach you what your Sacred Gift is and how to bring it to life. It's like discovering your superpower. And guess what? Money can be your utility belt in this heroic journey.

Don't worry if you don't know your Enneagram type yet; we'll get there soon enough. Just remember, discovering your type is also a journey. It's common to misidentify ourselves initially because we often see ourselves as we want to be, not as we are. You'll know when you've landed on your type because you'll cringe at what it reveals about you. If you're a bit more seasoned in life, you might have a harder time identifying yourself because you've already grown and matured, so try to channel your inner twentysomething when deciding your type. If you still need help after reading the type descriptions, there is an assessment you can take on my website at douglynam.com.

In the following chapters, we'll explore each Enneagram type in depth, examining their unique financial strengths and challenges. We'll look at how childhood experiences shape our money attitudes and learn how to leverage our personality traits for financial success. And who knows? You might just find yourself giving your wallet a much-needed therapy session.

CHAPTER THREE

WHAT KIND OF EGO ARE YOU DRIVING?

VROOM WITH A VIEW

You know how you can always spot your car, even in a crowded parking lot? That's because your car, like your ego, has its own unique traits. Maybe it's the dent from when you misjudged the distance to the garage wall or a snarky bumper sticker that annoys your neighbors. Whatever it is, it's distinctly yours.

Now imagine your ego is like a car. Yours is unique, but there are patterns or types of egos, just like there are types of cars. There are sedans, sports cars, and SUVs, and you drive a particular style of car, even though yours is different from every other car on the road. The Enneagram? Well, that's the user's manual for the type of car you drive, helping you navigate the highway of life without ending up in a ditch (metaphorical or otherwise). It's complete with a troubleshooting guide for when your emotional check engine light starts flashing.

But we're all stuck behind the wheel of our own ego-mobile, never able to step outside and get a good look at the model we are driving or the paint job. That's where the Enneagram comes in handy. It's also like a mirror that lets you see your vehicle from all angles, revealing those blind spots you never knew you had. (We all have them, and they're usually bigger than we'd like to admit.)

And let me tell you, discovering your Enneagram type can be about as comfortable as sitting on a cactus. It's like someone holding up a mirror and saying, "Hey, check out all your neuroses!" But don't worry, it's all part of the journey. After all, you can't fix a problem you don't know exists, right? But I haven't done my job if you don't have the urge to throw this book across the room at least once or scream at the walls while listening to it. Consider this your trigger warning.

"Enneagram" sounds like something you'd need a PhD to understand. Well, it's actually ancient Greek for "nine things drawn." *Ennea* means nine, *gramma* means drawn.[1] Not too hard, right?

Now picture a circle. Got it? Good. Now cut it up into nine even pie slices, one for each personality type. Each type is a whole spectrum or arc on the circle. Think of it like a color wheel, but instead of mixing blue and yellow to get green, you're mixing neuroses and quirks to get . . . well, all of us. It's a regular smorgasbord of human complexity!

At the center of this circle is your essence, soul, or whatever you want to call that sacred spark that allows you to have consciousness. Think of the Enneagram types as different models of cars in a cosmic dealership. When your soul first revved up in this world, it came with a ton of preloaded features, including a bunch determined by your DNA, but it also needed to be adaptable. So it scanned the environment in your early years, checking for potential hazards, much like a car's onboard computer assessing road conditions. It was looking for the biggest safety threats, akin to spotting a massive pothole or a Bridge Out Ahead sign. Was there a lot of yelling in your house? Emotional neglect? A pet goldfish that gave you the stink eye? Whatever the biggest, baddest threat was, it selected the right personality type from the Enneagram showroom—the vehicle best suited to help you navigate the terrain of your early years.

Here's where it gets interesting. The threats you encountered as a wee one triggered one of three core emotions: anger, fear, or sadness. These are the primary colors of the negative emotional world—all other icky feelings are different shades of these Big Three. We can then break the Enneagram down into three different triads based on anger, fear, and sadness (or shame and grief around one's identity).[2] (See Diagram 1.)

What kind of car are you driving?

Diagram 1

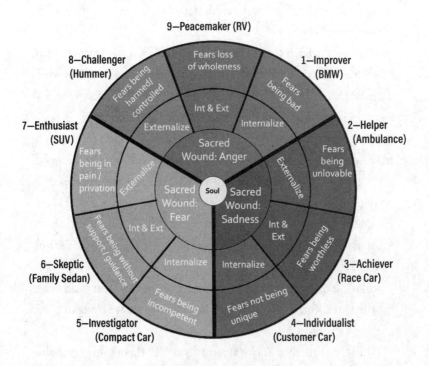

9—Peacemaker (RV)

8—Challenger (Hummer)

1—Improver (BMW)

7—Enthusiast (SUV)

2—Helper (Ambulance)

6—Skeptic (Family Sedan)

3—Achiever (Race Car)

5—Investigator (Compact Car)

4—Individualist (Customer Car)

Fears loss of wholeness

Fears being bad

Fears being harmed/controlled

Fears being unlovable

Fears being in pain / privation

Fears being without support / guidance

Fears being worthless

Fears being incompetent

Fears not being unique

Int & Ext

Externalize

Internalize

Externalize

Externalize

Int & Ext

Int & Ext

Internalize

Internalize

Sacred Wound: Anger

Sacred Wound: Fear

Sacred Wound: Sadness

Soul

This image is a cross-section of the 3-D double-coned Enneagram

Somewhere in early childhood, you were hit with one of these emotional tsunamis more than the others. You had to do something with all that pain, and so you either turned the pain inward (basically giving yourself an emotional wedgie), directed it outward (like an emotional food fight with the world), or did a bit of both. I call this emotional scarring your Sacred Wound, which is the basis of your personality.[3]

Your Enneagram type is like the perfect vehicle you chose to outrun the pain from your Sacred Wound. That pain creates your "greatest fear" (more traditionally called your basic fear), the thing that unconsciously terrifies you the most, and your Enneagram type is your personalized getaway car, designed to keep your greatest fear in the rearview mirror.

Those who fall into the anger triad picked a vehicle that gives them more control and empowerment; those in the sadness triad looked for a model that offers validation and connection; while folks in the fear triad chose a model that offers more security and certainty.

But here's the rub: While your emotional escape vehicle might have been perfect for navigating the treacherous roads of childhood, it's not always the best for adult driving. That fear you're constantly trying to outrun? Your car of choice can cause all sorts of fender benders and traffic accidents in your grown-up life. In fact, it's the basis for most of the suffering you'll experience in adulthood, aside from random tragedies.

We'll explore your Sacred Wound and greatest fear with more detailed precision in later chapters, but for now, we are going to go for a few test drives.

First, picture this: You're at a carnival, and there's this fun-house mirror. You know the one—it makes you look like a Picasso painting come to life. That's what I'm doing with the Enneagram descriptions throughout this book. I'm taking your personality traits and frequently stretching them to cartoonish proportions, partly for laughs, and partly to make a point. Of course, you're not actually a walking caricature (unless you're at Comic-Con, in which case, carry on).

So don't worry if you find yourself thinking, *That's not me! I don't have a secret lair where I plot world domination through extreme coupon clipping!* On the deepest level, the Enneagram is a fractal with infinite variety inside a firm structure, and we're only touching the top layer of the fractal in this book.

Also, personality traits aren't binary on/off switches. They're more like those fancy dimmer lights—you might have them turned up high in some situations and barely flickering in others. Your money monster might roar like Godzilla on payday and purr like a kitten when you're feeling zen. So as we dive into these descriptions, keep your sense of humor handy.

As statistician George Box said, "All models are wrong, but some are useful."[4] The Enneagram is a work in progress but still extremely useful. It won't explain all aspects of your personality, like why you are terrified of kittens and elevators, but it does provide a road map of your psyche.

Now strap in, because we're about to explore the nine different models in the Enneagram showroom. Whether you're driving a sturdy BMW (Type One), an all-terrain SUV (Type Seven), or a vacation-friendly RV (Type Nine), there's a place for you on this road trip. And who knows? You might even learn to parallel park your soul without dinging anyone else's karma.

Brief Descriptions of the Nine Types

Diagram 2

TYPE	SHORT DESCRIPTION
1-Improver (BMW)	Sacred Wound: Internalized Anger Greatest Fear: Being bad or defective Has a compulsive need to be perfect in everything they focus on, with a strong inner critic that fears being bad or defective. They run on anger directed internally at their imperfections, leading to resentment when things are not done "the right way." They are called the Improver because they see the flaws in everything and work tirelessly to correct them, especially in themselves. I playfully call them the BMW of egos: precision-engineered, but they need a lot of maintenance. Their inner critic makes Simon Cowell look like a pushover.
2-Helper (Ambulance)	Sacred Wound: Externalized Sadness Greatest Fear: Being unlovable Has a compulsive need to help or rescue others because they fear being unlovable and look to others to shower them with affection and praise because of their good deeds. They experience a profound, outwardly directed sadness (or shame) at not feeling lovable by the world. They are called the Helper because they compulsively offer assistance to those in need in order to win approval. They are like ambulances, coming to the rescue with sirens blaring: "Love me! Appreciate me!" Just don't expect them to rescue themselves anytime soon.
3-Achiever (Race Car)	Sacred Wound: Internalized and Externalized Sadness Greatest Fear: Being worthless Has a chronic need to win social approval through carefully curated accomplishments because they fear being worthless and use their accomplishments to validate their worthiness. An inwardly and outwardly directed sadness (or shame) fuels their sense of worthlessness in their own eyes and in the eyes of others. I call them Race Cars because they're always zooming toward the next achievement, leaving their authentic selves in the dust.

4-Individualist (Custom Car)	Sacred Wound: Internalized Sadness
	Greatest Fear: Not being unique or having an identity
	Has a compulsion to be unique and different from everyone else because they fear not having a unique identity. They habitually look to stand apart and stand out to assert their individuality. Inwardly directed sadness (or shame) fuels their experience of not having special significance in the world. Called the Individualist because they have to be different from the crowd in almost everything they set out to do. If life's a highway, these folks are determined to be the most unique, customized vehicle on the road. They're so scared of blending in that they'd rather break down on the shoulder than look like everyone else.
5-Investigator (Compact Car)	Sacred Wound: Internalized Fear
	Greatest Fear: Being incompetent or unable to care for themselves
	Has a need to conserve their energy, withdraw from the world, and be extremely capable in their chosen field of expertise because they fear being incompetent. They have a deep fear that they direct inward, leaving them uncertain about their ability to meet life's challenges, so they become extremely self-reliant, often living inside their minds. Called the Investigator because they stand back and absorb information from the world without letting much out. I call them Compact Cars because they're quiet, efficient, have a small gas tank for social interactions, and can squeeze into tight mental spaces where others fear to tread.
6-Skeptic (Family Sedan)	Sacred Wound: Internalized and Externalized Fear
	Greatest Fear: Being without support or guidance
	Desires safety and security because they fear being without support or guidance. They compulsively look for structure and authority to guide them and have difficulty making decisions independently while paradoxically being mistrustful of authority. Sixes have inwardly and outwardly directed fears that leave them uncertain about their ability to navigate reality while also being reluctant to trust others. They typically have a committee of voices in their head offering advice, leaving them confused, indecisive, and skeptical. Sometimes called the Loyalist because once they commit to a person, institution, or idea, they are reluctant to change their mind because their commitment was hard to achieve. I call them the Family Sedan because they want every safety feature known to humanity, plus a few they invented themselves.

7-Enthusiast (SUV)	Sacred Wound: Externalized Fear
	Greatest Fear: Being in pain or privation

Has a compulsive need for new and fulfilling experiences because they fear being in pain or privation. Since pain is experienced in the present moment, they always look ahead and plan the next exciting adventure to avoid the here and now and to ensure their desires are constantly being satiated. They are driven by fear that they externalize, pushing them outward into the world in search of distractions. Called the Enthusiast because they are so excited about whatever is coming next. I call them SUVs because they're ready to go anywhere and do anything, as long as it's not dealing with their pain in the present moment.

8-Challenger (Hummer)	Sacred Wound: Externalized Anger
	Greatest Fear: Being harmed or controlled

Has a compulsive need to push against the world's boundaries because they fear being harmed or controlled. They assert their will to control their environment before it controls them and are highly sensitive to betrayal or injustice. Eights run on externalized anger that is always challenging limitations and boundaries. For that reason, they are called the Challenger. Like a Hummer, they'll run over or through almost any obstacle—just don't expect them to be fuel-efficient with their opinions.

9-Peacemaker (RV)	Sacred Wound: Internalized and Externalized Anger
	Greatest Fear: A loss of wholeness from conflict

Has a compulsive need for peace and calm because they fear a loss of wholeness should they express their anger. Nines have a volcano of rage inside them that they want to avoid confronting because it could blow them apart, so they always seek peace, often at any price. They have internalized and externalized anger that they never want to encounter, which is why they are also called the Peacemaker. The RV of egos, they're often found parked at the emotional campground, chilling out while the world zooms by.

Before you start thinking this is some kind of cosmic car show where certain models are better than others, let me set the record straight. There's no such thing as a lemon in the Enneagram lot. Each type is simply a different vehicle, custom-designed by the universe for a specific kind of road trip. Sure, some might be better for off-roading, while others excel on the highway, but they're all part of the divine dealership, if you catch my drift.

The beauty of the Enneagram is that it's got more levels than a multistory parking garage, which we'll explore later. You can always move up to higher levels of emotional health. (Or down, but let's aim for up, shall we?) The goal isn't to trade in your type but to become the souped-up, deluxe version of yourself.

The Enneagram isn't just a diagnostic tool; it's an invitation to the most thrilling road trip of your life. Once you've tamed your inner monsters and tuned up your finances, you'll be ready to hit the highway of life with style and freedom. With a little extra cash in your pocket, you can take your unique gifts on the ultimate road trip, making your presence and life a blessing for everyone you meet along the way.

What Type of Driver Are You? Anxious or Avoidant?

So, what kind of financial driver are you? To find out, let's do a quick review of the Attachment Theory of Money. Are you the anxious type, white-knuckling the steering wheel of your financial life with the gas pedal to the floor, ready to throw down in road rage if the stock market sneezes or you get charged ten dollars for a bottle of water at the airport? Or are you more of the avoidant type, cruising in the slow lane,

What Is the Enneagram?

Diagram 3

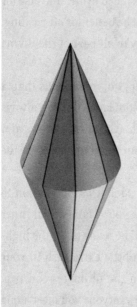

- The Enneagram is a well-researched and robust personality system comprising nine distinct archetypes, each with unique traits and challenges.

- In Greek, "Ennea" means nine and "gramma" means drawn, hence Enneagram translates to "nine things drawn together."

- Think of it as a user's manual for your ego—it helps you understand the psychological vehicle you're driving through life.

- The system shows how your personality developed to protect you in childhood and why those same protective patterns might now be causing problems in adulthood.

- Each type has a specific path to personal growth, tied to their individual strengths and weaknesses.

- While each type has clear patterns, there's infinite variety within each type—like a fractal with endless unique expressions inside a firm structure.

- Although it has ancient roots, the modern Enneagram was first developed through the work of Oscar Ichazo and Claudio Naranjo, both pioneers in the field of psychology.

pretending that retirement is as fictitious as the tooth fairy, and thinking unpaid credit card debt is an acceptable lifestyle choice?

There's also a third option, which we discussed earlier, that I like to call the "Financial Frankenstein's Monster"—a jumbled mess of money styles in different categories of your financial life. Most folks I've met are anxious in some areas and avoidant in others. But here's the thing: To build real wealth, you've got to master what I call the Four Pillars of Finance: earning, saving, investing, and giving. It's like driving a car with four wheels—you need all of them working together, or you won't get very far.

You might be an anxious earner and saver but avoidant of investing and charitable giving. One minute, you're anxiously counting pennies; the next, you're avoiding your retirement statements and donation appeals like they all have Covid. Some of you out there might be earning money like crazy, living large, and donating like a modern-day Robin Hood, but saving and investing? You'll get to those someday. Others might be squirreling away every penny, investing like Warren Buffett's protégé, but giving back to the community? Maybe that's a weakness.

Here's a fun fact: The money-anxious types actually have a head start in this financial adventure. They're already on the road, even if they're driving recklessly and playing bumper cars. The money-avoidant types? They're still in the parking lot, trying to figure out which key goes in the ignition. For those of you with the jumbled style? You're driving in circles or slamming on the gas and brake simultaneously.

Of course, there is a fourth option: being healthy, happy, and secure in all aspects of your financial life. But those people don't buy these types of books.

Remember, folks, becoming a true money master isn't about perfection—it's about finding that sweet spot where you're comfortable in all areas of your finances.

So, what's it gonna be? Are you ready to take control of your financial life and start driving toward fiscal health, or are you going to keep playing chicken with your bank account? The choice is yours.

The Attachment Theory of Money: Are You an Anxious or Avoidant Driver?

MONEY-ANXIOUS

These folks white-knuckle their financial lives with a lead foot on the gas pedal and are prone to road rage when they hit traffic or potholes. While they often achieve financial success, their constant anxiety can make the journey miserable for both themselves and their loved ones.

MONEY-AVOIDANT

These souls prefer to stick to financial side roads, stay in the slow lane, or idle indefinitely at rest stops. While often capable and accomplished in other areas of life, they neglect financial responsibilities like budgeting or planning for retirement rather than face the negative emotions that money matters trigger.

JUMBLED STYLE

These drivers can't decide whether to accelerate or brake, switching between money anxiety and avoidance depending on the financial terrain such as earning, saving, investing, and giving. They might be confident earners but terrified investors, or compulsive savers who avoid charitable giving. With one foot on the gas and one on the brake, their financial journey is more stop-and-go than cruise control.

Overview of the Money Monsters and Money Masters

MONEY MONSTERS AND MASTERS

1-IMPROVER (BMW)

Money Monsters

The Prude (money-avoidant): Needs to feel perfect and morally pure, so they demonize money instead of feeling bad about themselves. They can't tolerate being bad at dealing with money, so they do a moral tap dance and make dealing with money bad instead. The Improver then becomes prudish about finances, negatively judging others with a more robust financial life. They've put their wallet in a chastity belt and judge money like it's the devil's pocket lint.

The Pious (money-anxious): Needs to be perfect and is fearful of making mistakes, so they obsess over their finances, becoming tightfisted and neurotically attentive to detail. Will judge themselves and others harshly for any mistakes. They drive the financial highway of life with their hands clutching the wheel in perpetual road rage and honk aggressively at anyone who violates the slightest traffic rule. They're one budget mistake away from a complete meltdown.

Money Master

The Poised (money-secure): Has a robust financial life, is attentive to detail, but understands that everything belongs and is intrinsically good just as it is, including themselves. They are emotionally poised and financially stable, not getting upset or disappointed by the vicissitudes of life. They stop worrying about their own perfection and give generously of their time, talent, and treasure to help relieve the world's suffering, but without judgment, resentment, or anger. They've got their financial ducks in a row but understand that life's not a perfect balance sheet.

2-HELPER (AMBULANCE)

Money Monsters:

The Bleeder (money-avoidant): Puts others' financial needs and desires above their own, neglecting their personal goals. The avoidant Helper bleeds out their money or time in service to others to feel needed and wanted. They stop at every traffic accident and fender bender and will even take hitchhikers to their destination but never get anywhere themselves.

The Bonder (money-anxious): Uses their resources to bond with people and make them codependent, enslaving others financially to maintain a steady flow of gratitude and appreciation. They rescue victims along the road, but never let them out of the ambulance. They're like the financial equivalent of Annie Wilkes, the villain from the Stephen King novel *Misery*.

Money Master:

The Beloved (money-secure): Is financially stable and learns to love the world unconditionally without needing to give or receive anything in return. They set healthy boundaries on their time, talent, and treasure by not overextending themselves. When they do give to others, absolutely no strings are attached. At their highest level, they bring genuine, *unconditional* love and compassion into the world.

3-ACHIEVER (RACE CAR)

Money Monsters

The Burier (money-avoidant): Applying ostrich economics at its finest, they stick their head in the sand and refuse to deal with their finances to avoid feeling ashamed about their financial illiteracy or mistakes. Or they race away from their money problems, going quickly in the wrong direction rather than facing their issues.

The Blinger (money-anxious): Accumulates the trappings of wealth to look successful and to assuage their shame and lack of self-worth. Their financial life is like a Hollywood set—it looks great from the outside, but it's all plywood and paint behind the scenes.

Money Master

The Builder (money-secure): Instead of trying to look good in the eyes of others, they use their abundant talent and resources to selflessly build something of lasting value and significance. With a robust and healthy financial life, things like money, status, and power are no longer used to win validation, but as tools for building something in service to the greater good. They've traded their racing trophies for a road map to a better world.

4-INDIVIDUALIST (CUSTOM CAR)

Money Monsters

The Flop (money-avoidant): The Flop is averse to conforming to societal norms and expectations and rebels against prudent financial practices like making money. Their financial life is a total flop, and their car is always broken down and barely roadworthy. Their financial rebellion is less "stick it to the man" and more "stick it to my own bank account."

The Flinger (money-anxious): Accumulates resources and money to express their unique identity. They fling money at art, beauty, or any form of personal expression that will help them to stand out and stand apart. They're living proof that you can't take it with you, but you can sure wear it out the door.

Money Master

The Flame (money-secure): Uses their wealth and talent to bring beauty, truth, and creative expression into existence as a gift to others rather than for themselves. They light up the world with glorious magnificence, burning brightly without burning out.

5-INVESTIGATOR (COMPACT CAR)

Money Monsters

The Moot (money-avoidant): Sees money as irrelevant and unnecessary, preferring simplicity and minimalism to maintain their radical independence. The Moot neglects material pursuits and has decided that money is beneath them, but so is paying rent, apparently.

The Miser (money-anxious): Anxious about being dependent on others or running out of resources, the Miser becomes extremely tight-fisted and greedy to maintain their independence. Ebenezer Scrooge in human form. They've stuffed their Compact Car so full of resources that there's no room for passengers—or joy.

Money Master

The Midas (money-secure): Embodies the virtue of nonattachment and gives generously from their vast store of knowledge, talent, and treasure to serve a suffering world without neglecting their own needs. When they learn to share their gifts and wisdom fearlessly, everything they touch turns to gold. But unlike the myth, their wealth nourishes the world. They're the Warren Buffett of wisdom and generosity.

6-SKEPTIC (FAMILY SEDAN)

Money Monsters

The Paralyzed (money-avoidant): Gripped by fear and anxiety, unsure of what to do, they become paralyzed by indecision. They are stranded on the side of the road, looking for directions, not knowing which way to go. Their spirit animal is a deer caught in headlights—if that deer also had an anxiety disorder and a PhD in worst-case scenario thinking.

The Puppet and the Pugilist (money-anxious): Gripped by anxiety about financial uncertainty, combined with a fear of being unprepared for emergencies, they become hyper-prudent or puppets to conventionality, doing whatever they can to obtain financial security. If their security is threatened, like Dr. Jekyll and Mr. Hyde, they flip from being extremely compliant into fierce fighters or pugilists who knock down anyone or anything threatening their safety. They stay with traffic and carefully follow the crowd but lean on their horn and scream out the window if anyone cuts them off.

Money Master

The Pioneer (money-secure): Offers support and guidance to others rather than seeking it for themselves. They've found their inner compass and are boldly and fearlessly blazing trails for others to follow. They're the Lewis and Clark of personal finance.

7-ENTHUSIAST (SUV)

Money Monsters

The Gorger (money-avoidant): Unable to control their appetite for experiences and adventures, they sacrifice long-term financial stability for immediate gratification. Money is often spent on indulgences, which they gorge themselves on, leading to financial difficulties. They're consuming experiences like there's no tomorrow, and at their rate, there might not be—financially speaking.

The Grabber (money-anxious): Fearful of being unable to satisfy their desires and scared of deprivation, they hungrily grab money and resources. They've turned their SUV into a financial hoarder's paradise on wheels, complete with a rooftop cargo carrier and a towed camper.

Money Master

The Grounded (money-secure): Experiencing profound inner peace and contentment, they no longer restlessly seek external stimuli to fill an inner void but find fulfillment in the present moment from their internal resources. Financial security becomes a tool for serving and fulfilling the needs of others, bringing joy and delight to the world. They've found that the ultimate adventure is inner peace.

8-CHALLENGER (HUMMER)

Money Monsters

The Detonator (money-avoidant): Hates being controlled by money or financial constraints, so they detonate any prudent limitations. The Hummer rams through reasonable financial boundaries and blows up budgets like they're in a Michael Bay movie of personal finance.

The Dominator (money-anxious): Wants extreme control over their financial life and the lives of others, so they obsess over money. They dominate every aspect of their financial lives, harming their relationships and personal growth. The Hummer runs over anything and anyone to secure what they want, leaving carnage in their wake.

Money Master

The Dynamo (money-secure): Uses their extraordinary strength and ample resources to defend and protect others from harm, bringing justice into the world. They're like Robin Hood, if Robin Hood had a 401(k), a diversified portfolio, and a really good understanding of long-term capital gains tax.

9-PEACEMAKER (RV)

Money Monsters

The Spud (money-avoidant): Is a couch potato who avoids engaging with financial matters to maintain a sense of peace and harmony. Their financial RV is permanently parked in the land of blissful ignorance and never goes anywhere.

The Dud (money-anxious): Feeling anxious or stressed about money, the Dud engages in a flurry of activity, but never confronts their real issues out of fear of conflict. The results from all their efforts tend to be duds. Their RV drives in circles, creating a lot of dust, but gets nowhere fast.

Money Master

The Doer (money-secure): Rather than placid peace from nonaction, they courageously bring true harmony into the world through assertive action. Instead of avoiding problems, they bravely confront them and use their wealth to create the harmony that only arrives after a conflict is skillfully resolved. They're the financial equivalent of a martial arts master—powerful, balanced, and surprisingly zen.

Diagrams 4 and 5 show how these monsters and masters correlate with the Enneagram types.

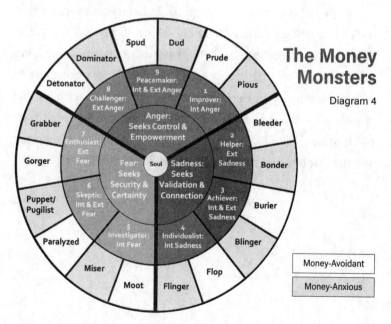

The Money Monsters

Diagram 4

The Money Masters

Diagram 5

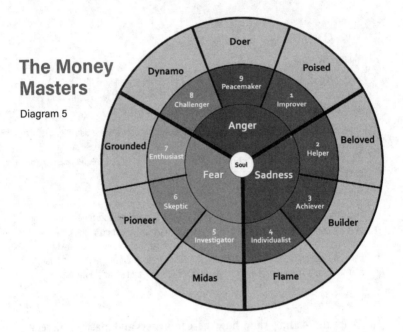

We've just taken a tour through the Enneagram showroom, and you've probably spotted your financial vehicle of choice. If not, again, there is an assessment you can take on my website at douglynam.com. But don't start revving those engines just yet. First, we're going to take a look at how your ego was built. We'll explore the assembly line of your past—the experiences and traumas that shaped your financial mindset. The ultimate goal? Transforming you from someone wrestling with money monsters to a bona fide money master.

CHAPTER FOUR

THE CHILDHOOD WOUNDING

WHEN YOUR EGO BECAME A GETAWAY CAR

Buckle up in your child safety seat, because we're about to take a wild ride down memory lane to figure out how you became your unique vehicle. It's like trying to solve a personality jigsaw puzzle, but instead of pieces, we've got a road trip through childhood traumas and coping mechanisms. Fun times, right?

There's a simmering debate in the personality world: Are we born with our Enneagram type factory-installed, or does life's bumpy road shape us? It's the classic nature versus nurture argument. I lean toward the "nurture" side of things, because even identical twins who share the same DNA often end up as different Enneagram types.[1] That doesn't mean there aren't any factory presets, but those seem to be adaptable. You might be destined to have leather seats and a great sound system, along with a noisy muffler and lousy shock absorbers, but those features can fit any vehicle.

Enter the Childhood Wounding Theory.[2] This theory supports the idea that your Enneagram type is essentially your childhood's greatest hits of suffering, remixed into a coping strategy to help you adapt and survive all that pain. Trauma is the master craftsman of our ego's defense mechanisms. While it's not the only thing that shaped your personality, it's the chisel that carved out your ego vehicle's protective chassis. We're all driving around with frames designed to help us navigate the psychological terrain that stressed us the most as kids.

A lot of this personality-shaping drama went down when you were too young to remember it. It's like your unconscious psyche was on a wild shopping spree in the cosmic car showroom, and by the time you woke up, you found yourself behind the wheel of your ego vehicle, doors locked, wondering how you got there.

Let me share a story that illustrates this point perfectly. David Foster Wallace told it best: "There are these two young fish swimming along, and they happen to meet an older fish swimming the other way, who nods at them and says, 'Morning, boys. How's the water?' And the two young fish swim on for a bit, and then eventually, one of them looks over at the other and goes, 'What the hell is water?'"[3]

Your Childhood Wounding is that water. It's the ocean you've been swimming in your whole life, shaping how you see everything, but you can't see it unless someone points it out because you've never experienced life without it.

Think of it this way: When you were born, you had a physical umbilical cord connecting you to your mom. Snip, snip, and you're physically separated. But emotionally? That's a whole other ball game. Your psyche had to go through its own "cutting the cord" process to individuate your personality from the caregivers you bonded with. This separation was necessary to stop being emotionally codependent on them. However, the process had to involve sharp negative emotions, because positive ones would only reinforce your connection to your caregivers. So, the biggest emotional threats in your childhood are what did most of the cutting.

This emotional cord-cutting is where the Childhood Wounding comes in. It's like your psyche's rite of passage, forging your unique personality by separating your ego from your parents, caregivers, and siblings, adapting itself to fit the environment it showed up in. Again, it's why even identical twins often end up as different models in the Enneagram showroom, and as a twin, I can see how this works. My brother and I had to differentiate from each other just as much as we had to differentiate from our parents.

The result of this cord-cutting? A hole in your psyche called the Sacred Wound. Sounds scary, but it's actually the birthplace of your self-awareness and emotional independence. However, whatever caused your Sacred Wound also created your greatest fear (or basic fear). Your psyche, being the clever little mechanic that it is, patches up this hole with your Shadow—all those dark, challenging parts of yourself you'd rather keep hidden from yourself and the world. This Shadow acts as a protective barrier, shielding you from your greatest fear while simultaneously driving most of your unconscious behavior.[4]

A more robust defense of this novel theory requires an entire book, but here's my basic claim: While these wounds might seem like factory defects, they're actually necessary for your ego to function. In fact, they are the chassis and engine for your ego. The silver lining? With some TLC and a good spiritual tune-up, these Sacred Wounds can transform into your unique and amazing gifts to share with the world.

Until we bring these wounds into the light and give them a good overhaul and refurbishment, they'll be driving us rather than the other way around. As Carl Jung aptly stated, "Until you make the unconscious conscious, it will direct your life and you will call it fate."[5] It's time to stop letting your Childhood Wounds be the GPS of your life journey, because while they were helpful in childhood, they are driving you into ditches as an adult, especially in your financial life.

Now, what was it that cut your psychological umbilical cord to create your Sacred Wound and the core structure of your personality? Not your average knife, my friends. We're talking about the sharpest emotional blades in the drawer: anger, sadness, and fear. As we briefly discussed earlier, these are the primary colors in the emotional pain box of life. Everything else? Just different shades of these Big Three.

Now, why are there only nine Enneagram types, you ask? Because the Big Three negative emotions (anger, sadness, and fear) are each processed in three possible ways (internally, externally, or both). *Boom!* Nine types. Your Sacred Wound is like your personality's birthright, and it comes with a free gift—your greatest fear! It's the foundation on which everything else is built.

Or think of it like mixing paint. The amount of red (anger), blue (sadness), and yellow (fear) in your childhood cocktail of pain determines where you land on the Enneagram color wheel. It's so simple it'll make your head spin.

For those familiar with the story of Adam and Eve, here's a fun one: Think of your time in the womb as your personal garden of Eden. You're in perfect unity with everything, blissfully unaware. Then *BAM!* You're kicked out of the garden and start becoming aware of good and evil. It's the original "fall," but instead of an apple, it's the development of self-consciousness that gets you kicked out of Paradise. And those angels with flaming swords blocking the entrance back to the garden? That's your psychological umbilical cord being cut, keeping you from strolling back into innocent bliss. That process is your sacred journey from "Thee to me," or how your soul became conscious and all the toils that go with it. Don't worry, though. In the next chapter, we'll look at how to build your own personal (metaphorical) stairway back to heaven, and no, you can't buy your way there.

Another way to say the same thing is that our journey through life begins in a state of unconscious unity, in the cozy cocoon of oneness with our environment in the womb.[6] Then life starts dealing its cards, and some of those hands are pretty rough. These experiences—let's call them "awareness awakeners"—are the cosmic coffee that jolts us into realizing, *Hey, I'm me, and everything else is . . . not me.* They then give us the tools to defend and protect "me" from everything that is "not me." Because let's face it, some of those "not me" things, if you aren't aware of them, will get you sent to the scrap heap in a heartbeat if you're not careful.

In psychological terms, this is called the "differentiation process" between you and the rest of reality. As we navigate these experiences, our ego structure begins to form. This development of self-awareness allows us to experience a conscious separation from our environment; without it, we couldn't survive or function in the world. (See Diagram 6.)

So, while it might be tempting to long for that original state of blissful unawareness, remember: These experiences allow us to grow, learn, and eventually write snarky comments on social media. After all, isn't that what being human is all about?

But for now, let's take a quick tour of the Sacred Wound souvenir shop. Looking again at Diagram 1, you can see how each type gets its own unique emotional backpack to carry around.

Type One, The Improver (BMW): These folks got their psychological umbilical cord snipped by a Sacred Wound of internalized anger, which makes them mad at themselves when they don't do things perfectly. This can also make them critical of others who don't live up to their high standards. It's like they've got a drill sergeant living in their head, constantly barking, "You're not good enough, soldier!" Their greatest fear? Being bad or defective. They work hard to suppress their anger by being good, and they're so busy polishing their halos that they sometimes forget to enjoy the ride.

Type Two, The Helper (Ambulance): Their psychological umbilical cord was cut by a Sacred Wound of sadness that they directed

The Childhood Wounding:
How Your Type Developed

Diagram 6

- The childhood wounding is how your psychological umbilical cord was severed, allowing your ego to differentiate from your caregivers and environment.

- This cord can only be cut by anger, fear, or sadness. These "Big Three" negative emotions are the primary colors in the emotional pain box of life—everything else is just different shades of these three.

- Your Enneagram type represents how your young psyche dealt with the anger, fear, or sadness that cut your psychological umbilical cord by internalizing, externalizing, or doing both with that emotional pain.

- Like choosing the right vehicle for difficult terrain, your personality type was your best childhood survival strategy.

- The childhood wounding, or Sacred Wound, is necessary to move from unconscious unity in the womb to conscious separation in adulthood.

- Your sacred wound isn't a flaw—it's the foundation upon which your entire personality is built. It's the chassis of your ego vehicle.

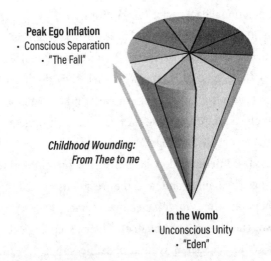

Peak Ego Inflation
- Conscious Separation
  - "The Fall"

Childhood Wounding:
From Thee to me

In the Womb
- Unconscious Unity
  - "Eden"

externally, creating their greatest fear of being unlovable. External sadness makes them feel grief or shame about how they think others perceive them, so they run around with their emotional sirens blaring, eager to rescue others from their problems to win the love their aching hearts so desperately desire. They're basically trying to earn gold medals in the Lovability Olympics. However, they deny their sadness and have difficulty acknowledging it because doing so would make them feel even more unlovable.

Type Three, The Achiever (Race Car): These speedsters got a double whammy of internal and external sadness for their Sacred Wound. Internal sadness makes them feel grief or shame about how they perceive themselves, and external sadness makes them feel grief or shame about how they think the world perceives them. This creates their greatest fear of being worthless, so they're always gunning for that next achievement, hoping it'll keep their leaky self-worth tank full. It's like they're constantly on stage, terrified of getting booed off, and so they work overtime to suppress their sadness through a never-ending to-do list of accomplishments.

Type Four, The Individualist (Custom Car): Their psychological umbilical cord was cut by a Sacred Wound of sadness that they directed internally, creating their greatest fear of not having a unique identity. Internal sadness makes them feel grief or shame about how they perceive themselves. They feel lost, as if they don't have a place in the world and don't know who they are. To compensate, they strive to be unique and stand apart in everything they do. These folks are so afraid of not having a unique identity that they'd paint their car purple and drive backward if it made them stand out. They embrace their sadness like it's a fashion statement and express it through wild mood swings.

Type Five, The Investigator (Compact Car): Their psychological umbilical cord was cut by a Sacred Wound of fear that they directed internally, creating their greatest fear of being incompetent. They are afraid they don't have the internal skills or talent necessary to survive a hostile world; as a result, they strive to be extremely competent at whatever they do. However, it takes a lot of work to be excellent in any discipline, so they can only pick a narrow range of things to engage with. They're reserved and taciturn by nature, but ask them about their areas of expertise, and they can talk your ear off. They work hard to suppress their fear by being capable and self-sufficient.

Type Six, The Skeptic (Family Sedan): Their psychological umbilical cord was cut by a Sacred Wound of fear that they directed internally and externally, creating their greatest fear of being without support or guidance. Their internally directed fear makes them scared to trust themselves, and their externally directed fear leaves them scared to trust others, so the world is a very scary place for them to live in. They don't know who to trust, so they become fiercely loyal when they find a person, group, institution, or ideology that makes them feel safe and secure. They embrace their fear through worst-case-scenario thinking and constant security-seeking behaviors.

Type Seven, The Enthusiast (SUV): Their psychological umbilical cord was cut by a Sacred Wound of fear that they directed externally, creating their greatest fear of being in pain or privation. Since pain and privation occur in the present moment, they always look enthusiastically forward to the next adventure or experience to get them out of the present moment. They deny their fear and have trouble acknowledging it. It's like they're trying to outrun their fear in an emotional around-the-world race.

Type Eight, The Challenger (Hummer): Their psychological umbilical cord was cut by a Sacred Wound of anger that they directed externally at the world, creating their greatest fear of being harmed or controlled. This makes them continually challenge boundaries and push against the limits of reality as a form of protection. They're the Enneagram's battering ram—if there's a wall, they'll find a way to knock it down, even if it's just to prove they can. It's like they're playing chicken with the universe, actively embracing and expressing their anger.

Type Nine, The Peacemaker (RV): Their psychological umbilical cord was cut by a Sacred Wound of anger that they directed internally and externally, creating their greatest fear of a loss of wholeness. They are angry internally for being unable to protect or care for themselves in childhood, and angry at the external world for not providing protection or meeting their needs either. Their anger is so intense that they want everything to be peaceful around them and to avoid confrontation. They're scared that acknowledging or expressing their anger will rip them apart, so they've turned peace-seeking into an extreme sport. However, they tend to be unconscious of their anger because they've installed the world's most effective denial system in their psyche.

Remember, your Sacred Wound is not bad—it is necessary for you to have an ego to drive around in and survive your childhood environment, even though the pain from it can sometimes be overwhelming. The key is learning to drive your ego with grace and dignity.

Understanding your Sacred Wound isn't about assigning blame or dwelling on past hurts. Although that's always fun, it's also futile. Rather, it's about gaining insight into the core of your personality structure. These wounds, painful as they may be, are integral to your development and individuation. They've forged your unique perspective on life and coping mechanisms to survive in a hostile world.

Moving forward, approach your Sacred Wound with compassion and curiosity. While we can't change the past, we can certainly work toward healing and integration. With awareness and effort, these wounds can transform into the source of your greatest strength and wisdom. As the 12-step program often says, "Forgiveness means giving up all hope of a better past."[7]

In the next chapter, we'll begin to unpack the user's manual for the Shadow Structure created by your Sacred Wound. This exploration promises to be enlightening, if occasionally uncomfortable. But hey, that's the price of admission for true self-understanding and, ultimately, a healthier relationship with ourselves, others, and yes, even our finances!

CHAPTER FIVE

A USER'S MANUAL FOR YOUR SHADOW

UNVEILING THE HIDDEN MECHANICS OF YOUR FINANCIAL BEHAVIOR

Welcome to the psychological auto shop. Grab your metaphorical wrench, because today we're going to pop the hood on your psyche and take a look at the intricate machinery driving your financial behaviors.

Now, cars are complicated, but we've understood how cars work for ages. However, we're still fumbling around when it comes to understanding egos. So if this chapter feels like you're trying to eat soup with a fork, don't sweat it. I'm cramming a PhD's worth of mind-bending concepts into a few pages here. I've done my darnedest to make it as easy to swallow as possible, but let's face it—understanding the darkest parts of your ego is about as simple as trying to assemble IKEA furniture while blindfolded and drunk. I promise that it will make more sense when we put this into practice at the end of the chapter, but we need to establish a framework first.

In keeping with our car metaphor, imagine your psyche as a beautifully complex automobile, cruising along on the highway of life. But hidden beneath that shiny exterior lies the Shadow Structure—the parts we'd rather not see or deal with but which are crucial to our functioning.

Now, don't let the word *shadow* spook you too much. Again, our psychological Shadow is like the chassis, engine, driveshaft, and fuel for our ego; it powers and controls everything. Without it, we'd be stalled on the side of the road of life, watching everyone else zoom by. It both motivates us and protects us as we navigate life's twists and turns, potholes, and occasional multicar pileups.

Most of the time, we're content to ignore this inner machinery. After all, if your car is running smoothly, why pop the hood? We're like those drivers who only open the manual when the check engine light comes on. But inevitably, after we've pushed our psychological vehicle too hard for too long without proper maintenance (hello, midlife crisis!), things start to break down. Only then are we willing to see what's been controlling our behavior all along.

The foundation of your Shadow Structure is the Sacred Wound, or the chassis of your ego, which we covered in the previous chapter. (It will help to follow along with Diagrams 7 and 8.)

Shadow Structure

Diagram 7   **Peak Ego Inflation**

First Half of Life
Path to Independence
"From Thee to me"

Structure of the Shadow
6) Ego Stress Response
5) Secondary Ego Addiction
(Stress Point)
4) Primary Ego Addiction
(Ego Fixation)
3) Worst Vice (Passion)
2) Greatest Fear (Basic Fear)
1) Sacred Wound

In the Womb

Shadow Structure by Type
Diagram 8

SHADOW STRUCTURE: ANGER TRIAD			
	TYPE 1	**TYPE 8**	**TYPE 9**
Money Monsters: Avoidant / Anxious	The Prude / The Pious	The Detonator / The Dominator	The Spud / The Dud
Ego Stress Response	Sorrow Anger + Melancholy = Sorrow (blocks Resentment)	Rigid Withdrawal Lust + Stinginess = Rigid Withdrawal (blocks Vengeance)	Security Seeking Sloth + Fear = Security Seeking (blocks Evasion)
Secondary Ego Addiction (Stress Point)	Melancholy	Stinginess	Fear
Primary Ego Addiction (Ego Fixation)	Resentment	Vengeance	Evasion
Greatest Vice (Passion)	Anger	Lust	Sloth
Greatest Fear (Basic Fear)	Being bad	Being harmed & controlled	Loss of wholeness & fragmentation
Sacred Wound	Internalized Anger	Externalized Anger	Int & Ext Anger

(Read each chart from the bottom up)

From your Sacred Wound springs your greatest fear—the engine of your ego. It unconsciously powers almost everything you do, like a V8 of anxiety under the hood. Just as a car's engine converts fuel into motion, your greatest fear transforms your deepest insecurities into action. It propels you forward, often in an attempt to outrun or over-compensate for your vulnerabilities.

SHADOW STRUCTURE: SADNESS TRIAD			
	TYPE 2	**TYPE 3**	**TYPE 4**
Money Monsters: Avoidant / Anxious	The Bleeder / The Bonder	The Burier / The Blinger	The Flop / The Flinger
Ego Stress Response	Revenge Pride + Vengeance = Revenge (blocks Flattery)	Elusion Deceit + Evasion = Elusion (blocks Vanity)	Co-Dependance Envy + Flattery = Co-Dependance (blocks Melancholy)
Secondary Ego Addiction (Stress Point)	Vengeance	Evasion	Flattery
Primary Ego Addiction (Ego Fixation)	Flattery	Vanity	Melancholy
Greatest Vice (Passion)	Pride	Deceit	Envy
Greatest Fear (Basic Fear)	Being unlovable	Being worthless	Having no identity or significance
Sacred Wound	Externalized Sadness	Int & Ext Sadness	Internalized Sadness

(Read each chart from the bottom up)

Connected to this engine is your "greatest vice" (or passion),[1] acting like the power train or transmission of your psychological vehicle. It's your primary coping mechanism, your habitual response to your greatest fear. Just like a car's power train converts engine output into wheel spin, your greatest vice transforms your deepest fears into real-world behaviors. It's your default way of engaging with the world.

SHADOW STRUCTURE: FEAR TRIAD		
	TYPE 5	**TYPE 6**	**TYPE 7**
Money Monsters: Avoidant / Anxious	The Moot / The Miser	The Paralyzed / The Puppet & Pugilist	The Gorger / The Grabber
Ego Stress Response	Indulgence Avarice + Planning = Indulgence (blocks Stinginess)	Self-Importance Cowardice + Vanity = Self-Importance (blocks Fear)	Frustration Gluttony + Resentment = Frustration (blocks Planning)
Secondary Ego Addiction (Stress Point)	Planning	Vanity	Resentment
Primary Ego Addiction (Ego Fixation)	Stinginess	Fear	Planning
Greatest Vice (Passion)	Avarice	Cowardice	Gluttony
Greatest Fear (Basic Fear)	Being helpless & incompetent	Being without protection or guidance	Being in pain or privation
Sacred Wound	Internalized Fear	Int & Ext Fear	Externalized Fear

(Read each chart from the bottom up)

Now you've got nine different power train options of vice to choose from, each one a unique blend of questionable coping mechanisms. There's the "Anger Automatic" for you Type Ones, the "Pride Power Steering" for Type Twos, and my personal favorite, the "Deceit Drive" for us Type Threes.

But wait, there's more! We've got "Envy All-Wheel Drive" for Type

Fours, "Avarice Acceleration" for Type Fives, and "Cowardice Cruise Control" for Type Sixes. For the thrill-seekers, try the "Gluttony Gearbox" for Type Sevens, "Lust Locomotive" for Type Eights, or if you're feeling chill, the "Sloth Suspension" for Type Nines.

Whatever it is, it's your go-to coping mechanism for dealing with this scary thing called reality. It might not always take you where you want to go, but it's sure going to take you for a ride.

Fueling this entire system is your primary ego addiction (or ego fixation)[2]—the psychological equivalent of gasoline. This isn't your garden-variety gasoline either; this is premium-grade psychological rocket fuel. This addiction is your main strategy for managing your greatest fear and greatest vice. It's your go-to strategy for keeping your fear-engine purring along and your vice-transmission powered up.

Chances are, you are so hooked on your primary ego addiction right now that you don't know how to function without it—or that you are even using it. In the Ego Addiction Emporium, we've got a smorgasbord of psychological petrol to choose from, each guaranteed to keep your neurosis-mobile running smoothly (or so you think).

For you Type Ones, we've got "Resentment Regular"—perfect for fueling those perfection binges. Type Twos, try our "Flattery Fuel"— it'll keep you compulsively helpful until you collapse. And for my fellow Type Threes, there's "Vanity Vapor"—because who doesn't want to look good while their life's falling apart?

We've also got "Melancholy Mixture" for the Type Fours, "Stingy Synthetic" for Type Fives, and "Fear Fluid" for Type Sixes. Type Sevens can fill up with "Planning Petrol," Type Eights have "Vengeance Diesel," and Type Nines can coast on "Evasion Ethanol."

Now, here's a dirty little secret—this stuff makes your worst vice feel like a superpower. It feels great, it feels right, but it's what will drive you into a ditch and cause most of the self-created suffering in your life. As addiction expert Timothy McMahan King said, "Addictions represent finite answers to infinite longings."[3] In other words, you're trying to fill the Grand Canyon with a garden hose. Spoiler alert: It isn't going to work.

Consuming too much of our primary ego addiction is like pushing our psychological engine into overdrive and redlining it. We're flooring the accelerator of our psyche, thinking we're outrunning our problems, but we're really just racing toward a breakdown. Under too much stress, the whole system starts to overheat.

Ironically, this is when our greatest fear—the very thing our ego has been desperately trying to avoid—starts to materialize. It's a psychological plot twist worthy of a *Black Mirror* episode: Our defense mechanism becomes the very thing that harms us! We're so busy trying to outrun our fears that we don't notice the engine smoking until it's too late.

When our primary ego addiction fails us, our psyche has a backup plan: the secondary ego addiction (or stress point).[4] It's like renting a car when you've crashed yours into a ditch.

Imagine your primary ego addiction suddenly can't handle the stress you're facing (often because your primary ego addiction caused that stress). Your ego, in its infinite wisdom, decides it's time for a change of strategy by renting a car from a different Enneagram type.

This borrowed coping mechanism isn't top-of-the-line. It's more like a junker with mysterious stains on the seats and a faint smell of old french fries. The key is that it operates very differently from your usual mode of behavior, potentially offering new ways to tackle your problems.

To operate this unfamiliar vehicle, you need to switch fuel sources, so you automatically adopt the primary addiction of another Enneagram type as your secondary ego addiction. Unfortunately, this doesn't make your greatest fear disappear. It's still very much present, acting as a turbocharger for this new system.

The result is a behavior pattern that is the inverse of your typical approach to life, or what I call your "ego stress response."[5] It's your psyche's way of hitting the reset button, creating a temporary fix for the issues your primary addiction couldn't solve.

Using your secondary ego addiction can be effective in the short term, getting you back on track when you're stuck. However, it's not a long-term solution. To shift our metaphorical gears, consider your secondary ego addiction as the psychological equivalent of chasing a tequila shot with an espresso—it's a jolt to your system that temporarily counteracts the effects of your primary addiction. But while it may keep you functioning, it comes with its own set of problems. Using it for extended periods of time is a sign of significant emotional stress and a red flag that you should seek professional help as soon as possible.

We can express this dynamic through a simple formula:

Worst Vice + Secondary Ego Addiction = Ego Stress Response (the antithesis of your Primary Ego Addiction)

In essence, when your primary coping mechanism becomes the source of your problems, or you face a problem it can't solve, you instinctively switch to a secondary strategy that creates opposite but equally challenging issues. Both primary and secondary ego addictions are ultimately maladaptive. It's a psychological balancing act where two negatives attempt to create a positive outcome.

It's important to note that our ego addictions are versatile tools we can deploy as needed, adjusting the dosage and duration to fit our circumstances. We might switch between our primary and secondary addictions more times in a day than we change our minds about lunch options.

Over time, these ego addictions can build our ego into such an impenetrable fortress that we feel isolated from others, the world, and even our spiritual connections. This "party of one" situation, where we feel completely alone in an empty universe, is called the Dark Night of the Soul.[6] It's about as fun as it sounds, and we'll dive into this cheery topic in the next chapter. After all, nothing says "fun read" like exploring existential crises, right? But I can make you a bright promise: This Dark Night is a critical turning point on your journey to becoming a true money master.

Understanding your Shadow Structure is like finally getting the user manual for your own brain. Remember, we're not here to judge or condemn our Shadow Structure. We're here to understand it, to shed light on the shadows, and maybe even to have a laugh or two along the way. After all, if we can't chuckle at our own psychological quirks, what can we laugh at?

Let's summarize the structure so far. The inverted steps, from 6 to 1, reflect the shape of the cone in Diagram 7:

Mechanics of the Shadow Structure

Diagram 9

STEP	SHADOW PART	DESCRIPTION	PURPOSE
6	Ego Stress Response	The behavior we engage in when our ego is stressed and our usual coping mechanisms fail us or don't fit the situation at hand. (It's the new direction your rental car is going in.)	Keeps the problems caused by your primary ego addiction from getting worse by blocking your primary ego addiction and potentially undoing some damage, but it is also maladaptive.

(Read each chart from the bottom up.)

5	Secondary Ego Addiction (Stress Point)	A negative behavior that, when combined with your greatest vice, creates the opposite traits of your primary ego addiction, or your Ego Stress Response. (It's like changing fuel sources by renting a different car.)	Activates automatically when your primary ego addiction either fails to protect you, creates too many problems, or you've simply overdosed on it.
4	Primary Ego Addiction (Ego Fixation)	Your most dominant negative behavior that motivates you. (The psychological equivalent of gasoline.)	Provides positive reinforcement for your greatest vice, putting it into action, and hiding it from your conscious mind.
3	Greatest Vice (Passion)	Your most negative characteristic. (The power train that converts your greatest fear into tangible behaviors and attitudes.)	A defense mechanism to prevent your greatest fear from coming true.
2	Greatest Fear (Basic Fear)	Anxiety or trauma response to the pain of your Sacred Wound. (The engine that drives your ego.)	Reaction to the greatest threats in your childhood environment.
1	Sacred Wound	The result of your Childhood Wounding through anger, fear, or sadness. (The chassis for your ego.)	How your psychological umbilical cord was cut. Allows independence and self-consciousness to form.

To show you how all this works in real life, let's go back Sarah and Mike, whom we met in chapter 1.

Type Three Sarah, if you remember, is a high-powered attorney with a corner office and a closet full of power suits that could fund a small country. Type Four Mike is an artist whose abstract paintings are as unpredictable as his income. On paper, the couple was living the American dream, but beneath the surface, their finances were a mess.

Sarah's Sacred Wound was forged in the pressure cooker of her hyper-competitive family. Growing up, her parents treated report cards like quarterly earnings reports for Fortune 500 companies and high school sports like the Olympics. This constant pressure to perform and the barrage of criticism that went with it created her Sacred Wound of internalized and externalized sadness. She felt grief or shame about how she perceived herself and grief or shame about how she thought others perceived her.

From this wound, Sarah's greatest fear roared to life: the terror of being worthless. This fear became the V12 engine of her psyche, constantly propelling her forward in a desperate attempt to prove her worth. It's as if she was perpetually afraid of being a rusty old clunker in a world of shiny Ferraris.

To protect herself from this fear, Sarah developed her worst vice: deceit. This deceit acted like her psychological transmission, translating her fear of worthlessness into a constant performance. She could subtly change personas in a heartbeat, always presenting the perfect image for every situation. This deceit drove her to seek external validation and make herself look good at all costs—even if it meant driving her finances off a cliff.

Fueling this entire system was Sarah's primary ego addiction: vanity. This wasn't garden-variety pride; this was industrial-strength, weapons-grade vanity. Sarah wore it like designer perfume to mask her insecurities and project an image of flawless success, deceiving others but mostly deceiving herself.

The combination of vanity and money anxiety led to Sarah's financial "Blinger" behavior. She'd work herself to the bone to make partner, only to blow it all on status symbols—designer clothes, flashy cars, lavish parties—not because she needed them but because they made her feel successful. Each purchase was like a billboard screaming, "Look how important and valuable I am!"

But when vanity led Sarah into a stress spiral and threatened to drive her career off a cliff, she'd unconsciously switch to her secondary ego addiction: evasion. Suddenly, our type-A achiever would transform into a master of avoidance, dodging responsibilities and hard truths. It was like she had traded her high-performance sports car for a beat-up RV from Type Nine and was hiding out at the campground.

This secondary addiction to evasion, combined with her worst vice of deceit, created her ego stress response of elusion. Sarah would find complex ways to avoid or elude reality, weaving a web of white lies and procrastination, complete with days spent in front of the TV mindlessly binge-watching *Game of Thrones* and eating ice cream. It was bizarre, but at least it gave her a temporary escape from her vanity and chronic need to appear perfect. It let her nervous system calm down until she could get her act together again.

Meanwhile, Mike's Sacred Wound was carved by the chisel of parental disapproval. Growing up in a family that valued practicality over passion, his artistic soul was constantly at odds with his environment. This led to a profound sense of being misunderstood and undervalued, creating his Sacred Wound of internalized sadness, or grief and shame about how he perceived himself.

Mike's greatest fear? Not having a unique identity. This fear became the turbo engine of his psyche, constantly pushing him to be different, special, unique—even if it meant financial ruin. He was like a custom car desperately trying not to blend in with modern traffic.

To combat this fear, Mike developed his worst vice: envy. He constantly compared himself to others, always found himself wanting, and pushed himself to stand out. This envy was like a faulty GPS, always telling him he wasn't where he needed to be.

Mike's primary ego addiction was then melancholy. He wore

his gloom like a beret, using it to withdraw from the world and feel uniquely misunderstood and different. It was the premium unleaded fuel for his artistic soul—moody, dark, and highly combustible.

This cocktail of melancholy combined with money avoidance turned Mike into a financial "Flop." He'd alternate between periods of intense creativity and productivity, followed by long stretches of artistic ennui, during which he'd avoid anything resembling responsibility. His spending was as erratic as his moods. One month, he splurged on expensive art supplies; the next, he was unable to help cover the household expenses.

When Mike's melancholy threatened to stall his emotional engine completely, he'd shift gears to his secondary ego addiction: flattery. Suddenly, our brooding artist would transform into a people-pleasing dynamo, acting like a Type Two Ambulance desperately seeking validation. This secondary addiction to flattery, combined with his worst vice of envy, created a potent cocktail of codependence. It was his ego's stress response, a way to temporarily block his primary addiction to self-isolating melancholy and force him to connect with others. Mike would suddenly dote on Sarah, expecting her to rescue him from his emotional doldrums even though it looked like he was trying to help her.

As their financial situation spiraled out of control, Sarah and Mike found themselves careening toward bankruptcy, complete with the vicious fights and marital strife that go with it. Their money monsters had taken the wheel, and they were headed straight for a fiscal cliff.

In this moment of crisis—bills piling up, creditors calling, their beautiful Victorian home at risk of foreclosure—Sarah and Mike crashed headlong into their collective Dark Night of the Soul. They were forced to confront the ugly truth: Their relentless pursuit of external validation and uniqueness had left them spiritually bankrupt long before they were financially so.

As we cruise into our next chapter, prepare yourself for a journey into the heart of darkness where those monsters hide. The road ahead might be bumpy, but the view at the end? Absolutely worth it.

CHAPTER SIX

DRIVING THROUGH THE DARK NIGHT OF THE SOUL

NAVIGATING THE POTHOLES OF YOUR PSYCHE

To become a money master, like a zen master, we've got to drag our Shadow kicking and screaming into the light. We can't afford to wait and pay attention only when it smacks us upside the head.

Now, I'm not going to lie to you. This chapter might be tougher to swallow than a mouthful of sand. It's going to bring up all those mistakes you'd rather forget and traumas you've been shoving into the back of your mental closet. But with a dash of humor, a sprinkle of self-acceptance, and a heaping helping of compassion, we'll get through this together. Just go easy on yourself!

Or maybe not? Maybe what you need is a good old-fashioned Marine Corps–style butt-kicking. Instead of coating everything in sugar like your typical self-help book, how about we make you feel worse for a bit? Sometimes a swift kick in the rear is just the motivation you need to make real change. It's like ripping off a Band-Aid—hurts like hell, but gets the job done.

Whatever your preference, remember, we're aiming for

personal growth here, not self-destruction. The goal is to get you into shape, not break you down completely.

I'll let you in on a little Marine Corps secret: Laughter wasn't just for fun; it was our secret weapon for self-improvement. Picture this: a bunch of jarheads huddled around, swigging beer and swapping stories about our epic screwups. We'd be cackling like a pack of deranged hyenas. Why? In the Marines, calling out someone's screwups wasn't just okay, it was our duty. After all, bonehead moves in combat get people killed. Our most lethal weapon against incompetence was a well-aimed zinger. Mess up, and you'd be roasted harder than a marshmallow over a campfire until you learned to laugh at yourself—and more importantly, learn from your mistake.

That, my friends, is what I call "driving through the darkness." It's facing your failures head-on, laughing in their face, and coming out stronger on the other side. You can't fake this. When you're doubled over, tears streaming down your face, snot bubbles threatening to burst as you recount your latest fiasco, there's no room for denial, anger, fear, or sadness. It's pure, unadulterated acceptance of your own stupidity.

If running into one's Shadow were an Olympic sport, I'd be a gold medalist. Not because I trained hard, mind you, but because I've face-planted into it so many times, I've practically mapped its entire topography with my forehead. The really funny part? The sheer, mind-boggling idiocy of my screwups. The aftermath? Not so funny. Even less funny is the pain I've caused others along the way.

There is no shortcutting this stuff. However, I finally see the pattern of how the Shadow works and can teach you a few tricks to help you sidestep a lot of unnecessary suffering, even if I'm still learning how to avoid those same problems along with you.

The first step in learning how to drive through the Dark Night involves staring down your ego addictions. Let's circle back to Sarah and Mike, our financial train wrecks from earlier. These two had to hit the fiscal equivalent of rock bottom—bankruptcy—before they could even look their money monsters in the eye. But here's where it gets good.

When they finally crashed and burned, then spent a little time in a pit of despair, they found the courage to laugh at their own stupidity. I'm talking full-on, tears-streaming-down-your-face, snorting-like-a-pig laughter. To commemorate this breakthrough, Sarah hung a ridiculously overpriced tapestry (purchased long ago) right above their fireplace. It was like their personal financial dunce cap, a constant reminder of what she *used* to do and how far they've come from financial screwups to money masters.

Now, as we dive headfirst into the double-cone 3-D Enneagram (see Diagram 10), remember this: Laughter is your North Star on this path of self-discovery. Trust me, it beats the alternative of losing your way in a labyrinth of self-pity. If it's any comfort, everyone around you has a Shadow to face, and you're not alone in your pain.

Structure of the Double-Cone Enneagram

In chapters 4 and 5 we explored the bottom half of the double-cone model I developed to explain why the Enneagram works. Let's review: Picture yourself floating in the womb, ego-free and blissed out, one with the universe. Then—*BAM!*—you're born, and reality hits you like a ton of bricks. Welcome to the world, kiddo.[1]

As you grow up, your Shadow Structure gets to work, feverishly building your ego. And to be clear: You need that ego. Without it, you'd be about as useful as a bartender at an Alcoholics Anonymous convention. But the more your ego expands, the further you drift from that original state of innocence. (See Diagram 10.)

Falling Upward
Outline of the Double-Cone Enneagram
Diagram 10

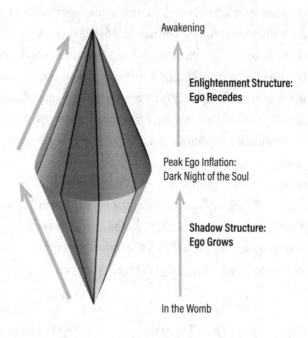

Awakening

Enlightenment Structure:
Ego Recedes

Peak Ego Inflation:
Dark Night of the Soul

Shadow Structure:
Ego Grows

In the Womb

This ego inflation keeps going until you peak at the widest part of the double cone. That's where you encounter the Dark Night of the Soul. Think of it as an existential pit stop—not exactly Disneyland, but a necessary evil on your journey of self-discovery. If you can muster the courage to let yourself break open here, your ego softens. You gain wisdom, compassion, and maybe even a sense of humor about yourself. With any luck, your ego deflates, and you inch closer to that elusive state of Enlightenment or Awakening.

On the other side of this Dark Night is the Enlightenment Structure—your personal road to healing and growth. It's the path you've got to navigate to soothe those Childhood Wounds that created your ego, kick those pesky ego addictions to the curb, and tame the money monsters lurking in the shadows of your psyche.

We'll explore the Enlightenment Structure in chapter 7, but first, it's crucial to understand the Dark Night of the Soul and how our ego addictions lead us there.

Now, let's be clear: The Dark Night isn't just a case of the Mondays or a funk that a pint of ice cream can fix. We're talking about a disconnection so profound that you feel like God has forsaken you completely, and you feel completely alone, trapped in a meaningless existence filled with pain. In this state, your ego and defense mechanisms are puffed up like a blowfish, keeping everything at bay.

As Mirabai Starr states in her translation of *Dark Night of the Soul* by St. John of the Cross, "The dark night is about being fully present to the tender, wounded emptiness of our own souls. It's about not turning away from the pain but learning to rest in it."[2]

The whole point of this experience is to make it through to the other side by letting your pain break open the wall of separation your ego has created. The goal is to turn inward, reconnect with your eternal essence, and reclaim that childlike innocence and bliss you had way back when. But this time, you're bringing along the wisdom, compassion, and unique gifts you've picked up along the way. It's like returning to the kindergarten playground full of joy, but with a PhD in Life, and the ability to serve and heal the world.[3]

Our True Self or highest self then begins to emerge. This process of transformation or "homecoming" is, perhaps, a psychological understanding of Jesus' statement, "Truly I tell you, anyone who will not receive the kingdom of God like a little child will never enter it" (Luke 18:17).

Simply put, the overall arc of your soul's journey begins in unconscious unity in the womb. Then your ego grows into full maturity to create conscious separation and independent self-awareness, but it doesn't know when to stop. Over time, your ego inflates so much that it separates you from everything and has to break open through suffering, causing the ego to recede and allowing more wisdom and compassion to form. If we do the work, our ego continues to recede until we arrive at our destination of conscious unity with everything and everyone, allowing the light of the Divine to shine more fully through us and our unique gifts. As Bertrand Russell said, "Only upon the firm foundation of unyielding despair, can the soul's habitation henceforth be safely built."[4]

Now, there are two ways to arrive at the Dark Night.

The first is the scenic route: This is the slow, steady drive up the Enneagram mountain until—oops!—a midlife crisis hits and you blow a gasket.

The slow, scenic route is the natural and healthiest trajectory for most people, like with Sarah and Mike. As we move steadily upward through the first half of life, or the bottom section of the double cone, we use our ego addictions to protect ourselves and navigate reality until our ego is so strong that it emotionally separates us from almost everyone and everything. The midlife crisis is a hallmark trait of the scenic route, when the things we strived so long and hard for to build up our self-image and ego fail to satisfy our deepest longings, creating an existential dilemma.

The second path to the Dark Night is the express lane: a swift, often brutal descent into the abyss as the result of trauma. Life loads you up with heavy circumstances your usual coping mechanisms can't handle, but you use them anyway. Following a significant ordeal, those of us in the express lane might overdose on our ego addictions in a misguided attempt at self-protection. This route is particularly treacherous because we often find ourselves on it when we're young and immature, with little more than our learner's permit for navigating life.

Although your Dark Night of the Soul may not be directly related to your finances, it inevitably impacts them profoundly, and there is often a strong correlation between the two. The quicker you can move through it by learning the lessons it has to offer and not repeating them, the stronger your financial life is likely to be.

Now let's shift our focus to Molly, a Type Eight (the Challenger, or Hummer), who took the express lane to the Dark Night.

At eighteen, Molly embodied the characteristic strength and assertiveness of a Type Eight. However, her world was shattered by a traumatic sexual assault.

In the aftermath, Molly's primary ego addiction—vengeance—manifested with passionate intensity. Her anger became a constant companion, volatile, and easily triggered by her post-traumatic stress. Every perceived slight elicited a disproportionate response, her rage burning hot and fast.

At twenty, this simmering anger erupted into violence. At a social gathering, impaired by alcohol and unprocessed trauma, Molly engaged in a physical altercation that resulted in serious injury to another person. The consequences were swift and severe: incarceration.

Prison life, where her greatest fear as a Type Eight of being harmed and controlled became a daily reality, plunged Molly even deeper into her Dark Night. The long-term financial repercussions of her felony conviction would cast a shadow over her future.

Yet, Molly's story took an inspiring turn. Rather than succumbing to the darkness, she chose to grapple with it. Determined to avoid returning to prison and wanting to help other women sidestep similar fates, Molly redirected her formidable Type Eight energy into education and advocacy.

With remarkable tenacity, she pursued and obtained a master's degree in social work. Molly transformed herself into a powerful advocate for women's rights, using her painful experiences as a catalyst for positive change rather than a source of perpetual anger.

Crucially, Molly learned to advocate for herself and others without resorting to violence. Using techniques we'll explore in the next chapter, she developed the ability to radiate compassionate strength, guiding others through their own Dark Nights with empathy and understanding.

The Dark Night of the Soul is an inevitable passage for those attuned to their inner struggles, manifesting as the realization of one's greatest fear. While external events often play a role, events alone don't throw us into the Dark Night; our response to them does. We tend to bear some responsibility for our deepest adult suffering by misapplying childhood coping strategies and overusing our ego addictions until they become liabilities rather than assets.

Most folks, when they first encounter the Dark Night, react like a cat that's been thrown into a full bathtub. They scramble, they claw, they'll do anything to get out of there. And who can blame them?

But do you know that feeling when you've been stumbling through life, half awake, bumping into furniture, and stubbing your toe on every emotional corner? Well, that's what happens when we refuse to face our Dark Night of the Soul. It's like we're zombies, and instead of searching for brains to eat, we're hungry for validation, control, security, or whatever our ego addictions are reaching for. The only solution is to face our darkness and let it break us open.

Now, I know what you might be thinking: *Breaking open sounds painful and messy. Can't I just stay in my comfortable cocoon of denial?* Well, sure you can. But the alternative isn't pretty. Trust me, I've been there. My greatest regrets aren't the times I faced my inner demons, but the times I let those demons run amok and hurt the people I love. As I said earlier in the book, every time I've seriously hurt someone I love, it was because I was acting out the worst aspects of my Enneagram type, and the same thing is true for every time someone has seriously wounded me.

As a Type Three, my ego addiction to vanity and the deceit that fuels it have caused most of the suffering in my life. Vanity keeps trying to soothe my greatest fear of being worthless, but I inevitably overdose on it and create problems that make me feel completely worthless when my vanity and deceit are exposed.

Here's the deal: We can either choose to break open now, on our own terms, or wait until life breaks us open forcibly. As we navigate these challenging roads, remember: The depth and duration of our Dark Night experience is, to a large extent, within our control. Will we retreat into denial or face our truths and evolve? The choice, as always, is ours.

Death doulas and hospice workers often talk about people experiencing "enlightenment at gunpoint"—that moment when the terminally ill suddenly let go of all their ego addictions and have a profound spiritual awakening. But why wait until we're staring down the barrel of mortality? Why not have our awakening now, when we still have time to enjoy it? As Stephen King wrote in *Doctor Sleep*, "We're all dying. The world's just a hospice with fresh air."[5] Besides, backing out of the Dark Night is like trying to un-ring a bell. You can pretend you didn't hear it, but that sucker's still vibrating.

And don't even get me started on some of these modern psychological approaches to dealing with it.[6] They're like those well-meaning but misguided parents who try to solve every problem by buying their kid a new toy. "Oh, you're in the Dark Night of the Soul? Here, have some happy pills and think positive thoughts!"

What we need are approaches that don't just yank us down and out of the Dark Night but help us navigate up and through it. Carl Jung even helped his patients *enter* the Dark Night by encouraging their egoism and forcing them into it.[7] Or, as William Blake said, "If the fool would persist in his folly he would become wise."[8]

So let's put on our big-kid pants, grab a flashlight, and venture into that Dark Night. It's time to face our shadows and emerge as the wonderful, fully realized versions of ourselves we were meant to be.

CHAPTER SEVEN

LETTING IN THE LIGHT

TURNING YOUR FINANCIAL HEADLIGHTS ON

Our ancestors knew a lot about the Dark Night and tried to teach us about it through story and myth, but we often dismiss the depth of meaning behind these stories because they sound magical and superstitious to modern ears.

For example, imagine you're the biblical prophet Jonah, minding your own business, maybe savoring a nice falafel on a deck chair as you enjoy an ocean cruise, sailing away as fast as you can from trouble, when suddenly—*BAM!*—you're tossed overboard and get swallowed by a giant whale. But here's the rub: This isn't just some freak marine biology incident. This is your ticket to spiritual maturity, whether you like it or not.

You see, that whale isn't just any old fish. It represents the Moby Dick of your psyche, the Jaws of your soul, the Free Willy of your existential crisis. And you're going for a ride.

For three days, you're marinating in whale stomach acid, which does wonders for your complexion but is absolute hell on your ego. But here's the beautiful part: When that whale finally upchucks you, you're not the same old Jonah. You're Jonah 2.0, new and improved, with a fresh worldview more in sync with the cosmic game plan. It's like being reborn, but instead of a midwife, you've got a whale.

This theme repeats throughout spiritual texts around the world, and we see it again in the Bible with Saul, soon-to-be Paul. This guy was cruising down the road to Damascus, probably thinking about which Christians to persecute next, when suddenly—*WHAM!*—he gets hit with the mother of all Dark Nights. We're talking literal blindness. It's like God said, "You want to be blind to the truth? Fine, let's make it official."

Here's the thing: Saul had to die for Paul to be born. It wasn't just a name change, it was a complete spiritual makeover. He went from being the biggest bully on the religious playground to the guy writing love letters to early Christian communities.

Paradoxically, the "fall" into the Dark Night always leads us upward if we let it. Richard Rohr's book *Falling Upward* masterfully elucidates this process, and as the thirteenth-century poet Rumi said: "Don't turn your head. Keep looking at the bandaged place. That's where the light enters you."[1]

Now let's break this metaphor down into two halves of life. (See Diagram 11.) The first half? It's all about you. You're building your ego like it's a masterpiece. School, job, romance, the whole shebang. And money? Money becomes your ego's best friend. It's like Miracle-Gro for your sense of separation from the rest of the world. Again, the first half of life is where all our money monsters are born and raised.

But then comes the Dark Night, and if you pass through it, you arrive at the second half of life. It's not about "me" anymore, it's about "we." You're no longer trying to be the star of your own reality show. Instead, you're realizing you're just one tiny, fabulous piece in this grand cosmic puzzle. Dr. Dan Siegal calls this the movement to Mwe, or Me + We.[2]

It is the transition from independence to interdependence, where we discover our True Self or higher self that the universe is calling us to become. When we enter the second half of life, we start developing a healthier relationship with ourselves, the world, and yes, money.

Falling Upward
Shadow Structure of the Double-Cone Enneagram
Diagram 11

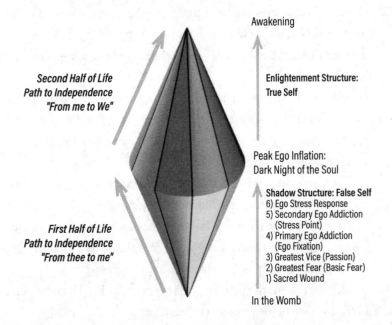

Awakening

Second Half of Life
Path to Independence
"From me to We"

Enlightenment Structure:
True Self

Peak Ego Inflation:
Dark Night of the Soul

Shadow Structure: False Self
6) Ego Stress Response
5) Secondary Ego Addiction
   (Stress Point)
4) Primary Ego Addiction
   (Ego Fixation)
3) Greatest Vice (Passion)
2) Greatest Fear (Basic Fear)
1) Sacred Wound

First Half of Life
Path to Independence
"From thee to me"

In the Womb

The Primary Path to Recovery

So how do we get out of this existential quagmire? Well, to be honest, there's no easy escape hatch, no "get out of Dark Night free" card. The only way out is through. And by through, I mean diving headfirst into the muck and mire of your own psyche. Fun times!

Don't get me wrong—this isn't an invitation to wallow in misery. We're not trying to win an Oscar for "Most Dramatic Existential Crisis." (Yes, I'm talking to you, Type Fours.) The goal here is to face your ego addictions head-on. You've got to own up to your part in creating this mess. It's time to take responsibility for your life, even when it feels like the universe is using you as its personal punching bag.

When you finally accept how your ego addictions and greatest vice are royally screwing up your life and causing suffering for the people you love, you'll naturally want to kick them to the curb. Besides, without them, there's a lot less suffering in your life, so things get lighter and easier.

You'll still have tough days, and suffering isn't going to disappear from your life. But—and this is the cool part—you'll be fulfilling your greatest hope. And that fulfillment? It's directly proportional to how well you overcome your ego addictions.

So what's the antidote to these pesky ego addictions? It's your primary recovery virtue—the yang to your addiction's yin, the peanut butter to your jelly, the . . . well, you get the idea. This virtue is your golden ticket out of the Dark Night and onto the path of Awakening.

So, are you ready to drive through your darkness?

If so, here are the primary recovery virtues I've identified that overcome each of the primary ego addictions:

The Primary Recovery Virtues
Diagram 12

ENNEAGRAM TYPE	PRIMARY EGO ADDICTION	PRIMARY RECOVERY VIRTUE
Type One: Improver or BMW	Resentment	Gratitude
Type Two: Helper or Ambulance	Flattery	Honesty
Type Three: Achiever or Race Car	Vanity	Modesty

Type Four: Individualist or Custom Car	Melancholy	Joy
Type Five: Investigator or Compact Car	Stinginess	Generosity
Type Six: Skeptic or Family Sedan	Fear	Faith
Type Seven: Enthusiast or SUV	Planning	Mindfulness (Being in the present moment)
Type Eight: Challenger or Hummer	Vengeance	Mercy
Type Nine: Peacemaker or RV	Evasion	Assertiveness

The goal here isn't to become an overnight saint. We're aiming for slow, incremental progress. The good news? The more you try to live with integrity, the easier life gets. It's like upgrading from a tricycle to a Harley. You'll still hit bumps in the road, but you'll look way cooler doing it.

When we dive deep into the Dark Night, our suffering cracks our ego open like a piñata. Breaking open is how we let the light of love in. It's a spiritual renovation. We're knocking down the walls of our old, addicted-thinking dungeon to make room for the God of our understanding. Is it messy? You bet. Mysterious? Absolutely. But when we surrender to the Divine in the Dark Night, we open ourselves to the light of compassion, forgiveness, and love. It's grace, the ultimate cosmic hug.

Now, I hate to break it to you, but most of us need multiple rounds in the Dark Night boxing ring before we fully embrace our primary recovery virtue. Some of us (ahem, yours truly) are tougher nuts to crack than a petrified walnut. We might need several Dark Nights, Weeks, Years, or even Decades before we finally let go of our primary ego addiction. It's like my friend who wanted to be a Navy Seal but didn't know how to swim, so he had to go through Hell Week three times before he finally passed. The great tragedy is for those who never learn they have ego addictions and spend way more time in the Dark Night than necessary.

In the classic midlife crisis, many people regress emotionally to behaviors from their earlier years to try and recapture their enthusiasm for life, or they make big external changes without addressing their inner woundedness. Both choices and their many variations push people back down on the Enneagram and merely reset the clock until they hit the Dark Night again down the road. Sadly, many repeat this process without ever getting to the second half of life, the other side of the double cone, where true wisdom and maturity reside. And then there are the people like me, who make it through to the other side of the Dark Night, only to fall back down into it again and again and yet again. Our ego addictions are hard to give up, and like substance addictions, we can easily relapse.

The Dark Night doesn't necessarily bring our worst pain, but rather the pain that really cracks us wide open. For instance, the loss of a child might plunge a parent into the Dark Night, but emerging on the other side could open them to the pain of every parent who's ever lost a child. It's a heavier burden, for sure, but now they might have the spiritual strength and compassion to bear it.

But accessing all that collective pain also opens us to all the collective love. They go together. It's like upgrading from a kiddie pool to the entire ocean—vast, deep, and a bit salty, but infinitely more profound and meaningful. Or as Ram Dass wrote, "Something in you dies when you bear the unbearable. And it is only in that dark night of the soul that you are prepared to see as God sees and to love as God loves."[3]

One of the greatest gifts of this journey? An increased capacity for compassion. We learn "to suffer with" others, which is what compassion means. However, it doesn't mean we're signing up for a lifetime of misery. It's more like becoming a spiritual sponge, able to absorb and hold both the pain and the joy of the human experience with grace and dignity.[4]

Remember: *Your heart never fully opens until it completely breaks.*

Faux Virtues

Picture this: You're trudging through the Dark Night, desperately seeking some light, when suddenly you spot what looks like a shining beacon of virtue. But surprise! It's actually your ego addiction's favorite snack in disguise, there to help fatten it up. These faux virtues are like spiritual junk food. They taste great going down but leave you with a nasty case of spiritual indigestion.[5]

Without proper discernment (and let's face it, in the Dark Night and in much of life, our discernment is about as sharp as a rubber knife), we're prone to cherry-pick sacred texts to pick out the tastiest bits from a spiritual buffet. "Oh look, a passage that justifies my ego addiction! Don't mind if I do!" We end up doubling down on our primary ego addiction faster than you can say "self-sabotage."

All sacred texts, to be enduring, must speak to all Enneagram types—which means some passages weren't meant for you! Take "Blessed are the meek" (Matthew 5:5). That's not a Snuggie blanket for our conflict-shy Type Nines; it's a spiritual kick in the pants for our bulldozer Type Eights. And just a few pages later, what about "I did not come to bring peace, but a sword" (Matthew 10:34)? That's not a battle cry for Eights to sharpen their blades; it's a wake-up call for Nines to stop hitting snooze on life's conflicts. So next time you're diving into your sacred text of choice, remember: Sometimes the passages that make you squirm are the ones you need most.

Now let's dive into the hit parade of faux virtues by type, otherwise known as excuses. It's like a rogue's gallery of spiritual traps, each one custom-tailored to turbocharge our ego addictions:

Type One: Honesty

"I'm not being critical about your mistakes; I'm just being honest." These folks could criticize a saint and call it constructive feedback. When an angry One goes full honesty mode, it's like being hit with a truth tornado—devastating, yet oddly precise.

Type Two: Generosity

"I'm not codependent; I'm selflessly giving!" Prideful Twos can smother you until you're gasping for air while making themselves martyrs.

Type Three: Assertiveness

"I'm not showing off; I just refuse to hide my light under a bushel!" A vain Three's humblebrag could make Narcissus look self-deprecating.

Type Four: Mindfulness

"I'm not wallowing; I'm deeply mindful of my emotions!" Fours can be so busy soaking in a pool of melancholy that they miss the No Swimming sign.

Type Five: Gratitude

"I'm not hoarding; I'm just grateful for my abundance!" Stingy Fives can squeeze a penny so hard that Lincoln begs for mercy. They're grateful for everything—except the concept of sharing.

Type Six: Modesty

"I'm not fearful; I'm respectfully vigilant!" Cowardly Sixes can turn uncertainty into a full-time job with excellent benefits.

Type Seven: Mercy

"I'm not overindulging; I'm being kind to myself!" Gluttonous Sevens can justify a shopping spree or wild party as self-care faster than you can say "overdraft fee" or "rehab."

Type Eight: Joy

"I'm not domineering; I'm passionately engaged!" When lusty Eights are having too much fun, it's like watching a bull in a china shop—if the bull thought breaking things was hilarious.

Type Nine: Faith

"I'm not avoiding conflict; I'm trusting the universe!" Slothful Nines will faithfully wait for divine intervention to solve their problems until their world falls apart.

Remember, spotting these faux virtues in action is half the battle. The other half is not laughing so hard at your friends when they use them that you fall off your spiritual path.

Enlightenment Structure

Unfortunately, our Shadow Structure contains more than one ego addiction, which means we need more than one recovery virtue. To make sense of this section, you'll want to follow along closely on Diagram 13.

When we start tending to our primary recovery virtue, it's like we're giving our ego some much-needed rest. This process begins to

Enlightenment Structure by Type

Diagram 13

ENLIGHTENMENT STRUCTURE: ANGER TRIAD			
	TYPE 1	**TYPE 8**	**TYPE 9**
Money Master	The Poised	The Dynamo	The Doer
Sacred Gift (Holy Idea)	Divine Perfection	Divine Justice	Divine Harmony
Greatest Hope (Basic Desire)	To experience their eternal goodness	To experience total freedom from harm and control	To experience complete wholeness and peace of mind
Greatest Virtue (Virtue)	Serenity Gratitude + Mindfulness = Serenity	Innocence Mercy + Honesty = Innocence	Right Action Assertiveness + Modesty = Right Action
Secondary Recovery Virtue (Relaxation Point)	Mindfulness	Honesty	Modesty
Primary Recovery Virtue	Gratitude	Mercy	Assertiveness
Faux Virtue	Honesty	Joy	Faith

(Read each chart from the bottom up)

ease the stress on our psychological system, opening up new possibilities for growth and transformation.

You might think your biggest stress-inducers are your overflowing inbox, that term paper you've been avoiding, or Janice from accounting who keeps giving you the stink eye. But most of your stress is actually coming from your ego addictions.

ENLIGHTENMENT STRUCTURE: SADNESS TRIAD			
	TYPE 2	**TYPE 3**	**TYPE 4**
Money Master	The Beloved	The Builder	The Flame
Sacred Gift (Holy Idea)	Divine Love	Divine Purpose	Divine Glory
Greatest Hope (Basic Desire)	To feel uncondi-tionally loved	To feel eternally valuable	To feel their eternal uniqueness
Greatest Virtue (Virtue)	Humility Honesty + Joy = Humility	Authenticity Modesty + Faith = Authenticity	Equanimity Joy + Gratitude = Equanimity
Secondary Recovery Virtue (Relaxation Point)	Joy	Faith	Gratitude
Primary Recovery Virtue	Honesty	Modesty	Joy
Faux Virtue	Generosity	Assertiveness	Mindfulness

(Read each chart from the bottom up)

They're sneaky little gremlins. They're the ones whispering, "Look how important you are with all these emails." Or, "Who needs to start that paper now? Future you can handle it." Or, "You better show Janice who's boss!"

Your ego addictions are the master puppeteers, pulling your strings and making you dance to their tune, all while convincing you it was your

(Read each chart from the bottom up)

ENLIGHTENMENT STRUCTURE: FEAR TRIAD			
	TYPE 5	TYPE 6	TYPE 7
Money Master	The Midas	The Pioneer	The Grounded
Sacred Gift (Holy Idea)	Divine Truth	Divine Trust	Divine Fulfillment
Greatest Hope (Basic Desire)	To know they are completely capable and competent	To know eternal protection and guidance	To know complete satisfaction
Greatest Virtue (Virtue)	Non-attachment Generosity + Mercy = Non-attachment	Courage Faith + Assertiveness = Courage	Contentment Mindfulness + Generosity = Contentment
Secondary Recovery Virtue (Relaxation Point)	Mercy	Assertiveness	Generosity
Primary Recovery Virtue	Generosity	Faith	Mindfulness
Faux Virtue	Gratitude	Modesty	Mercy

idea in the first place. Your Shadow has you programmed not to notice these shenanigans. Welcome to the wacky world of your psyche, folks.

The next time you're feeling stressed, take a moment to peek behind the curtain. You might just catch your ego addictions in the act, trying to make you feel important, procrastinate, or pick fights with poor Janice in accounting.

But as soon as we flex the muscle of our primary recovery virtue, our stress eases, our ego kicks back into the hammock, and we've suddenly got extra energy and strength to flex our secondary recovery virtue (or relaxation point).[6]

When these two recovery virtues join forces, this dynamic duo creates your greatest virtue (or your virtue),[7] which is basically your personal superpower against your Shadow. Start living in harmony with your greatest virtue and watch your greatest vice and greatest fear get knocked down faster than the villain in a superhero movie.

Then, surprise! Your greatest hope that you've unconsciously always longed for is no longer a far-off dream in a fairy tale, but a tangible reality that you can at least taste if not feast on. Experiencing the magic of your greatest hope then starts the process of healing your Sacred Wound.

I know it sounds more complicated than quantum physics because sometimes it is. But here's the CliffsNotes version: You've got two recovery virtues to practice, and they work together to create a super-virtue that heals the trauma from your childhood. Once you soothe those old wounds, the anger, fear, or sadness that's been feeding your ego addictions and money monster(s) starts to starve. And that's when your inner money master can finally emerge from its cocoon, ready to fly.

Let's switch gears and apply this to our trusty car metaphor. Picture this: You're so fed up with all the fender benders and traffic tickets your ego addictions have caused, you're ready to park your ego in the garage and never drive again. But life's highway beckons, and you have to drive something.

So what do you do? You head back to the Enneagram showroom and borrow the luxury version of another type. But not just any type; you pick the ride that purrs along on the fuel of your primary recovery virtue. And because it's a luxury vehicle, it comes with a dual fuel system, like a hybrid car, and you also get its primary recovery virtue—which becomes your secondary recovery virtue. Using both of these fuel systems is what powers your greatest virtue and cures your greatest vice. (My apologies for overworking the car metaphor, but it's better than mixing metaphors.)

Let's look once again at Sarah and Mike Johnson. She's a Type Three, the Achiever or Race Car, zooming around in her legal business like she's auditioning for *Fast and Furious: Corporate Edition*. Her ego addiction to vanity and evasion had her taking on clients faster than a cheetah on Red Bull, all to make herself look good while making promises she couldn't keep. This behavior was partially responsible for Sarah and Mike needing to file for bankruptcy when her business collapsed.

But Sarah, bless her heart, finally got sick of her own BS. Her Race Car lifestyle had driven her straight into a ditch, and she was tempted to leave the highway of life to become a hermit. But instead of giving up, she decided to try on a little modesty—her primary recovery virtue—for size.

Now, the Race Car runs about as well on modesty as a Ferrari does on maple syrup. So Sarah's ego went car shopping and came back with a luxury Family Sedan borrowed from Type Six. But to really make this new ride purr, she also needed to adopt the Six's primary recovery virtue: faith. For a Type Three, faith means trusting the universe enough to let down their masks and stop performing. This became Sarah's secondary recovery virtue.

By practicing modesty and faith together, Sarah unlocked her highest virtue: authenticity. And wouldn't you know it, authenticity turned out to be the cure for Sarah's deceit, which had fueled her vanity and created most of the suffering in her life.

By borrowing that Family Sedan, Sarah started acting more like a loyal Type Six, achieving goals to serve and protect others. She didn't change her Enneagram type, because she still drove the Family Sedan like a Race Car driver, but now she had room for passengers. It turned out that having company for the ride by thinking more of others was way more fun than driving alone in a hot rod.

In the real world, this meant Sarah stopped trying to be a narcissistic one-woman show and started building something bigger than herself. She turned her legal practice into a socially responsible B Corp and hired a diversely talented team that matched her clients' needs and complemented her own weaknesses. And within a few years, her business doubled. It turns out that being ethical and team-focused is good for the bottom line. Surprise!

Most of all, by embodying her authentic True Self, she finally fulfilled her deepest hope: to feel eternally valuable. Only by dropping the fake masks based on deceit could she feel valued for who she truly is—a beloved child of the God of her understanding. You see, the masks we wear don't just keep the world at bay; they keep the Divine out too.

Her husband, Mike, the Type Four Individualist, was stuck in a rut deeper than the Mariana Trench. His Custom Car ego was sputtering along on envy and a tank full of melancholy. He'd been so busy trying to be unique that he'd painted himself into a corner of artistic despair and financial ruin.

Picture this: Mike sitting in his studio, surrounded by half-finished canvases and overdue bills, wondering if he should just give up and get a real job. His moping around the house and leaving dirty dishes in the sink all day had Sarah ready to kick him to the curb.

In this pit of despair, Mike was forced to face the ugly truth: His addiction to melancholy wasn't making him special; it was making him broke and miserable. His envy of other artists and his fear of not having a unique identity? They turned him into a caricature of the "tortured artist."

In the depths of his Dark Night, Mike finally had a breakdown and cracked open. After plenty of tears and a few weeks stuck in bed, he started to take responsibility for his troubles and his rocky marriage and stumbled upon his primary path to recovery: joy.

Mike started small. He forced himself to find one tiny moment of joy each day. Maybe it was the way the light hit his coffee mug in the morning, or the satisfying squish of paint between his fingers. At first, it felt fake. Then, slowly, like rusty gears starting to turn, Mike began to genuinely enjoy these little moments.

As he practiced joy, something magical happened—the stress on his ego started to ease. As it did, he was able to access his secondary path to recovery: gratitude. He started appreciating the fact that he could create art at all, that he had a roof over his head (even if it was leaking), and that he had a beloved wife who hadn't left him (yet) and wonderful children (who sometimes got suspended from school).

Joy and gratitude worked together, creating Mike's highest virtue: equanimity. Suddenly, Mike wasn't on an emotional roller coaster all day. He had found balance, seeing beauty in the ordinary, and— miracle of miracles—actually finishing his paintings. It was like trading his clunky old Custom Car for a luxury BMW from Type One and taking it for a joy ride.

With this newfound equanimity, Mike's greatest fear of not having a unique identity started easing up because he wasn't so envious of others. He found something beautiful inside him that was always there and always will be, regardless of anything he (or anyone else) does, because he was finally able to see the glory of the Divine shining through all things. Most importantly, he experienced the glory of the Divine flowing through himself. This fulfilled his greatest hope—to feel his eternal uniqueness.

His art began to reflect this new perspective. And wouldn't you know it, his art sales took off. It turns out that people respond to joy and gratitude more than tortured pseudo-profundity. Who knew?

Mike started managing his finances with the same balanced

approach he applied to his art—no more feast-or-famine cycles. He and Sarah set up a budget, paid off their debt, started saving for rainy days, and began investing.

Mike's journey from financial flop to money master wasn't a straight line. It was more like his art—messy, unpredictable, but ultimately beautiful. He learned that being financially responsible didn't mean selling out; it meant giving himself the freedom to create without constant money stress.

In the end, Mike became the kind of artist he always dreamed of being—authentic, successful, and yes, unique. Not because he was trying to be different, but because he had finally found his place in the world and was truly able to be himself.

So there you have it:

Primary Recovery Virtue + Secondary Recovery Virtue = Highest Virtue (and a cure for your worst vice)

It's like a mathematical formula for spiritual growth.

By the time you finish reading this book, you'll have a clearer understanding of your Enneagram type's virtues and can start practicing them more robustly.

Sacred Gift: Your Cosmic Treasure Chest

Imagine you've just emerged from the Dark Night of the Soul, a bit dazed and confused, but finally living your most authentic life yet. Congratulations! You've been trying to live in integrity with your highest virtue, and boy, does it feel good to have your greatest hope fulfilled, at least a little bit. But there's more.

Your highest virtue is like the key to a treasure chest. Inside that chest? Your Sacred Gift. Think of it as your cosmic superpower, your spiritual X factor, the piece of the Divine plan that only you can place on the board game of life.[8] As St. Catherine of Siena is believed to have said, "Be who God meant you to be and you will set the world on fire."[9]

Sarah Johnson, our reformed Type Three, used to be all about the mask-wearing, people-pleasing, vain dance of inauthenticity. And any praise she got for her false masks rang hollow, leaving a gaping void in her soul. When she finally embraced authenticity (her highest virtue), something magical happened. Sarah felt seen and valued for who she truly was.

Living authentically allowed Sarah to manifest her Sacred Gift: Divine Purpose. Now, don't roll your eyes at the "Divine" part. I'm not talking about growing a beard and living in a cave (unless that's your thing, in which case, rock on). For Type Threes like Sarah, Divine Purpose means finding meaning and direction in life that isn't about impressing others or collecting gold stars. It's about seeing the intrinsic worth and value in everyone and everything, just as it is. It's also about using their unique talents to build something meaningful, to bring more love into the world, and to help others do the same.

The Sacred Gift of Type Threes is to help show everyone that they are valuable, worthy, and cherished because they have a tangible Divine Purpose for being. As Nietzsche said, "If you have a *why* for life, you can get by with almost any *how*."[10] Threes bring the Sacred Gift of "why" more fully into our lives.

Think of it as cosmic community service, but way cooler. And every type has a Sacred Gift—an expression of God in the world—whether it is Divine Justice as Type Eights or Divine Harmony as Type Nines.

The more Sarah lived her Divine Purpose, the more connected she felt to the God of her understanding. It was like getting a cosmic thumbs-up, a celestial high five, and a heavenly hug. She felt reconnected to her original unity or essence. She also gained the wisdom to navigate the world with less vanity and deceit, living in communion with the world.

Her husband, Mike, learned to manifest his Sacred Gift of Divine Glory. For our beloved Fours, Divine Glory isn't about being the most unique snowflake in the blizzard (though they'd probably win that contest without even trying). It's something far more profound and, dare I say, universal.

Divine Glory for a Four is about recognizing and reveling in the inherent beauty and wonder in everything around them—yes, even the mundane stuff they'd usually consider beneath their notice. When a Four embodies Divine Glory, they become a walking, talking celebration of the universe's intrinsic beauty, living in conscious unity with the world. They're no longer trying to prove their uniqueness or depth through their carefully curated aesthetic or by standing apart from everyone else. Instead, they're radiating the message that everything—yes, even that mass-produced IKEA lamp—has a unique beauty.

It's as if they've traded in their artisanal, small-batch, cold-pressed melancholy for a megaphone that broadcasts, "Look at the wonder of existence!" to everyone they meet. And the kicker? They include themselves in that wonder, no longer feeling like the odd one out in the grand tapestry of life.

Divine Glory allows Fours to see the Divine artistry in every person, every situation, every moment. They become ambassadors of awe, poets of the extraordinary in the ordinary, and believers in the inherent beauty of every soul they encounter. Who knew that connecting and finding common ground with others could be more fulfilling than being tragically misunderstood?

The Money Connection

Now, here's the million-dollar question (pun absolutely intended): What does all this have to do with money? Everything, my friend. Everything. When you embody your Sacred Gift, you're not just connecting with your deepest self but plugging into the Divine Wi-Fi. You are working with the cosmic game plan, not against it.

When you embody your Sacred Gift, money becomes a tool to amplify your cosmic superpower. It's no longer about impressing the Joneses or filling that void in your soul with another Amazon Prime purchase. Instead, it becomes fuel for your mission, a resource for your Divine assignment. The universe has a funny way of helping out, and miraculous synchronicities start to occur. I'm not saying life will always be easy, but you have a better reason to move forward in life, and that's significant.

Think about it: Having enough money to meet your security needs (plus a little extra for those fancy coffee drinks) gives you the stability and resources to start healing our fractured world. And if you're rolling in dough? Well, you can heal an even bigger crack. As Vicki Robin said, "How you spend your money is how you vote on what exists in the world."[11]

But perhaps the greatest gift money can provide is time! When you're not constantly grinding for that paycheck, you have the luxury of caring about the big issues. There's a reason affluent folks staff most nonprofit boards—they have the time to show up and make a difference.

So, here's my advice: Strive for affluence. Not for the fancy cars or the ability to bathe in champagne, but for the time and energy to heal the specific crack in the world that you were born to fix!

And if you're already wealthy? Well, my friend, you know what you need to do next. (Hint: It involves using your resources for something bigger than a gold-plated yacht. Although, if you figure out how to use a gold-plated yacht to save the world, I'm all ears.)

Now feast your eyes on Diagrams 14 and 15. They tie the whole Enneagram shebang together. They're like the Rosetta Stone for your psyche. Take a good, long look. Seriously, stare at them like they owe you money. If you're a visual learner like me (and let's face it, who doesn't love a good chart?), these will help you build a mental map to money mastery. So get comfy, and let's decode your path to fiscal enlightenment.[12]

Falling Upward
The Double-Cone Enneagram
Diagram 14

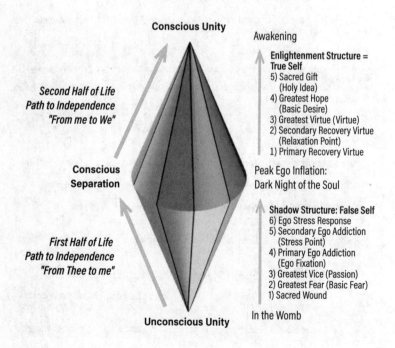

Conscious Unity

Awakening

Second Half of Life
Path to Independence
"From me to We"

Enlightenment Structure =
True Self
5) Sacred Gift
   (Holy Idea)
4) Greatest Hope
   (Basic Desire)
3) Greatest Virtue (Virtue)
2) Secondary Recovery Virtue
   (Relaxation Point)
1) Primary Recovery Virtue

Conscious
Separation

Peak Ego Inflation:
Dark Night of the Soul

Shadow Structure: False Self
6) Ego Stress Response
5) Secondary Ego Addiction
   (Stress Point)
4) Primary Ego Addiction
   (Ego Fixation)
3) Greatest Vice (Passion)
2) Greatest Fear (Basic Fear)
1) Sacred Wound

First Half of Life
Path to Independence
"From Thee to me"

Unconscious Unity

In the Womb

Putting It All Together
Diagram 15

PUTTING IT ALL TOGETHER: ANGER TRIAD		
ENLIGHTENMENT STRUCTURE		
	TYPE 1	**TYPE 8**	**TYPE 9**

	TYPE 1	**TYPE 8**	**TYPE 9**
True Self: Money Master	The Poised	The Dynamo	The Doer
Sacred Gift (Holy Idea)	Divine Perfection	Divine Justice	Divine Harmony
Greatest Hope (Basic Desire)	To experience their complete goodness	To experience complete freedom from harm and control	To experience complete wholeness and peace of mind
Greatest Virtue (Virtue)	Serenity Gratitude + Mindfulness = Serenity	Innocence Mercy + Honesty = Innocence	Right Action Assertiveness + Modesty = Right Action
Secondary Recovery Virtue (Relaxation Point)	Mindfulness	Honesty	Modesty
Primary Recovery Virtue	Gratitude	Mercy	Assertiveness
Faux Virtue	Honesty	Joy	Faith

SHADOW STRUCTURE		

	TYPE 1	**TYPE 8**	**TYPE 9**
False Self: Money Monsters	The Prude / The Pious	The Detonator / The Dominator	The Spud / The Dud
Ego Stress Response	Sorrow Anger + Melancholy = Sorrow	Rigid Withdrawal Lust + Stinginess = Rigid Withdrawal	Security Seeking Sloth + Fear = Security Seeking
Secondary Ego Addiction (Stress Point)	Melancholy	Stinginess	Fear
Primary Ego Addiction (Ego Fixation)	Resentment	Vengeance	Evasion
Greatest Vice (Passion)	Anger	Lust	Sloth
Greatest Fear (Basic Fear)	Being bad	Being harmed & controlled	Loss of wholeness & fragmentation
Sacred Wound	Internalized Anger	Externalized Anger	Int & Ext Anger

(Read each chart from the bottom up)

PUTTING IT ALL TOGETHER: SADNESS TRIAD

ENLIGHTENMENT STRUCTURE

	TYPE 2	TYPE 3	TYPE 4
True Self: Money Master	The Beloved	The Builder	The Flame
Sacred Gift (Holy Idea)	Divine Love	Divine Purpose	Divine Glory
Greatest Hope (Basic Desire)	To feel unconditionally loved	To feel completely valued	To feel their total uniqueness
Greatest Virtue (Virtue)	Humility Honesty + Joy = Humility	Authenticity Modesty + Faith = Authenticity	Equanimity Joy + Gratitude = Equanimity
Secondary Recovery Virtue (Relaxation Point)	Joy	Faith	Gratitude
Primary Recovery Virtue	Honesty	Modesty	Joy
Faux Virtue	Generosity	Assertiveness	Mindfulness

SHADOW STRUCTURE

	TYPE 2	TYPE 3	TYPE 4
False Self: Money Monsters	The Bleeder / The Bonder	The Burier / The Blinger	The Flop / The Flinger
Ego Stress Response	Revenge Pride + Vengeance = Revenge	Elusion Deceit + Evasion = Elusion	Co-Dependance Envy + Flattery = Co-Dependance
Secondary Ego Addiction (Stress Point)	Vengeance	Evasion	Flattery
Primary Ego Addiction (Ego Fixation)	Flattery	Vanity	Melancholy
Greatest Vice (Passion)	Pride	Deceit	Envy
Greatest Fear (Basic Fear)	Being unlovable	Being worthless	Having no identity or significance
Sacred Wound	Externalized Sadness	Int & Ext Sadness	Internalized Sadness

(Read each chart from the bottom up)

PUTTING IT ALL TOGETHER: FEAR TRIAD

ENLIGHTENMENT STRUCTURE

	TYPE 5	TYPE 6	TYPE 7
True Self: Money Master	The Midas	The Pioneer	The Grounded
Sacred Gift (Holy Idea)	Divine Truth	Divine Trust	Divine Fulfillment
Greatest Hope (Basic Desire)	To know they are wholly capable and competent	To know complete protection and guidance	To know complete satisfaction
Greatest Virtue (Virtue)	Non-attachment Generosity + Mercy = Non-attachment	Courage Faith + Assertiveness = Courage	Contentment Mindfulness + Generosity = Contentment
Secondary Recovery Virtue (Relaxation Point)	Mercy	Assertiveness	Generosity
Primary Recovery Virtue	Generosity	Faith	Mindfulness
Faux Virtue	Gratitude	Modesty	Mercy

SHADOW STRUCTURE

	TYPE 5	TYPE 6	TYPE 7
False Self: Money Monsters	The Moot / The Miser	The Paralyzed / The Puppet & Pugilist	The Gorger / The Grabber
Ego Stress Response	Indulgence Avarice + Planning = Indulgence	Self-Importance Cowardice + Vanity = Self-Importance	Frustration Gluttony + Resentment = Frustration
Secondary Ego Addiction (Stress Point)	Planning	Vanity	Resentment
Primary Ego Addiction (Ego Fixation)	Stinginess	Fear	Planning
Greatest Vice (Passion)	Avarice	Cowardice	Gluttony
Greatest Fear (Basic Fear)	Being helpless & incompetent	Being without protection or guidance	Being in pain or privation
Sacred Wound	Internalized Fear	Int & Ext Fear	Externalized Fear

(Read each chart from the bottom up)

CHAPTER EIGHT

BECOMING A MONEY MASTER

ACCELERATING YOUR JOURNEY
TO FINANCIAL FREEDOM

Becoming a money master isn't just about crunching numbers or mastering spreadsheets. It's about embarking on a hero's journey of self-discovery and transformation. There are five fundamental steps on this path, and while they're simple to list, they require the courage and persistence of a hobbit venturing to Mordor. This quest follows the archetypal pattern laid out by Joseph Campbell in his book *The Hero's Journey*[1]—a narrative structure that underpins countless stories, from Luke Skywalker's galactic adventures to Harry Potter's magical quests.

I like to think of these steps as the most incredible adventure of my life—and trust me, I know a thing or two about adventures. In the chapters ahead, we'll tailor this journey to each Enneagram type, providing a personalized road map to financial mastery. But for now, let's unfurl the map and take a bird's-eye view of the terrain we'll be traversing. Don't worry if it looks daunting—remember, every hero feels a little overwhelmed at the start of their quest. The key is to take that first step. So, are you ready to answer the call to adventure?

STEPS TO BECOMING A MONEY MASTER				
1	**2**	**3**	**4**	**5**
Acknowledge the pain from your Childhood Wounding.	Stop reacting out of the anger, fear, or sadness that created your money monsters.	Learn to be less anxious or avoid-ant about money by confronting your money monsters.	Build a strong financial life by earning, saving, and investing ethically.	Use your money and your talents as tools to love and serve a suffering world.

Steps to Becoming a Money Master

1. Acknowledge the pain from your Childhood Wounding.

Confronting the demons of your past is no walk in the park, but it's necessary if you want to become the protagonist of your own financial epic.

At first, you might feel like Frodo when Gandalf tells him he needs to destroy the One Ring. Your initial reaction might be, "Nope, not doing that, thank you very much." Now, I get it. You might not be ready to charge headfirst into your psychological Mordor just yet. But if you see how unresolved trauma is impacting your life (and your wallet), then it's time to get moving.

The next step? Find your Gandalf. Or your Dumbledore. Or your Yoda. Whatever floats your boat. The point is, you need a guide. This could be a therapist, a counselor, a support group, or even a trusted friend. Just like Frodo needed the Fellowship, you need a support system. Trust me, trying to navigate this trauma journey alone doesn't end well.

A familiar saying applies: "When the student is ready, the teacher will appear." That means the teacher is always there, but you won't see them until you start looking. (If you're curious about working with me, more information is available at douglynam.com.)

One technique that helped me was creating a trauma timeline. Picture it like a map of your life's battles. Get a big whiteboard, a roll of paper, or a spreadsheet and start charting out the major hurts, betrayals, and catastrophes you've experienced. Look for patterns. What keeps coming back?

- How did your childhood experiences shape your Enneagram type?
- How has your Enneagram type created unnecessary suffering in your life?
- What childhood or young adult issues first triggered your money anxiety and/or avoidance?
- How have those money issues created unnecessary suffering in your adult life?

When I did this, it took me a full week in seclusion, and I had a therapist guiding me through the process. It was exhausting but illuminating. Be patient with yourself. This isn't a sprint; it's a marathon. And it's okay if you walk.

If you can't afford a therapist, reach out to trusted friends, clergy members, or support groups. Your fellowship might include financial professionals too—CPAs, lawyers, accountants, or investment advisors. Just make sure they're fiduciaries, legally bound to act in your best interests. Perhaps join a support group like Alcoholics Anonymous, Narcotics Anonymous, Debtors Anonymous, or reach out to the Anxiety and Depression Association of America (ADAA). There are lots of options out there, so go looking for your people.

Once you've assembled your Fellowship and created your map, you're ready to step out of your comfort zone and into new psychological territory. It's time to leave the Shire of your familiar patterns and start your adventure toward financial mastery.

This first step isn't easy, but by acknowledging your wounds, you're not just setting the stage for financial health—you're embarking on a journey of personal growth and self-discovery.

2. Stop reacting out of the anger, fear, or sadness that created your money monsters.

To overcome the anger, fear, or sadness that birthed our money monsters, we need to embark on a daily practice of contemplation and compassion. Think of it as going to the gym, but for your psyche. Just like you wouldn't expect six-pack abs after one sit-up, don't expect to conquer your ego addictions overnight.

Contemplation is about shining a spotlight on those ego addictions and the Sacred Wound behind them that are wreaking havoc in your life. It's like being your own private investigator, and you're uncovering the ways you sabotage yourself. Set aside time each day for quiet reflection. This could be traditional meditation, a contemplative walk, or even journaling. The key is consistency. I've found priceless guidance from The Way meditation app by Henry Shukman and from his book *Original Love: The Four Inns On The Path of Awakening*.

There are more meditation apps than soda flavors, so maybe find one that tickles your fancy. Personally, I've found the Wheel of Awareness meditation practice Dr. Dan Siegel developed to be helpful.[2] Or, if you're old school, sit in silence, focus on your breath, and try to be in the present moment for a few minutes each day. It's harder than it sounds, but it gets easier over time.

One of my quirky routines is to stand in front of a large whiteboard in my home office and jot down all my ideas and problems, dumping them out of my head so I can stop ruminating on them. Then I play connect-the-dots to see what patterns emerge and how my sadness, ego addictions, and other bad habits are contributing to my issues. It's just another style of journaling. With my mind a bit freer, I then do a contemplative sit for ten to twenty minutes to try and soothe my grief. Then I go back and look at the board again to see what pops out. If you don't have access to a whiteboard, get a stack of supersized sticky notes and use them as wallpaper to create one, or tape up sheets of paper. If you're an overachiever, they now sell whiteboard wallpaper and whiteboard paint you can use to cover an entire surface.

As you begin your practice, focus on your primary ego addiction. Get curious about it. What purpose has it served? Where did it come from? How is it both helping and hindering you? Remember, these addictions developed as survival strategies. They're not the enemy—they're more like overprotective babysitters armed with tasers who haven't realized you've grown up and don't need them anymore. Most importantly, how does the anger, fear, or sadness behind your primary ego addiction create unnecessary suffering for you and those you love?

Don't neglect your secondary ego addiction either. Notice when it shows up and what triggers it. What's it trying to accomplish? Understanding both addictions will help you navigate stressful situations more skillfully.

Once you've identified these patterns, it's time to start cultivating your core virtues. These are your primary and secondary paths of recovery that lead to your highest virtue. Think of them as spiritual muscles you need to strengthen. How can you incorporate them into your daily life? Consider creating a personal mantra or prayer that acknowledges your addictions and affirms your virtues, and then recite it each morning and evening. If you need help, I've written a nondenominational prayer for each type and included it in each type-specific chapter.[3]

I also recommend having a picture of your childhood self to look at as you meditate or recite your daily prayer. It's that wounded inner child crying out inside you who needs to be comforted, protected, and reparented.

Speaking of prayer, find a spiritual practice that resonates with you. It's essential to have something to keep you from spiraling into an existential crisis every time life gets tough. It doesn't have to be a traditional religion, but those come with built-in support networks and well-established practices, which can be very helpful. It could also be meditation, time in nature, yoga, ecstatic dance, or any practice that connects you to something larger than yourself. The goal is to have an anchor and support system when encountering your Dark Night(s) of the Soul.

The next crucial step in this process is cultivating self-compassion. You didn't choose your childhood circumstances or how your psychological umbilical cord was cut. Work on forgiving yourself for the coping mechanisms you developed to survive. You were just a kid trying to get by without an instruction manual. Cut yourself some slack. Your money monsters are just manifestations of that scared and wounded inner child, desperately crying out for some TLC.

Try to extend this compassion to your caregivers too. As the cliché goes, hurt people hurt people, and all of us are deeply wounded, including those who helped raise us. Understanding their Enneagram types can provide insight into their behaviors and motivations, making their inevitable mistakes more forgivable. They were probably just overgrown kids themselves, fumbling through parenthood. Understanding their Enneagram type might help you see them as the flawed, complex humans they are rather than the villains in your personal narrative. If you can, take a hard look at your grandparents and have some sympathy for the struggles your parents had to overcome.

Finally, focus on integrating your primary and secondary virtues into your routine. This is where the rubber meets the road. It's not enough to understand your patterns—you need to actively work on changing them. Start small and be consistent. Remember, you're aiming for progress, not perfection.

This journey isn't easy, but it's infinitely worthwhile. By facing our ego addictions head-on, we improve our financial lives and move toward becoming our truest, most authentic selves. It's a path that requires courage, persistence, and a sense of humor.

So, are you ready to roll up your sleeves and get to work? Your future self—the one free from the tyranny of ego addictions and money monsters—is waiting. Let's not keep them waiting too long, shall we?

HEALING THE CHILDHOOD WOUND	
Contemplation **Uncover the** **Unconscious Wounds**	· Meditation · Therapy · Prayer · Journaling · Spiritual direction · Yoga · Time alone in nature · Dance
Compassion **Forgive the Wounding**	· Self-care of your wounded inner child · Go deep into your spiritual tradition · Explore your parents', caregivers', and siblings' Enneagram types

3. Learn to be less anxious or avoidant about money by confronting your money monsters.

Let's dive deeper into the heart of our financial hero's journey. This next step is where the hero faces their greatest challenge. Here's where we face our financial Balrog, our monetary Voldemort. Behind all our money anxiety or avoidance lurks our greatest fear. But here's the kicker—you can't conquer this fear with brute force or sheer will-power. Trying to strong-arm your fear is like trying to put out a fire with gasoline. It only makes things worse.

Instead, we need to take a page out of St. Francis's playbook. Do you know the tale of the Wolf of Gubbio?[4] It's not just a quaint story—it's a powerful metaphor for dealing with our inner demons. It goes something like this:

Picture this little Italian town called Gubbio. They've got a serious wolf problem—we're talking a full-on furry nightmare that terrorizes folks and turns sheep into snacks. The townspeople are losing their minds, trying everything to eliminate this four-legged menace.

Enter St. Francis, the original animal whisperer. He hears about this canine calamity and thinks, *Hey, maybe we should chat with the big bad wolf instead of trying to turn it into a rug.* I know, crazy idea, right? But Francis was always a bit . . . out there.

So, Francis moseys on up to the wolf's den, flashing the Sign of Peace like he's at a sixties love-in. The townspeople are watching, probably taking bets on how long before Francis becomes Alpo. But here's the kicker—the wolf doesn't attack. Instead, it slinks out like a dog who just got caught eating the Thanksgiving turkey, all submissive with its tail tucked.

Francis then starts chatting up the wolf. His exact words are something like, "Hey, Fang Face, you've been a real pain in the town's collective backside and scared the pants off of everyone. But I want to make peace between you and these fine folks. How about we make a deal and you promise to stop using them as chew toys?"

And get this—the wolf nods! I swear I'm not making this up. It's like a scene from a Disney movie, minus the singing woodland creatures.

Francis promises the wolf that if it stops its reign of terror, it won't have to dumpster dive for dinner and will be fed by the townsfolk. And wouldn't you know it? It works! The wolf becomes the town's furry mascot, the people start leaving out food instead of running away screaming, and everyone lives happily ever after.

It shows that sometimes all it takes is a little communication and a lot of guts to solve even the hairiest of problems. And hey, if it works for wolves, maybe it'll work for taming those money monsters too!

Picture your money monster as that fearsome wolf. It's been terrorizing your financial village for years. Your first instinct might be to attack it, to try and destroy it. But that's not the way.

St. Francis approached the wolf with the Sign of Peace—with love and forgiveness. That's our first lesson. We need to approach our money fears with compassion, not condemnation. Beating yourself up over past financial mistakes just reinforces your anger, fear, or sadness.

The second key point is that the wolf submitted because it sensed that St. Francis was unafraid. It's our fear that gives our money monsters power. When we face our financial fears with vulnerable courage, they begin to lose their grip on us.

Here's the truth, folks: That ravenous wolf of financial anxiety or avoidance? It's really just a scared and traumatized child howling for comfort. The more we attack it, the louder it howls and the more damage it does. But when we approach it with understanding and compassion, we can begin to tame it.

And here's where the magic happens: Once tamed, all that fierce energy causing havoc in our financial lives can be integrated and harnessed for good. That's how we become true money masters. It's how we transform our Sacred Wound into our Sacred Gift.

This process isn't easy. It requires patience, persistence, and a whole lot of self-compassion. You might need to dig deep into your past, uncover old wounds, and face uncomfortable truths. But remember, every hero's journey has moments of darkness before the dawn.

As you work through this step, try to cultivate an attitude of curious compassion toward your financial fears and behaviors. Instead of berating yourself for overspending or avoiding your bank statements, ask yourself what need that behavior is trying to meet. What is your inner wolf really howling for?

To make this transformation a practical reality with your money, we're going to get up close and personal with your anxious or avoidant money mindsets. Don't just skim the surface here—we're talking deep-sea diving into your financial psyche. Where do money monsters show up in how you earn, save, invest, and give? Take a good, hard look at how your anxious or avoidant mindsets play out in each area. You might find some surprising contrasts.

For example, you might have an anxious money monster controlling you when it comes to earning money but an avoidant one when trying to save money. Or perhaps you are anxious about investing but avoidant around giving. Or maybe you're so avoidant around earning money that you are stuck in a dead-end job, so you never have the luxury to save, invest, and give. We'll go deeper into your money monsters in the chapters dedicated to each type, making this process much easier.

Once you've mapped out your money monster traits in each category of earning, saving, investing, and giving, it's time to pair each trait with a corresponding action step to becoming a money master. You want to make these countermoves when your money monster starts to take control. Why not turn this into a visual masterpiece? Create a "Money Monster to Money Master" transformation chart. Make it colorful, make it bold—heck, make it so eye-catching that you can't help but look at it every day. For examples and a template, please check out my website at douglynam.com.

Go wild with this. Plaster it on your wall or stick it on your fridge. Surround yourself with reminders of your journey from financial chaos to money mastery, complete with practical action steps. And while you're at it, how about creating a good budget and financial plan?

Next, try this helpful exercise: Write a letter to money as if it were a person. What would you say? How has your relationship been? Be honest about your fears, your resentments, your expectations. Then write a response from money to you. What might it say if it could speak? It's like couples therapy, but you're working on your relationship with your bank account. It might sound a bit odd, but I dare you to try it.

So, are you ready to face your wolf? To approach it not with a sword, but with an open heart? It's time to transform those money monsters from fearsome foes into powerful allies on your journey to financial mastery. The path may be challenging, but the rewards— both financial and personal—are immeasurable.

4. Build a strong financial life by earning, saving, and investing ethically.

This next step is where we start to see some real, tangible changes in our financial lives.

Let's tackle what I call the Holy Trinity of Finance: earning, saving, and investing. (We'll come back to giving in step five.) Think of these as the three pillars of your financial cathedral that we'll build together, brick by brick. I've only outlined the basics here, but if you need help becoming financially literate and need more detailed action steps, please see my first book, *From Monk to Money Manager*. It will give you all the nuts and bolts for managing your money and becoming wealthy, with entire chapters on these topics. I apologize for the brevity of this section, but here is where a more traditional finance book is helpful. There just isn't enough room to thoroughly cover all that content, but here is a quick overview.

First up, earning. It might be time to level up your skills if you're not bringing in enough dough. This doesn't necessarily mean going back to school for a fancy degree (though it could). It might mean learning a new trade, developing a marketable talent, or finding your "right work"—a calling that energizes rather than drains you. Remember, you're not just looking for a paycheck; you're looking for purpose. If you're stuck in a soul-sucking job, start plotting your escape. It might take time, but your future self will thank you. It's important to align your income with your Enneagram strengths, which will be covered in the later chapters. Harness your unique Enneagram superpowers into super-earning potential. Also, try to develop multiple income streams if possible.

Now let me toss a curveball your way: Consider dipping your toes into the entrepreneurial waters. Starting a business isn't for the faint of heart, but if you've got a skill or passion that solves a problem for people, why not monetize it? It's not easy to do, but the payoff can be astronomical.

Next, let's talk about saving. This is where many of us stumble, but it's crucial. Start with a budget—think of it as a map for your money. Armed with a good budget, you'll need to practice mindful spending because you'll always be broke if you spend everything you earn. Before making a purchase, ask yourself if it aligns with your values and long-term goals. As Morgan Housel said in *The Psychology of Money*, "When you define savings as the gap between your ego and your income, you realize why many people with decent incomes save so little."[5] Then focus on building up an emergency fund of at least six months of expenses for those "uh-oh" moments life throws at you. After that, tackle debt like a knight slaying a dragon. I also strongly recommend trying to own a home if that aligns with your goals.

Plenty of apps and tools exist to help you automate all parts of your financial life and will make this process much easier. Use them! They're like having a squire to help you manage your financial kingdom. It is also important to continuously educate yourself about personal finance; knowledge truly is power in the realm of money.

Finally, investing. This is how we build long-term wealth, folks. Aim to save and invest at least 15 percent of your pre-tax income for retirement. The power of compound interest is like magic—the earlier you start, the more powerful the spell. Every great fortune was built through the power of compound interest in some form. To make this work, you'll need a sound financial plan, and there are apps for that as well, or consider hiring an investment advisor.

Here's a nugget of wisdom that might surprise you: Ethical investing isn't just good for your conscience; it can be good for your wallet too. Environmentally and socially responsible investments with good governance (ESG) often perform as well as, or better than, conventional investments.[6] Plus, you're helping to create the kind of world you want to live in. Win-win!

Just remember to review and adjust your financial plan regularly—as your life changes, your money strategy should evolve with it. You'll also need an estate plan, including wills, powers of attorney, and a living will, which may require a lawyer, but again, there are good apps for those things as well.

Remember, building a strong financial life isn't about getting rich quick. It's about making consistent, ethical choices that align with your values and long-term goals. It's about creating a life of purpose and impact, not just accumulating wealth for its own sake.

So, intrepid financial adventurer, are you ready to start building your financial cathedral? Remember, every brick you lay, every disciplined habit you form, is a step toward becoming a true money master. Now go forth and prosper—ethically, of course.

TAKING ACTION	
Earning	· Career development / right work · What is your calling?
Saving	· Budgeting · Savings plan: emergency fund, education, health care · Debt management · Use technology to automate everything possible
Sustainable Investing: ESG-Environmental, Social, Governance	· Retirement: Invest at least 15 percent of your salary · Homeownership · Entrepreneurial endeavors
Giving	· Philanthropy · What unique skills and talents can you offer the world? · Get involved

5. Use your money and talents as tools to love and serve a suffering world.

This is where we transform our financial journey from a personal quest into a force for good in the world. The ultimate goal of our hero's journey isn't to hoard wealth like a dragon on its pile of gold. No, the true purpose is to return to our community, bearing gifts that can heal and transform. We've tamed our money monsters not just for personal gain, but to wield our abundance as a force for love and service.[7]

Think about it: What's the point of accumulating wealth if not to make a positive impact? Those who amass riches without addressing their inner demons often end up projecting their unresolved issues onto the world, creating more problems.

So, how do we go about this? First, get your hands dirty. Before you start writing checks, invest your time and talents in causes you care about. This gives you invaluable insider knowledge and helps you understand where your contributions can make the most impact. It's about being a participant, not just a patron.

Remember, the world doesn't need more vanity projects or ego-stroking donations. It needs thoughtful, committed individuals willing to roll up their sleeves and engage with real issues. Don't be the wealthy donor who's more interested in seeing their name on a building than in creating meaningful change. As Brian Portnoy said in *The Geometry of Wealth*, "In life and literature, the good guys fight for others. The bad guys fight for themselves. Heroes have context."[8]

As you embark on this phase of your journey, consider starting small and local. Look for needs in your immediate community. Maybe you can support a local food bank, mentor underprivileged youth, or help fund a community garden. These grassroots efforts often have a more direct and visible impact than donating to large, impersonal organizations.

Also, don't underestimate the power of your unique skills and experiences. Perhaps your journey to financial mastery has given you insights that could help others struggling with money issues. Consider offering financial-literacy workshops or one-on-one mentoring. Your hard-won wisdom could be the lifeline someone else needs.

Remember, too, that giving back isn't just about money. It's about sharing your time, your knowledge, your compassion. Sometimes, the most valuable thing you can offer is a listening ear or a word of encouragement to someone struggling.

And here's a powerful truth: When we heal ourselves, we become agents of healing by bringing our Enneagram Sacred Gift to the world. Serene people reveal the inherent perfection in all things. Humble folks teach us unconditional love. Authentic souls help us uncover our life's purpose. Those who've found equanimity unveil life's glory.

Nonattached individuals show us the truth. The courageous teach us to trust. Content people offer fulfillment. Innocent hearts demand justice. And those who've mastered right action create harmony wherever they go.

By becoming a money master, you're not just changing your own life—you're gaining the power to be a force for good in the world. Your financial success becomes a catalyst for spreading love, showing compassion, and healing the unique crack in the world that you were born to repair.

CHAPTER NINE

TYPE ONE—THE IMPROVER (BMW)

HOW TO STOP CRITICIZING YOUR BANK STATEMENT AND START ENJOYING LIFE

Type Ones are the well-intentioned perfectionists of the Enneagram family. These folks have a deep-seated desire to be good—scratch that, to be perfect—in everything they set their sights on. It's as if they've been cosmically appointed as the quality-control managers of the universe, constantly fine-tuning the details of life. Practical, conscientious, and hardworking, they live according to high internal standards and have a strong sense of purpose. Like human excellence detectors, they can spot areas for improvement in themselves, others, or systems with remarkable speed, which they then strive to reform or perfect. I affectionately call them the BMWs of ego consciousness—precision-engineered, but requiring a fair bit of maintenance.

Take my friend Carl, a classic Type One. I once invited him to a fancy restaurant, and he immediately noticed a slightly crooked painting on the farthest wall. Instead of savoring his artisanal, farm-to-table culinary masterpiece, he gave the

Type One Ego Map: The Improver or BMW

ENLIGHTENMENT STRUCTURE	
MONEY MASTER	**THE POISED**
Sacred Gift (Holy Idea)	Divine Perfection
Greatest Hope (Basic Desire)	To experience their complete goodness
Greatest Virtue (Virtue)	Serenity Gratitude + Mindfulness = Serenity (cure for Anger)
Secondary Recovery Virtue (Relaxation Point)	Mindfulness (Primary Recovery Virtue for Type 7)
Primary Recovery Virtue	Gratitude
Faux Virtue	Honesty
SHADOW STRUCTURE	
MONEY MONSTERS: AVOIDANT / ANXIOUS	**THE PRUDE / THE PIOUS**
Ego Stress Response	Sorrow Anger + Melancholy = Sorrow (blocks Resentment)
Secondary Ego Addiction (Stress Point)	Melancholy (Primary Ego Addiction for Type 4)
Primary Ego Addiction (Ego Fixation)	Resentment
Greatest Vice (Passion)	Anger
Greatest Fear (Basic Fear)	Being bad or defective
Sacred Wound	Internalized Anger

(Read the chart from the bottom up.)

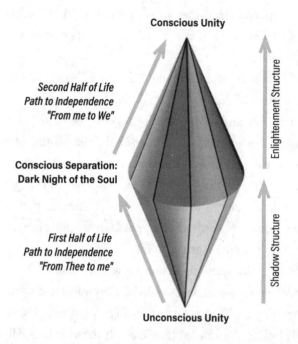

Conscious Unity

Second Half of Life
Path to Independence
"From me to We"

Conscious Separation:
Dark Night of the Soul

First Half of Life
Path to Independence
"From Thee to me"

Enlightenment Structure

Shadow Structure

Unconscious Unity

poor waitress an earful. I'm sure in Carl's mind, he was just helping them improve their ambiance. Ones can be demanding of others only because they hold themselves to even higher standards. As children, Ones often internalized the message to "Be a good boy or girl," which their young minds translated as: "Don't you dare mess up or make a mistake, or the world might just fall apart." Talk about a heavy burden for little shoulders!

The psychological umbilical cord of the One was cut by anger at feeling criticized or condemned in childhood, especially around moral issues, which they directed inward at themselves for not being perfect. This Sacred Wound of internalized anger fuels their need to improve everything, giving rise to their motto: "Excellence in all." It also creates their greatest fear of being bad, defective, or corrupt, driving them to

TAMING YOUR MONEY MONSTER

be virtuous and principled in all they do. For a One, everything should be done "the right way"—and they're more than willing to show you exactly what that means.

Now, here's where it gets interesting. This fear of being bad creates their greatest vice of anger, which is not the same as their Sacred Wound of internalized anger. Their vice of anger is their motivator, keeping them from becoming the "bad" person they fear. Think of it as their inner drill sergeant, always on duty to maintain ship-shape behavior. But here's the kicker—they're so wary of this "bad" anger that they'll go to great lengths to avoid triggering it through perfectionistic behavior. In other words, they try not to let anything happen that will send their inner drill instructor into a rage.

And what happens when perfection proves impossible? Their primary ego addiction to resentment sneaks in. They might find themselves thinking, *Why can't everyone just get their act together?* while simultaneously feeling frustrated at their inability to single-handedly fix themselves and the universe.

In essence, Type Ones smolder with repressed anger and resentment, all in the noble pursuit of being "good." It's a challenging path, but it leads to an interesting life.

When their resentment explodes, Ones often shift gears to their secondary ego addiction: melancholy. This creates deep sorrow and serves as their emotional fire extinguisher. When the flames of resentment threaten to consume their carefully constructed facade of perfection, or after they've reached their limit, their ego stress response is to douse themselves in sorrow. It's their temporary escape from the confines of their own rigid standards, allowing them a moment of self-indulgence.

In essence, they're borrowing a Custom Car from Type Four.

The formula for this process looks like this:

Anger (greatest vice/passion) + Melancholy (secondary ego
addiction/stress point) = Sorrow (ego stress response)

So, when you see a Type One suddenly waxing poetic about the sorry state of the world instead of trying to fix it, you'll know what's up. They're not just feeling blue; they're taking a vacation in the land of the Fours, where moody self-indulgence is the national pastime and sighing is an Olympic sport. It's their way of saying, "I'm not angry, I'm just . . . disappointed."

As unpleasant as it sounds, melancholy is the best short-term antidote to their resentment. If they can't allow themselves some idiosyncratic and self-indulgent behavior, their resentment could become so intense that they grievously damage themselves or others. However, they don't become a Four; they only look like one until their resentment abates, when they can return to their primary ego addiction. At their healthiest, Ones discover inner peace and embody true serenity. They learn to express genuine gratitude for life's blessings, imperfections and all. It's a beautiful transformation to witness, as they move from rigid perfectionism to a more balanced and accepting view of the world.

Type One Money Monsters

The Prude: Money-Avoidant

Because Type Ones have a compulsive need to be perfect in everything they do, if they can't be good at something, they'd rather not deal with it. But like it or not, we must deal with money, which puts the money-avoidant Type One in an awkward situation. They have to justify their avoidance as something inherently good, or they will feel flawed and imperfect. Without a philosophical framework to rationalize their behavior, every time they open their wallet, a Type One will be triggered by their fear of being bad or defective.

So what's a Type One to do? Simple: Turn money into the villain in their morality play. These folks transform their financial fumbling into a virtue, painting money as the root of all evil. Suddenly, their inability to handle a 401(k) becomes a badge of honor. Their avoidant behavior is the "perfect" way to relate to something inherently awful. It's a brilliant but perverse twist of moral logic.

Unfortunately, the avoidant Type One can demonize those of us who have a healthy relationship with money. Hence, I call this money monster the Prude. To maintain their sense of virtue, the Prude projects their anger and resentment onto money and economic systems rather than confronting a personal flaw. Their "cheaply" acquired moral superiority lets them look down on others with their virtue intact.

As mentioned earlier, I knew a monk who took pride in the fact that he never touched money or credit cards. Ironically, that forced everyone around him to work harder and deal with money more often to care for him. However, his "virtue" was spotless, regardless of his prudish behavior's impact on others.

Instead of learning to use cash like a superhero's tool for good, Ones treat it like kryptonite. This attitude might keep them safe from the temptations of wealth, but it also keeps them broke and powerless. So, a Prude sits on their moral high horse, looking down on those trying to make a difference with their dirty, dirty money.

Remember, Ones, it's okay to be imperfect with money. In fact, learning to navigate finances with grace and purpose could be your next big self-improvement project. Who knows? You might find that mindfully managing money is another way to bring more order and goodness into the world. And isn't that what you've been aiming for all along?

Traits of the Prude

Abundance Allergy: They treat abundance like it's radioactive. These folks break out in hives at the mere thought of having more than they "need." God forbid they enjoy their success—that might lead to dancing, and we all know where *that* leads. A patient, understanding therapist can help them see that a spa day won't lead to eternal damnation.

Financial Fundamentalist Syndrome: These folks have more unbreakable financial rules than a regulatory handbook. While having principles is admirable, being too rigid can lead to missed opportunities and unnecessary stress. Perhaps it's time to experience the concept of "financial yoga"—learning to bend a little before breaking. They might try having a "Flexible Finance Friday" once a month, where they intentionally (and safely) break one or two financial rules. This doesn't mean running up a credit card, but maybe having an impromptu date night. It's not financial anarchy; it's learning to breathe.

Voluntary Vow of Poverty Complex: Some Prudes turn frugality into an extreme sport, believing that if they're not financially suffering, they're sinning. While being mindful of spending is great, this self-imposed austerity can lead to an aversion to earning, spending, or investing, even when appropriate. How about budgeting for a small "joy fund" each month? It's not frivolous; it's financial self-care. Your inner miser might grumble, but your overall well-being will thank you.

The Fiscal Pharisee Phenomenon: Our Prude friends can sometimes appoint themselves as the financial morality police, ready to condemn others for enjoying their money. They'd give Jesus tips on how to judge the money changers. Instead of criticizing, try this: When you feel the urge to critique someone's spending, write that thought down, then find one positive aspect of their financial choice. It's like mindfulness practice for financial tolerance.

Financial Perfectionism Paralysis: Some money-avoidant Ones are so concerned about making the perfect financial move that they often make no move at all. They're like deer caught in the headlights, frozen by the fear of making mistakes. Here's a gentle suggestion: Try embracing the "perfectly imperfect" approach to finance. Start small—maybe make one financial decision each week within a five-minute time frame. No overthinking allowed. Remember, sometimes *done* is better than *perfect!*

Compulsive Donation Syndrome: While generosity is beautiful, some Prudes might give away their last penny to prove they're not attached to money, only to find themselves in a bind later. How about creating a structured giving plan? Allocate a specific percentage of income for donations each month. It's not being stingy; it's sustainable generosity or simply tithing.

Remember, dear Prudes: Money doesn't make you bad, but being a sanctimonious pain in the wallet just might. It's how you use it that matters. Developing a healthier relationship with finances doesn't mean compromising your values—it means aligning your resources with your principles to create positive change in the world.

The Pious: Money-Anxious

When a Type One becomes anxious about money, their perfectionism kicks into overdrive, making them incredibly diligent and, well, a tad controlling. The Pious isn't just good with money—they're exceptionally, meticulously, perhaps overwhelmingly excellent at it.

On the flip side, these folks are often at the mercy of their inner critic, who provides a nonstop commentary of self-judgmental thoughts, resentments, and critiques about their finances. Both exacting and impatient, they make stellar accountants and CFOs. But beware—force them to deviate from their carefully crafted budget, and you might find yourself receiving a fire-and-brimstone sermon.

While the Pious are often in excellent financial shape, they sometimes struggle to find joy or satisfaction in their fiscal prowess. They become so focused on doing everything "right" that they may miss out on the simple pleasures of financial well-being. In their world, money doesn't just talk—it lectures, critiques, and occasionally gives a TED Talk on fiscal responsibility.

Living with a Pious isn't easy because they will likely refuse to compromise their irrationally high accountability standards in moments when love, compassion, and common sense suggest a gentler approach. At their worst, this level of fixation on perfection creates a money monster that can alienate loved ones, destroy friendships, and ruin marriages.

I once worked at a company where the business manager was a Pious Type One, and he'd reject expense forms if the staple wasn't in the right spot. I once filled out the same form three times for a measly $7.50.

This anxiety exists to protect the Pious from their greatest fear: being bad. Since they think money is good, any mistakes they make with it are not just bad but make them bad people. And other folks who are bad with money are also bad people. In their world, a missed bill isn't just a mistake—it's a moral failure.

If you find yourself living or working with the Pious, remember: Their money behavior isn't just about the bottom line; it's about being good. With patience and understanding, you might help them see that true financial wisdom includes balance and flexibility. Just don't expect miracles overnight.

Traits of the Pious

Perfection Paranoia: These folks balance their checkbook like they're crossing Niagara Falls on a tightrope. They worry incessantly about making mistakes or falling short of their own high standards. For a fix, set up a "Mistake Jar." Every time you catch yourself obsessing over a tiny financial error, drop in a dollar or IOU or transfer a few bucks to a savings account. Use the accumulated funds for a guilt-free treat. It's like training yourself to associate mistakes with rewards—take that, Pavlov!

Control-Freak Fever: They guard their money with the intensity of a squirrel guarding its last acorn in winter. These folks often feel it's their moral duty to police everyone else's wallets too. Your spending habits become their personal crusade. Family budgeting or boardroom meetings are 10 percent discussion and 90 percent Spanish Inquisition. For a hack, try instituting a monthly "Financial Free-for-All" day. Let your partner or kids make a financial decision without your input. Start small—maybe they choose where to order takeout. Baby steps.

Fiscal Flogging: These folks whip themselves for making money mistakes. To counter this, it's time to embrace the "good-enough" philosophy. Aim for 95 percent perfection and celebrate when you hit 80 percent, or when you stop all the self-mortification. Or maybe create a "Financial Forgiveness" ritual. Write down your money mistakes on a piece of paper, then dramatically burn it.

Keeping Up with the Loans-es: The Pious are constantly peeking over the fence at the neighbor's financial grass, convinced it's greener and better fertilized. Sometimes it's just Astroturf financed at 29.99 percent APR. Comparison fuels their anxiety and sense of inadequacy, exacerbating their resentment. Here's a radical idea: Start a gratitude journal. Every time you catch yourself comparing your own finances to someone else's, write down something about your finances you're grateful for.

Killjoy Accounting: These folks are so busy being responsible that they forget that money *can* actually buy happiness—it's called ice cream. Try using your abundance to bring more joy to your life and those you love. It can be a beautiful spiritual practice. Allocate a small "Fun Fund" in your budget. Use it for something purely enjoyable, no practical justification needed. Your loved ones will thank you.

Budget Obsession Disorder: These accountants' budgets have more categories than an Amazon drop-down menu. It might be time to simplify. Try consolidating categories or even budgeting for spontaneity. It might feel uncomfortable at first, but it could bring some much-needed flexibility to your financial plan.

Coupon Crusader Complex: They're convinced financial ruin lurks behind every unclipped coupon or unnegotiated bill. They'll drive fifty miles to save a nickel on gas, convinced they're financial geniuses. While being frugal is great, it's important to consider the value of your time too. Before driving across town for a deal, ask yourself: "Is this worth it?" Calculate your hourly rate and see if the savings justify the effort. You might find you're better off staying home and binge-watching financial videos on YouTube.

Monetary Messiah Complex: The Pious can preach the gospel of fiscal responsibility with more zeal than a televangelist. Each week, try confessing to someone a financial mistake and the lesson you learned. It's a great way to stay humble and connect with others over shared experiences.

Remember, money is a tool to help us live our best lives, not a measure of our intrinsic worth. Balancing responsibility with flexibility and joy can lead to a healthier, more fulfilling relationship with finances.

A Money Master—The Poised

Picture our Type One friends cruising down the highway of life in their meticulously maintained ego-mobile carrying suitcases stuffed with resentment and sorrow. Life, in its infinite wisdom (and occasional mischief), will eventually lead them into the Dark Night of the Soul. It's not a fun destination, but trust me, the spiritual Wi-Fi there is incredible.

In this place of radical vulnerability, they're forced to face their inner Hulk and admit their imperfection. But welcoming imperfection can offer a new experience of goodness, because the most beautiful music often comes from improvisation and the occasional wrong note.

If they allow themselves to break open, they discover a profound truth. They realize they don't need to earn love (or money) through perfection. The Divine, in its infinite compassion, already sees Ones as perfect. It's a bit like a parent smiling at a child's wobbly first steps—the imperfection is part of the beauty.

As they embrace this truth, they can cultivate gratitude, which is their primary recovery virtue.[1] The language of gratitude is the appreciation for life as it is, not as they think it should be. A gentle stream of gratitude can slowly erode mountains of resentment, helping them count their blessings rather than counting others' faults.

By shifting gears from resentment to gratitude, their ego stress takes a backseat because they aren't living their life out of so much anger. They can feel more connected to everyone and everything. Without the stress of anger and resentment holding them back, they have easier access to their secondary recovery virtue, which is mindfulness. With this shift, they start to experience life more like a Type Seven on vacation—present, joyful, and open to adventure.[2] It's like trading in their BMW for a sporty SUV that can better handle the off-road detours in their financial life.

Mindfulness in the present moment, free of efforts to fix things in the future or worry about mistakes in the past, when combined with gratitude, produces the highest virtue for a Type One—serenity.

Their secret formula is:

Gratitude (primary recovery virtue) + Mindfulness (secondary recovery virtue/relaxation point) = Serenity (greatest virtue/virtue)

Serenity is like yoga for the soul, stretching them out of their rigid financial posture into a more flexible money mindset to become the Poised.

True serenity arises from detaching from ego-driven desires and realizing that the world is impermanent and subject to constant change. This is perfection in motion. It involves a profound acceptance of the present moment and surrendering to the flow of life, trusting that everything is unfolding according to Divine Perfection, not how uptight Ones think the world should be run.

Through breaking open their egos in the Dark Night of the Soul, healthy Ones finally see the Divine Perfection inside themselves—a perfection that includes all their mistakes—and recognize this same perfection flowing through all of existence. Seeing the world through this new lens, in loving, conscious unity with all, transforms how they view life's struggles. Their Sacred Gift of Divine Perfection helps them see that everything belongs and has value, exactly as it is. Like master artists appreciating both light and shadow, they help others recognize the inherent worth in all things—even life's messy, imperfect moments. Where others see chaos, they perceive a deeper order, revealing the sacred worth in everything from pocket change to grand endeavors. They stand calmly poised in life's beautiful complexity, showing us that true perfection includes our flaws and the struggle to overcome them. From this place of acceptance, they can use their problem-solving expertise, wealth, and resources to make the world a little bit better—not from anger, resentment, judgment, or melancholy, but from love, acceptance, and compassion.

For those anxious about money, arriving at serenity is about gently loosening their grip on control. For those who avoid money, it's about approaching money with curiosity rather than fear and striving for more abundance and wealth. In both cases, it's about finding a harmonious balance in their finances, making peace with the ebb and flow of their financial life.

A wise and accomplished Improver told me that he prays for one humiliation each day, some small or large embarrassment, so that he can learn to laugh at himself and see the Divine Perfection even in his stupidity. After all, our imperfections keep us humble.

However, Ones should be careful not to fall through the trapdoor of their faux virtue: honesty. Too much honesty for Ones is like a get-out-of-jail-free card for their inner critic. "I'm not judging, I'm just providing necessary feedback!" they insist, as everyone around them suddenly develops an urgent need to be anywhere else.

Becoming a Money Master—The Poised

Please be sure to read (or review) the chapter 8 overview of these five steps before you get started here.

Acknowledge the pain from your Childhood Wounding.

For you Type Ones, this step is like opening a box of memories more organized than Marie Kondo's closet, but far less joyful. It's time to confront the demons of your past that turned you into the walking, talking embodiment of a rule book.

Picture little you, trying to color inside the lines of life, only to have every tiny mistake magnified like it's being examined by the world's most judgmental microscope. Maybe you had parents who treated your report card like it was a referendum on their parenting skills. "An A-minus? Why not an A-plus? Are you even trying?"

Or perhaps you were the "good child" in a chaotic family, thinking if you could just be perfect enough, you'd fix everything. Spoiler alert: You couldn't, but I bet you're still trying.

Some of you grew up with a constant chorus of "Why can't you be more like . . . ?" ringing in your ears. Nothing like a little comparison to fuel that internalized anger, right? And let's not forget about those moral or religious purity codes that made you feel like every tiny mistake was going to bring the wrath of the heavens upon your head.

You probably got praised for being "good" and responsible. But instead of feeling proud, you internalized the pressure, and your trophy got heavier every day. Now, I know you'd rather alphabetize your spice rack than delve into these messy emotions, but trust me, it's necessary.

I know you love organization—put this skill to use in making your trauma timeline (see chapter 8). Use a whiteboard or spreadsheet to map out those moments when you felt that crushing weight of perfectionism, including around money. When did you first feel that your worth was tied to your behavior? Look for patterns. Maybe you'll notice that every time you made a mistake, you were met with disappointment instead of support. Or perhaps you'll see how often you sacrificed your own needs to maintain the image of the "perfect" child.

My client Olivia grew up in a household where money was in short supply. As the eldest child of a large family, she had to set a good example for her siblings and bear the responsibility of helping raise them. She spent her entire childhood convinced by her parents that she would end up living in a van down by the river if she splurged on an outfit that didn't come from a thrift shop. But through some good old-fashioned detective work (and a few therapy sessions), she was able to trace that money anxiety back to her parents' issues, not her own inherent failings. Just because she grew up in scarcity and a hypercritical environment didn't mean she had to live in that fear and pinch pennies forever.

Remember, confronting trauma isn't about blaming anyone. It's about understanding how these experiences shaped your relationship with yourself, others, and yes, money. Be gentle with yourself as you do this. You're not judging your past self but seeking to understand and heal.

As you assemble your "fellowship" of helpers, just make sure they're not enablers of your perfectionism. You need allies who can lovingly point out when you're being too hard on yourself.

Once you've assembled your team and created your map, you're ready to step out of your comfort zone and into new psychological territory. It's time to leave the land of "shoulds" and "musts" and start your adventure toward financial mastery. And who knows? You might even learn to appreciate a little chaos along the way. Just a little, though. Let's not get too crazy.

Stop reacting out of the anger that created your money monsters.

To overcome the anger that birthed your money monsters, a daily practice of contemplation and compassion will be useful. Think of it as polishing your psyche to a mirror shine. Just like you wouldn't expect a spotless house after one swipe of the duster, don't expect to conquer your ego addictions overnight.

Contemplation for Ones is about shining a spotlight on those ego addictions that are wreaking havoc in your life. It's like being your own financial auditor, but instead of tracking down every penny, you're uncovering the ways you sabotage yourself with unrealistic standards. Set aside time each day for quiet reflection. This could be traditional meditation, a contemplative walk, or even journaling. The key is consistency—and Ones excel at that.

One practice that might appeal to your detail-oriented nature is a "perfection inventory." Get a large whiteboard or a stack of paper and start listing out all the ways you think you *should* be perfect in life and with money. Then, next to each item, write down the reality of the situation. This exercise can help you see the gap between your ideals and reality, and maybe even find some humor in your impossibly high standards.

As you begin your practice, focus on your primary ego addiction: resentment. Get curious about it. What purpose has it served? How is it both helping and hindering you? Remember, this addiction developed as a survival strategy. It's not the enemy—just the best your childhood self could manage without any training or tools.

Don't forget your secondary ego addiction to melancholy—and the sorrow it produces. Notice when it shows up and what triggers it. It's the understudy to your resentment, ready to take center stage when your critical inner voice gets too exhausted from all that resenting.

One powerful technique is the "self-forgiveness ritual." Light a candle, play some soothing music, and write yourself a letter acknowledging the money pain you've carried. Validate the frustration, anger, and endless striving for perfection—and then consciously choose to let it all go. Tear up the letter, bury it, or burn it. The act of physically releasing those feelings can be freeing.

Once you've identified these patterns, it's time to start cultivating your core virtues: gratitude and mindfulness. These are your primary and secondary paths of recovery that lead to your highest virtue of serenity. Think of them as spiritual muscles you need to strengthen. How can you incorporate them into your daily life?

Consider starting and ending your day with this prayer for serenity:

Divine Perfection, open my heart to your flawless love and soothe the restless anger within my heart. Grant me the strength to embrace gratitude and mindfulness, trusting in your infinite grace. Help me to release my addictions to resentment and melancholy so that I may use my gifts to serve and love you with steadfast serenity through those around me.

Don't forget the crucial step of cultivating compassion for yourself and the people who raised you. And when you begin to integrate new habits into your routine, give yourself a lot of grace. It's going to take time to learn to live comfortably with imperfection.

Learn to be less anxious or avoidant about money by confronting your money monsters.

To take things up a notch and to make this transformation a practical reality with your money, we're going to get up close and personal with your Prude and Pious mindsets by making a detailed "Money Monster to Money Master" transformation chart. (You can find examples on my website at douglynam.com.) How do prudishness and piety show up in your earning, saving, investing, and giving habits right now? The trauma timeline you created is about your past; your money monster chart is about the present. Identifying these places will form a minefield map of your financial world, with every coordinate triple-checked so you know where not to tread.

Take a good, hard look at how these mindsets play out in each area. Some surprising contrasts may appear. For example, you might catch yourself in constant Prude mode when it comes to spending— always judging every purchase as either morally pure or tainted. But when it comes to investing, you're more of a Pious, obsessively checking your portfolio with the dedication of a monk at prayer.

Or perhaps you're a master at earning and following the rules, but when it comes to actually enjoying your money? You can't even imagine it.

Now, here's where it gets exciting (in a perfectly controlled way, of course). Once you've mapped out your money monster traits in each category of earning, saving, and investing, it's time to pair each trait with its countermove or opposite action step. What practical things can you do to overcome each of them? Use the suggestions in this chapter to jump-start your ideas. Make it colorful (but tastefully so), make it bold (within reason)—heck, make it so impeccably designed that you can't help but look at it every day and think, *Now* that's *what financial perfection looks like.*

Go meticulously wild with this. Surround yourself with these reminders of your journey to money mastery, complete with practical action steps that would make a project manager weep with joy.

Remember, becoming a money master isn't about dampening your natural drive for improvement—it's about channeling it into financial fulfillment. We're not trying to turn you into a sloppy spender, but into a financially poised paragon of real virtue.

Try this exercise as well: Write a letter to money as if it were a person. What would you say? How has your relationship been? Be honest about your fears, your resentments, your expectations. Then, write a response from money to you. What might it say if it could speak?

So take a deep breath, channel the best of your Type One energy, and get ready to turn those money monsters into your greatest allies on this perfectly plotted financial quest. Who knows? Budgeting might just become your new form of meditation, bringing you one step closer to that elusive state of financial serenity.

Build a strong financial life by earning, saving, and investing ethically.

Okay, Type Ones, let's put that incredible work ethic of yours to good use! You're the Energizer Bunny of productivity but with better posture and a stronger moral compass.

When it comes to earning, your attention to detail and high standards can be a real asset. You might excel in careers that require precision and integrity, like accounting (where your love for perfectly balanced books can shine), quality control (where your eagle eye for imperfections is celebrated), or ethical consulting (where your strong moral compass can guide others). Your ability to spot inefficiencies and improve systems could make you an excellent process-improvement specialist or operations manager. You can be the superhero who fights inefficiency and moral ambiguity.

For saving, your natural inclination toward discipline is another superpower. You're like a financial Boy Scout—always prepared. Set up automatic transfers to your savings account, but also allow for some flexibility. Maybe create an I'm-Only-Human Fund—a small amount set aside each month that you're allowed to spend on anything, even if it's not "perfect."

When it comes to investing, your thorough nature can be a great asset. You're likely to do extensive research before making investment decisions, which can lead to wise choices. You're like a financial detective, leaving no stone unturned. Consider ethical investing that aligns with your values—this can help you feel good about where your money is going. Remember, no investment is perfect, and that's okay.

Here's a challenge for you: Make one financial decision this week without overthinking it. Maybe it's buying a stock you've been eyeing, or saying yes to a slightly pricier but much nicer piece of clothing. The world won't end if it's not the absolute perfect choice, I promise. Think of it as financial skydiving—scary, but exhilarating!

Your gift for precision and attention to detail is like having a financial superpower—use it wisely as you craft your financial plan. This natural talent for spotting what needs refinement, combined with your capacity for disciplined action, makes you uniquely suited for building lasting wealth. Where others see a boring budget spreadsheet, you see a masterpiece waiting to be perfected.

Use your money and talents as tools to love and serve a suffering world.

This is where you can really shine, Type Ones. Your desire to improve the world can now be backed by financial resources. It's like being Batman, but instead of cool gadgets, you've got a heart of gold and a perfectly balanced checkbook.

Your superpower is your ability to see how things could be better and your drive to make it happen. You have a keen eye for spotting inefficiencies and stupidity, and the determination to address them. This makes you excellent at identifying causes that need support and finding effective ways to help.

Consider using your talents to help nonprofits streamline their processes, or to develop more efficient systems for delivering aid. Your attention to detail could be invaluable in ensuring that charitable funds are used effectively and ethically.

Remember, Divine Perfection eternally resides inside you and all things. As Richard Rohr discusses in his book *The Wisdom Pattern*, the perennial cycle of the world is the movement from order to disorder and then to reorder.[3] Everything moves through this cycle, and your gift is to help facilitate the transition from disorder to reorder, improving things a little bit in the process. This is part of the Divine Perfection you are called to facilitate with serene loving-kindness, with the understanding that perfection always lies in the present moment, in the mess, and to not judge it with anger or resentment, or to wallow in sorrow. The disorder is all part of the perfection!

Prudence's Story

Prudence wasn't just organized; she was a label maker with legs. Her life was meticulously arranged, managed, and maintained. Her parents had hammered home the importance of being "good" with the subtlety of a sledgehammer, leaving Prudence with the unshakable belief that one misstep would be catastrophic.

This Childhood Wounding cut her psychological umbilical cord with a Sacred Wound of internalized anger. Prudence was quietly angry at herself for never quite hitting the bull's-eye of perfection and silently seething at a world that seemed hell-bent on chaos. This anger, carefully concealed behind a mask of prim propriety, fueled her greatest fear: being bad or defective.

To keep this fear at bay, Prudence developed her worst vice: anger. She was angry at others for their apparent lack of standards, but mostly at herself for never quite measuring up. But anger is a "bad" emotion to feel, so she worked hard to avoid triggering her anger by compulsively trying to improve everything and everyone around her.

But reality is a harsh mistress. When things didn't go according to her plans, she covered her anger with her primary ego addiction to resentment, which justified her anger and made her feel virtuous when she criticized herself or others.

When it came to money, Prudence was the Pious on steroids. She tracked every penny. Suggesting an unplanned purchase was like proposing a dance party in a library—it just wasn't done.

At work, Prudence's perfectionism was cranked up to eleven. She critiqued her colleagues' emails, reorganized the company filing system without being asked to do so, and once spent an afternoon adjusting everyone's desk chairs to "optimal ergonomic height." Her coworkers avoided her.

When her resentment at all the problems around her piled up, she found herself in melancholy funks, lamenting the pitiful state of the world, wondering how any Divine plan could allow such a mess.

When the company faced downsizing, Prudence was certain her impeccable work would save her. But her boss, exhausted from

Prudence's constant nitpicking and complaints about others' subpar work, decided that team morale would improve significantly in her absence. Prudence was the first to go, her severance package handed to her in a folder she immediately noticed was slightly askew.

As if unemployment wasn't enough of a kick in the teeth, Prudence's long-term boyfriend decided he couldn't handle her "intensity" and left her for a free-spirited yoga instructor. Then Prudence discovered her identity had been stolen, temporarily tanking her credit score. Her meticulously crafted financial fortress didn't just crumble; it exploded.

Prudence spiraled into her Dark Night of the Soul. As her savings dwindled and her life disintegrated, she found herself face-to-face with her deepest fears. She felt like a failure, a bad person who couldn't keep a job or maintain a relationship. Her resentment reached toxic levels, poisoning her self-esteem and what few relationships she had left.

In her desperation, Prudence unconsciously turned once again to her secondary ego addiction: melancholy. She didn't just wallow in self-pity; she swan-dived into a pool of sorrow, convinced the universe had a personal vendetta against her.

During this pity party she hit rock bottom. She found herself sitting on the floor of her half-empty apartment, surrounded by self-help books, eating peanut butter straight from the jar with her last clean spoon.

But as Prudence sat there, mascara streaking her face, something inside her snapped, and she allowed herself to begin to examine the ways she was creating her own suffering. It was as if the universe had finally managed to knock some sense into her with a cosmic two-by-four.

Slowly, Prudence began to practice gratitude, her primary path of recovery. At first, it felt as awkward as wearing shoes on the wrong feet, but slowly, she began to appreciate the small things: a sunny day, a kind word from a friend, the fact that she could still afford instant ramen.

As she cultivated gratitude, Prudence naturally became more mindful, her secondary path of recovery. She started to notice the present moment instead of fretting about the future or berating herself about the past.

Over time, with many fits and starts, and a few more trips into the Dark Night, this combination of gratitude and mindfulness led Prudence to her highest virtue: serenity. She began to accept things as they were, imperfections and all. Her budget became a guideline rather than a torture device. She even allowed herself to buy brand-name cereal once in a while.

As Prudence embraced serenity, she discovered her Sacred Gift of Divine Perfection. She realized that true perfection isn't about flawlessness, but about wholeness. Everything, including her mistakes and struggles, was part of a perfect whole.

With this new perspective, Prudence rebuilt her financial life. She landed a job at a cutting-edge tech company developing AI-assisted diagnostic tools for oncologists. Her attention to detail and drive for improvement was now invaluable in fine-tuning algorithms that could mean the difference between life and death for cancer patients. But she learned to harness that superpower without anger, judgment, or resentment toward herself or her colleagues.

Prudence's journey from the Pious to the Poised wasn't smooth or easy. There were plenty of bumps, detours, and the occasional U-turn. But in the end, she learned that true mastery, financial or otherwise, isn't about creating the perfect plan and flawlessly executing it. It's about finding serenity in the face of life's inherent messiness and using one's talents to create positive change in the world.

Most importantly, she fulfilled her greatest hope: to experience her complete goodness. She was finally able to feel her perfection as a beloved child of God who is seen and loved unconditionally.

CHAPTER TEN

TYPE TWO—THE HELPER (AMBULANCE)

HOW TO STOP BUYING EVERYONE'S LOVE AND START SAVING FOR YOUR OWN DANG SELF

Type Twos are often called the Helper (I call them the Ambulance of egos) because they love to rescue those in distress and always seek ways to be of service. They're like a warm hug wrapped in a friendly smile, with a side of "Can I get you anything?" They tend to be kind and charming and deeply attuned to the emotions of others.

They are also chronic people-pleasers who engage in complex emotional games to get their needs met. These seemingly selfless saints are actually running a covert emotional operation. They're not just giving freely; they're giving to get love.

Somewhere along the way, their psychological umbilical cord got snipped by a hefty dose of sadness through neglect, rejection, or straight-up abandonment. They externalize that sadness and feel profound grief or shame about how they think others perceive them. That insecurity creates their deepest fear that they are unlovable, and to assuage that fear, they work hard to get others to like them.

Type Two Ego Map: The Helper or Ambulance

(Read the chart from the bottom up.)

ENLIGHTENMENT STRUCTURE

MONEY MASTER	THE BELOVED
Sacred Gift (Holy Idea)	Divine Love
Greatest Hope (Basic Desire)	To feel unconditionally loved
Greatest Virtue (Virtue)	Humility Honesty + Joy = Humility (cure for Pride)
Secondary Recovery Virtue (Relaxation Point)	Joy (Primary Recovery Virtue for Type 4)
Primary Recovery Virtue	Honesty
Faux Virtue	Generosity

SHADOW STRUCTURE

MONEY MONSTERS: AVOIDANT / ANXIOUS	THE BLEEDER / THE BONDER
Ego Stress Response	Revenge Pride + Vengeance = Revenge (blocks Flattery)
Secondary Ego Addiction (Stress Point)	Vengeance (Primary Ego Addiction for Type 8)
Primary Ego Addiction (Ego Fixation)	Flattery
Greatest Vice (Passion)	Pride
Greatest Fear (Basic Fear)	Being unlovable
Sacred Wound	Externalized Sadness

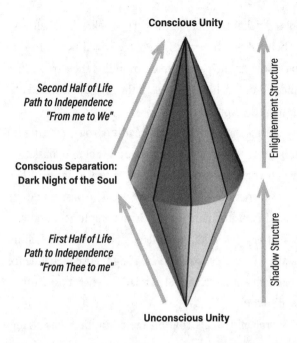

Conscious Unity

*Second Half of Life
Path to Independence
"From me to We"*

**Conscious Separation:
Dark Night of the Soul**

*First Half of Life
Path to Independence
"From Thee to me"*

Enlightenment Structure

Shadow Structure

Unconscious Unity

Unfortunately, this longing to be appreciated and seen makes them prone to codependence, and sometimes they can be intrusively "helpful." Twos thrive on the constant flood of positive emotions from the gratitude their generosity produces. Rather than teaching a hungry person how to fish, they'd sometimes prefer to give someone a fish daily, complete with a side of tartar sauce and a "You're amazing!" note.

While Twos instinctively see the needs and emotions of others, they often struggle to acknowledge their own needs or directly ask for what they want. Because they often deny their own desires, they can run themselves into the ground through endless acts of service in their relentless attempt to earn love.

To prevent their greatest fear of being unlovable from becoming a concrete reality, Twos embrace their worst vice: pride. They take pride in what a good and delightful person they are—look at how selflessly and nobly they behave! But this pride is a double-edged sword. In Type Twos' quest to be seen as the paradigm of lovability, their true center of being becomes obscured, hidden beneath the carefully curated persona they present to the world.

Accurately seeing their pride would be disastrous, making the Two feel bad about themselves and, therefore, unlovable. To mask their pride, they develop a primary ego addiction to flattery to ensure others validate them. It's a complex form of seduction. The best way to get someone to compliment and care for you is to compliment and care for them first. Flattery gives the Two a feel-good rush while helping them appear selfless and altruistic and creating their codependence. The Two is dependent on the stream of accolades they get from others and can't live without it.

The dirty secret of Twos is that all their kindness has strings attached. If you don't reciprocate their kindness as expected, beware! Hell hath no fury like a Two scorned.

When their flattery stops working effectively or they overdose on it, they don't receive the love and attention coming back to them that they think they deserve, and they fall back to their secondary ego addiction: vengeance. By embracing vengeance, the Two becomes aggressive and assertive about demanding what they want. It's like watching a cuddly teddy bear suddenly grow claws and fangs.

When Twos aren't honest about their needs and have overextended themselves to help others who don't give back the way a Two expects, they trade their Ambulance in for a Hummer. Vengeance is the primary ego addiction for Type Eight, and combining it with the Two's worst vice of pride can turn them into an apocalyptic destruction machine.[1] A Type Two will not only feel justified in their revenge, but they'll also be convinced the punishment is for your own good. It's like they're saying, "I'm going to teach you a lesson about appreciating my kindness, and you're going to thank me for it later!"

However, their means of revenge might not be obvious. They might suddenly become ill to demand attention, gossip behind your back, pick a fight, or send you on a guilt trip—regardless, you are going to suffer.

As frightening as the vengeance of a Two can be, it temporarily blocks their ego addiction to flattery and prevents them from further overextending themselves for others, forcing them to examine their own needs, however unhealthy their methodology.

The formula for this transformation is:

Pride (greatest vice/passion) + Vengeance (secondary ego addiction/stress point) = Revenge (ego stress response)

When healthy, Twos embody a deep humility that isn't afraid to ask forthrightly for what they need and honestly accept the help and love they deserve. At their best, they help others without any expectations or strings attached to their generosity and learn to love unconditionally. But first, they must learn that they are loved unconditionally as a beloved child of the God of their understanding, which is the only cure for their constant need for approval from others.

Despite their complexities and struggles, Type Twos are remarkable individuals. Their capacity for love and compassion is unparalleled, and when Twos learn to direct that love inward as well as outward, they become a force for genuine good in the world.

Remember, if you're a Two, you're already worthy of love—no strings attached. Your value isn't measured by how much you give or how many people you help. You're lovable just as you are because you're a fractal piece of the Divine.

Money Monsters

The Bleeder: Money-Avoidant

The Bleeder's deepest desire is to be loved and admired for their service. Bleeders tend to drain themselves dry by giving too much of their money or time away in service to others. They're like a financial hemophiliac with a paper-cut fetish. Warm, friendly, and self-sacrificing, they enjoy being indispensable and having others depend on them. They get an ego boost from helping others, often martyring themselves to feel cherished.

While appearing selfless, the Bleeder's generosity comes with strings attached to their deep desire to feel needed, which temporarily wards off their chronic fear of being unlovable or unwanted. At their worst, these strings become choke chains, creating bitterness and animosity in relationships.

A senior monk in my community, an unhealthy Type Two, collected wounded people, taking them under his care and helping them with all their problems. His inability to set healthy boundaries on his charity was one factor in the monastic community's bankruptcy. While his actions appeared altruistic and heroic, the more he gave, the more praise and adulation he craved. Any disruption to the influx of gratitude and affection made him quite angry.

Bleeders unconsciously think that money, time, and resources can buy the love they need to heal their emotional wounds. While charitable giving is one requirement to becoming a money master, giving comes *after* earning, saving, and investing. It's not the starting line. The Bleeder's excessive generosity can make it difficult to accumulate wealth.

Traits of the Bleeder

Love-for-Sale Syndrome: Bleeders can treat others like emotional vending machines. They shove dollars, gifts, or a five-course meal into people, hoping to get a hug in return. They're subconsciously trying to buy affection. While their generosity is admirable, true affection isn't bought. Here's a tip: Next time you feel the urge to splurge on a friend, offer to listen to them over a cup of coffee (that they buy). You might be surprised how much more valuable your presence is than your presents.

Self-Neglect Sabotage: Watch in awe as Bleeders magically make their financial needs disappear by not acknowledging them. Sound familiar? Maybe swallow that pride and call a financial planner instead. Or set up a "Me Fund"—a separate savings account that you pay into monthly as if it were a bill. Just as you wouldn't dream of skipping out on your rent, make regular deposits into this account. Or add to an IRA with a future view toward retirement. This isn't selfish; it's self-preservation.

Endless Enabling: Marvel at a Bleeder's ability to consistently bail out financially irresponsible friends and family with no expectation of changed behavior. If this is you, try to channel your inner tough-love guru. Offer to help these money-suckers create a budget. If they refuse, well, sometimes the most loving thing you can do is let people face the consequences of their actions. They won't change if they don't have to.

Altruism Addiction: Applaud as the Bleeders donate their last dollar to every cause that crosses their path. They're saving the world, one overdraft fee at a time. Who needs retirement savings when you've got a heart of gold and a wallet full of lint? Instead, try the "True Cost of

Giving" exercise. Each time you're about to make a generous financial gesture, pause and write down three numbers: the dollar amount, your current bank balance, and how much you need for your own basic needs and future security. Be radically honest—is this giving coming from a place of genuine abundance, or are you sacrificing your own stability to feel needed? If it's the latter, that's not generosity—it's financial self-sabotage dressed up as love.

Monetary Muzzling: These folks are quieter than a mime in a silent movie about their money issues and struggle to speak their truth, preferring to suffer like martyrs. Avoiding financial discussions won't make money issues disappear. It may help to practice financial assertiveness in front of a mirror. Start small: "I'd like to discuss our household budget." Work your way up to: "I think I deserve a raise." Remember, your needs are just as important as everyone else's. Treat discussing money like exposure therapy—the more you do it, the easier it gets.

The Self-Discounting Dilemma: These Bleeders undervalue their worth and the amazing gifts they have to offer the world, which can leave them broke. Lowballing the value of your services and talents is like putting yourself on permanent clearance. Remember, you're a limited edition—price accordingly. Look up the going rates for your skills and services. Then, the next time you're tempted to offer a discount, imagine me standing behind you with a bullhorn shouting, "You're worth every penny!" Because you are.

Retail Therapy Addiction: When burnout hits, Bleeders find themselves on shopping sprees that are misguided forms of pampering. Instead of maxing out their credit card, they should try maxing out on self-care that doesn't involve spending. How about finding a quiet corner with a cup of homemade tea and a gratitude journal? Create a list of free or low-cost activities that boost your mood. Maybe it's a nature walk, a bubble bath, or a chat with a friend. Next time you're tempted to shop away the blues, consult your list instead.

The Let-Go-and-Let-God Delusion: These folks avoid long-term financial planning, believing that if they take care of others now, the universe will magically take care of them in the future. Hint: God provides, but often through our own efforts. God won't work a miracle to solve a problem you have the power to fix. Remember, even the manna-receiving Israelites had to go out and gather it. Start with a basic retirement calculator to see what you need to save. Think of it as partnering with the Divine. You have a part to play.

Remember, dear Twos, taking care of your finances is a form of self-care. By nurturing your financial health, you'll be better equipped to help others in the long run.

The Bonder: Money-Anxious

Some of the most severe abuse I've witnessed has been perpetrated by wealthy but money-anxious Type Twos. Their deep-seated desire for love, when combined with financial resources and power, can transform them into a particularly destructive force. These individuals, whom I call Bonders, often initiate relationships by rescuing and supporting people through their struggles, but with hidden expectations.

The Bonder creates a situation where their target becomes financially and psychologically dependent on them, effectively binding their quarry into a form of indentured servitude. Once this dependency is established, the Bonder exploits their prey to serve their own emotional, physical, or sexual needs. Bonders can even manipulate their targets into gratifying the bonders' desires while convincing themselves they are helping their victim and acting from pure altruism. After everything they've sacrificed, why shouldn't they be repaid with a little gratitude?

Linda was a wealthy Type Two client who turned financial manipulation into an art form. She'd spot friends or family members struggling financially and swoop in like a fairy godmother with her checkbook. Starting with small expenses like car repairs, she'd escalate to larger "gifts" like paying for private school tuition.

The kicker? Linda would remind them of her generosity at every turn. "Oh, you can't make it to my birthday dinner? After everything I've done for you?" The tragic irony? Everyone walked on eggshells around her, grateful but resentful, trapped in a web of financial codependency that served neither them nor her.

True generosity comes without strings attached. So stay kind and stay generous, but for the love of all that's financially holy, my dear Twos, keep it clean and strings-free.

Traits of the Bonder

Cash-Stash Syndrome: These money-anxious folks work overtime to make money to give to their victims but hug their wallet tight everywhere else. "Oh no, what if I run out of cash and can't buy love anymore?" Instead of hoarding money for love-buying, create a "Love Fund" with a twist. Go ahead and set aside a portion of your income for spontaneous acts of kindness. Then take this challenge: Don't spend more than twenty dollars on any single act. This forces you to get creative with your giving. Bake cookies, write heartfelt notes, or offer your time and skills. You'll quickly realize that the most meaningful gestures often cost the least.

Where's-My-Parade Disorder: These Bonders give out money and gifts but get grumpy when people don't worship the ground they walk on. It's like, "Hey, I bought you a Christmas present, kid, now love me forever!" Instead of giving gifts that scream "Love me!" try giving anonymously. Leave an envelope of cash in a struggling coworker's desk drawer. Pay for the person behind you in the drive-thru. Donate to a GoFundMe without leaving your name. The secret joy of knowing you've helped someone without them knowing it was you can be far more satisfying than any parade. Plus, it's excellent karma.

Predatory Puppeteering: If you thought emotional codependency was fun, wait till you see financial codependency. These Bonders are like master puppeteers, using their money to pull everyone's strings. Instead of wielding money to control others, use it to empower them. If you want to help a friend start a business, consider investing in equity instead of just giving them money. This way, their success becomes your success. Or better yet, offer your skills and connections instead of your cash. Teaching someone to fish is always better than buying them a fish market.

The I-Wanna-Be-Mr.-Beast Complex: Instead of trying to out-donate everyone in exchange for admiration, focus on becoming a savvy philanthropist. Research charities thoroughly, looking for those with the highest impact per dollar donated. Then, when you make a donation, share the research that led to your choice rather than the amount you gave. "I chose this charity because 95 percent of donations go directly to the cause" sounds better than "Look at my big check!" Remember, it's not about the size of the donation, it's about the impact.

Self-Flagellation Fixation: Money-anxious Twos flaunt their self-sacrifices as a way of demanding love. They go without new clothes or three square meals, explaining things are tight, while they fund the dreams of others. Start investing in your own dreams. For every dollar you put toward someone else's goal, put a matching amount into your own dream fund. Want to learn to paint? Take a cooking class? Start your own business? Your dreams are just as valid as anyone else's.

Remember: Money can't buy happiness, but it sure can buy a whole lot of codependency! Maybe it's time for our dear Bonders to invest in something truly valuable—like a good therapist and a crash course in healthy boundaries.

A Money Master—The Beloved

Listen up, you beautiful, generous Type Two lovebugs, and grab your emotional first aid kits because we're about to dive deep into the heart of your helper syndrome.

You've been so caught up in proving your worth by helping others that you've hidden your True Self behind a mask of flattery and pride. It's like you've been starring in a one-person show called *Love Me, Please!* complete with jazz hands and a showstopping number about self-sacrifice. The love and affection you've earned through your masterful manipulations might have felt good in the moment, but deep down, you know it's all been a bit hollow.

Here's a truth bomb: Constant people-pleasing and ego-driven tendencies will drain you and toss you straight into the Dark Night of the Soul. It's like your emotional gas tank has run dry after years of filling everyone else's. And that's when your deepest fear of being unlovable rushes in to fill the void.

Realizing that you've rarely, if ever, been loved and accepted for who you truly are—that's a hard pill to swallow. But as painful as that realization may be, it's a necessary step toward healing and wholeness. If you can get real and break free of those ego addictions, you're on the path to enlightenment.

Now, let's talk about your primary path to recovery: honesty. I know, I know, you're thinking, *But Doug, I'm always honest!* Well, my friend, that flattery you've been dishing out? That's not honesty. That's manipulation wrapped in a compliment sandwich. It's time to tell the truth—not just to others, but to yourself. What do you really think and feel about the people and situations you find yourself in? And can you communicate those thoughts with clarity and purpose? Most importantly, can you directly ask for what you want and don't want without all the pretense?

Now let's talk about joy—your secondary path of recovery. Joy for a Two is like water for a plant—essential for growth and vitality. But we're not talking about the fleeting happiness you get from helping others (although that's nice too). We're talking about the deep, soul-nourishing joy that comes from within.

It's time to trade in your Ambulance for a luxury Custom Car borrowed from your Type Four friends. Take that bad boy for a spin down the highway of self-expression.[2] Maybe you'll discover a passion for painting, or realize you've got a knack for competitive dog grooming. The key here is to focus on activities that feed your soul, not your need for external validation. It's about finding beauty and creativity within yourself, rather than constantly seeking it in the reactions of others. Think of it as emotional self-sufficiency—you're no longer dependent on others for your happiness.

As you practice honesty and cultivate joy, something magical happens. These two virtues combine to create your highest virtue: humility. But we're not talking about the self-deprecating, "shucks, it was nothing" kind of humility. We're talking about the quiet confidence that comes from truly knowing and accepting yourself. It's about telling it like it is and feeling good about it.

With humility, you no longer need to prove your worth through endless giving. You can set boundaries without feeling guilty. You can receive as well as give, knowing that you're worthy of love and care without manipulating others into meeting your needs. It's like discovering you've had superpowers all along, and those superpowers are about being authentically you.

Your spiritual practice is to find joy in the daily wonder of life and existence without giving or getting anything in exchange. When you integrate joy with honesty, your greatest virtue, humility, shines forth and cures that pesky pride. It's like finally taking off those uncomfortable shoes you've been wearing to impress others and realizing you can dance better barefoot.

Remember, your magic formula for growth is:

Honesty (primary recovery virtue) + Joy (secondary recovery virtue/relaxation point) = Humility (greatest virtue/virtue)

When living with integrity and in alignment with your highest virtue of humility, your Sacred Wound starts to heal, and your grief at feeling unlovable transforms into your Sacred Gift of Divine Love—a love that accepts others *unconditionally*, without expecting anything in return, giving freely and abundantly.

When you experience and offer Divine Love to others, nothing more is required. Divine Love isn't earned and doesn't demand anything from others. Instead, it stems from recognizing the inherent worth of every person—yourself included.

Just be careful of your faux virtue, generosity, which can spin you right back into the ego trap you're trying to escape.

When a Type Two masters the art of Divine Love, the floodgates of abundance and blessing start to flow. You become this Beloved figure, radiating authentic love and healing the world around you just by being present. It's like unlocking the cheat code to life—miracles start happening left and right. That's when you'll finally experience your greatest hope: to feel completely loved for who you truly are.

This is how you move from being a Bleeder or a Bonder to becoming the Beloved—a Two who loves unconditionally, including yourself.

You'll find that your financial decisions are no longer driven by a need to buy affection or secure relationships. Instead, you'll use your resources in a way that reflects your authentic self and values.

Remember, this journey isn't about becoming a different person. It's about becoming more authentically you. And let me tell you, the real you is pretty darn awesome—no flattery required.

Becoming a Money Master—The Beloved

Please be sure to read (or review) chapter 8, which provides an overview of these five steps, before you get started here.

Acknowledge the pain from your Childhood Wounding.

Okay, Twos, it's time to stop being a Bleeder or a Bonder and become the Beloved you were born to be by tending to your Childhood Wounds.

Many Twos report growing up in households where their worth seemed tied to their usefulness. "What a good helper you are!" might have been the highest praise they received, teaching them that love was conditioned on their ability to meet others' needs.

Some Twos might have had a parent who was emotionally needy or unstable, forcing them into a caretaker role at a young age. Imagine a little girl comforting her sobbing mother after her dad left, or a boy learning to tiptoe around his father's volatile moods and substance abuse. These kids learned that their own needs had to take a backseat to keep the family functioning.

In other cases, Twos might have grown up in large families where individual attention was scarce. They figured out that the best way to get noticed was to be helpful, to anticipate others' needs before they were even expressed.

The common thread in all these scenarios is a child who learns that their own needs and feelings are secondary—or even irrelevant—compared to those of others. They internalize the message that to be loved, they must be needed.

This is where the externalized sadness comes in. These little Twos start to feel embarrassed of their own needs and emotions, a pain that cuts their psychological umbilical cord. They begin to see themselves as unlovable and feel ashamed or sad about how they think others perceive them. Instead of feeling worthy of love just for being themselves, they feel they must earn it through constant giving and self-sacrifice.

It's like they're constantly auditioning for the role of Lovable Person, never quite believing they've landed the part. This externalized sadness and grief becomes the lens through which they view all their relationships, always questioning whether they're "good enough" to deserve love and connection.

Our adult Twos then enter the world with this emotional baggage, their psychological umbilical cord severed by the sharp knife of neglect and conditional love. They're like emotional tightrope walkers, constantly balancing between their desperate need for love and their shame about having needs at all.

But here's the beautiful twist in the Two's story: This very wound, when acknowledged and healed, becomes the source of their greatest strength. Their capacity for empathy, their intuitive understanding of others' needs, their ability to create deep connections—all of these admirable qualities are rooted in that original wound.

So remember, Twos, your desire to help others isn't a flaw—it was a brilliant survival strategy. We're just updating that strategy to include taking care of yourself too.

The first step is to acknowledge that hurt. Without judgment, get curious about where those money monsters came from. What beliefs did you inherit? Where do you tend to get caught in unhealthy patterns of money anxiety or avoidance? It's time to get a journal and write your story down or create a trauma timeline of all the betrayals, abandon-ments, and rejections that created your money monster. What was it about your childhood environment that made you feel so unlovable? And for goodness' sake, have a little compassion for yourself! You're not broken; you're human.

Stop reacting out of the sadness that created your money monsters.

To overcome the sadness and grief that birthed your money monsters, embark on a daily practice of contemplation and compas-sion. Think of it as going to the emotional gym, but instead of lifting weights, you're lifting your self-worth. You wouldn't expect to bench-press three hundred pounds after one workout, so don't expect to conquer your ego addictions overnight.

Contemplation for Twos is about shining a spotlight on your pride and flattery, as well as on the Sacred Wound of externalized sadness behind them that is wreaking havoc in your financial life. Set aside time each day for quiet reflection. This could be traditional medita-tion, a contemplative walk, or even journaling about your feelings (yes, your own feelings, not everyone else's or their drama). Only in solitude can you let go of your chronic codependence.

Create a self-care "map." Jot down all the ways you take care of yourself each day, no matter how small. Then, see what patterns emerge. How often are you putting yourself first? How does it feel when you do? This can help you break the pattern of prioritizing others' needs over your own and work on being more emotionally independent.

As you begin your practice, focus on your primary ego addiction: flattery. Get curious about it. Why do you feel the need to constantly please others? How is this addiction both helping and hindering you? Remember, this addiction developed as a survival strategy. It's not the enemy—but it is causing a lot of suffering for you now. Most importantly, how does the sadness or shame behind your flattery addiction create unnecessary suffering for those you love?

Don't neglect your secondary ego addiction to vengeance either. Notice when it shows up and what triggers it. Understanding both addictions will help you navigate stressful situations more skillfully, especially when you feel unappreciated or taken advantage of.

Once you've identified these patterns, it's time to start cultivating your core virtues: honesty and joy, which will lead to your highest virtue of humility. Think of them as spiritual muscles you need to strengthen. How can you incorporate them into your daily life? Maybe start finding joy in activities that are just for you, not for others' benefit.[3]

Consider creating a personal mantra or prayer that acknowledges your addictions and affirms your virtues, such as this Humility Prayer:

Boundless Love, open my heart to your unconditional acceptance and heal the sadness that binds my heart. Bestow upon me the courage to speak honestly and live joyfully, anchored in your unwavering grace. Help me relinquish my addictions to flattery and vengeance, so I may humbly love and serve you through those around me.

Perhaps have a picture of your precious childhood self to look at as you recite your prayer. That wounded child is still crying out and needs to be comforted, protected, and reparented. Remember, little you deserved unconditional love and care without having to earn it through constant giving and people-pleasing.

Speaking of spiritual practices, find one that resonates with you. It's essential to have something to keep you from spiraling into an existential crisis every time someone doesn't appreciate your efforts. A built-in community of support can be very helpful for connection-seeking Twos.

Don't forget the crucial step of cultivating compassion for yourself and the people who raised you. And when you begin to integrate new habits into your routine, give yourself a lot of grace. Remember, learning to love yourself takes time, patience, and practice. But eventually, you'll stop needing others' approval to feel worthy.

Learn to be less anxious or avoidant about money by confronting your money monsters.

Picture this: Your money monster isn't a terrifying beast, but a needy puppy that's been following you around, constantly demanding attention and treats. You've been feeding it your self-worth, your time, and yes, your hard-earned cash. It's time to train that puppy!

For you Twos, your greatest fear isn't about money itself—it's about being unlovable. Your money monsters, the Bleeder and the Bonder, are just manifestations of this fear. The Bleeder drains your resources dry in service to others, while the Bonder uses money to create codependent relationships.

Now let's channel our inner St. Francis and approach these monsters with compassion. Remember the Wolf of Gubbio? St. Francis didn't try to destroy the wolf—he made peace with it. That's your mission, should you choose to accept it (and let's face it, you Twos never say no to a mission).

Start by acknowledging your money monsters. "Hello, Bleeder. Hi there, Bonder. I see you're trying to make me lovable by giving everything away or by buying people's affection. Thanks for your effort, but I've got this covered now."

Next, let's create that "Money Monster to Money Master" transformation chart. You can find examples on my website at douglynam.com. Grab your favorite colorful pens (I know you have a stash for making those heartfelt cards) and let's get creative.

For earning, ask yourself: "Am I undervaluing my work because I feel guilty charging for my services?" Or are you working overtime without compensation just to be "helpful"? Your action step might be to practice saying, "My time and skills are valuable" in the mirror daily.

For saving, consider: Do you have trouble saving because you always put others' needs first? Your countermove could be setting up an automatic transfer to a savings account named "Self-Love Fund."

Are you avoiding investing because it feels selfish? Try reframing it as "investing in my ability to help others long-term."

And for giving, the trickiest area for you generous souls, ask yourself: "Am I giving to feel worthy, or out of genuine desire to help without any expectation or hidden agenda?" Your action step might be to set a giving budget and stick to it, knowing that firm boundaries are a form of love too.

Now, let's write that letter to money. "Dear Money, I know we've had a complicated relationship. I've used you to buy love and approval. I've given you away to feel worthy. But I'm ready for a healthier relationship . . ."

And money's response? "Dear Two, you are worthy of love just as you are. You don't need to buy anyone's affection or drain yourself dry to be lovable. Let's work together to create security and abundance, so you can help others from a place of fullness, not depletion."

Remember: You *are* lovable, just as you are, without giving away all your resources or creating financial codependency.

As you work through this, cultivate curious compassion toward your financial behaviors. When you feel the urge to overspend on a gift or undercharge for your services, pause and ask yourself: "What am I really seeking here? Is it love? Approval? A sense of worth?" Then remind yourself: "I am worthy of love, just as I am."

Your goal isn't to silence your Bleeder or Bonder, but to integrate them. Transform that Bleeder energy into thoughtful generosity that doesn't leave you drained. Let the Bonder teach you about creating genuine connections that aren't based on financial transactions.

This journey isn't about becoming a penny-pinching miser. It's about finding a balance where you can be the caring, generous soul you are, while also taking care of yourself. It's like the airplane oxygen-mask principle—you need to secure your own mask before helping others.

So, my beloved Twos, are you ready to make peace with your money monsters? To transform them from needy puppies into loyal companions on your financial journey? Sometimes you'll want to fall back into old patterns. But remember, every time you set a healthy financial boundary and value yourself and your resources, you're one step closer to becoming the money master you're meant to be.

And hey, once you've mastered this, think of all the genuine, strings-free help you'll be able to offer. Now *that's* a future worth investing in!

Build a strong financial life by earning, saving, and investing ethically.

Don't worry, we're not going to turn you into a miserly Scrooge—we're just going to make sure you have enough in your love tank to keep spreading that Two magic around. Let's dive into the Holy Trinity of Finance: earning, saving, and investing, Two-style!

First up, earning. You Twos have a superpower that's practically made for bringing home the bacon—your incredible ability to connect with people and intuitively understand their needs. It's time to monetize that empathy! Consider careers or side hustles in fields like counseling, coaching, human resources, or customer service. Your natural talent for making others feel valued and understood is worth its weight in gold.

Here's a curveball for you: Have you ever thought about starting your own "caring" business? Maybe a concierge service for busy families, a pet-sitting empire, or a wellness coaching practice? Your ability to anticipate needs and go the extra mile could set you apart in the entrepreneurial world. Just remember, it's okay to charge for your services—you're not any less caring just because you're making a living!

Now let's talk about a tricky subject for you Twos—saving. I know, I know, the idea of keeping money for yourself when others might need it probably makes you break out in hives. But here's the thing: You can't pour from an empty cup. Think of saving as creating a reserve of love that allows you to help even more in the future.

Start with a "Self-Love Fund"—create an account for your future well-being. Set up automatic transfers to a savings account (let's call it your "Helper's Hideaway" or "Two's Treasure Chest") to build up an emergency fund covering six months of expenses. This safety net ensures you can keep going when life throws you a curveball.

When it comes to mindful spending, before making a purchase, ask yourself: "Is this helping me become a more effective helper in the long run?" This reframe can help you balance your natural generosity with necessary self-care.

Now, on to investing—the area where many Twos feel like fish out of water. Here's where your desire to improve the world can shine. Look into investments that align with your values and can help you take more responsibility for the broader issues you care about. Socially responsible investing allows you to grow your wealth while supporting causes you believe in. It's like planting a money tree in a garden of good!

Aim to invest at least 15 percent of your pre-tax income for retirement into an IRA or 401(k). I know it might feel selfish, but remember: A financially secure you is a you who can help others well into your golden years. Think of compound interest as your silent helper, working tirelessly to grow your ability to care for others.

Consider setting up a "Giving Fund" as part of your investment strategy. This can be a separate account where you invest money earmarked for future charitable giving. It's a beautiful way to align your financial growth with your desire to help others.

Don't forget to review and adjust your financial plan regularly. Life changes and your money strategy should evolve too. And yes, you need an estate plan—think of it as your final act of care, ensuring your loved ones are provided for and your favorite causes supported even after you're gone.

Remember, dear Twos, building a strong financial life isn't about becoming a coldhearted money hoarder. It's about creating a sustainable foundation that allows you to care for yourself and others in the long term. It's about recognizing that your financial health is not separate from your ability to help. A financially healthy Two is a force of love to be reckoned with!

Use your money and your talents as tools to love and serve a suffering world.

For you Twos, this step is like coming home. It's what you've been yearning for all along—a way to help others that's sustainable, impactful, and doesn't leave you emotionally and financially drained. You've tamed your Bleeder and Bonder money monsters, and now it's time to unleash your Beloved money master on the world!

First things first, let's channel that amazing Two intuition of yours. You have an uncanny ability to sense others' needs—now it's time to use that superpower for good. Before you start throwing money at causes, get your hands dirty. Volunteer, attend community meetings, really listen to the people you want to help. Your empathy is your secret weapon here—use it to understand where your contributions can make the most impact.

Remember, you're not just a checkbook with legs (although your generosity is legendary). You're a force of love incarnate, and that's what the world really needs. Don't just donate to the local food bank—organize a community fundraising dinner where you can connect with people one-on-one. Your ability to make others feel seen and valued is worth more than any dollar amount.

As you embark on this giving journey, start small and local. Look for needs in your immediate community that speak to your heart. Maybe it's mentoring a struggling single parent, or starting a support group for caregivers. These grassroots efforts allow you to see the direct impact of your love and resources, which I know is important to you Twos.

Now, let's talk about your unique skills. You've mastered the art of caring for others while also caring for yourself—that's huge! Consider offering workshops on "Sustainable Giving" or "Self-Care for Caregivers." Your journey from compulsive helper to balanced giver is invaluable wisdom that could help countless others avoid burnout.

Remember, giving back isn't just about money. It's about sharing your time, your knowledge, your legendary Two compassion. Sometimes, the most valuable thing you can offer is a listening ear or a heartfelt hug to someone who's struggling. Never underestimate the power of your presence.

And here's the beautiful part: As a money master Two, you're not just changing lives, you're teaching the world about unconditional love. Your Sacred Gift of Divine Love is exactly what this suffering world needs. You're showing people they are worthy of love and care, just as they are, without having to earn it or prove themselves.

By becoming a money master, you gain the power to love the world more effectively than ever before. You're no longer trapped in cycles of giving until you're depleted or entangled in codependency. Instead, you're modeling healthy, sustainable love—and that's revolutionary.

So, my dear Two, as you reach this final step, ask yourself: "How can I use my abundance to spread more love in the world? How can my financial journey become a testament to the power of unconditional love?" The world is crying out for the kind of love you have to give—and now you have the resources to give it sustainably and powerfully.

Go forth, my beautiful Two, and let your love flow abundantly. You're not just a money master now—you're a love master, and the world is so much better for it. Remember, every act of genuine care, every moment of undivided attention you give, every resource you share wisely—it's all part of your grand love revolution. And let me tell you, it's a revolution we all need.

Now get out there and love the world like only a financially savvy, emotionally balanced, radiantly loving Two with healthy boundaries can. The world is waiting for your magic!

Sophia's Story

Sophia's journey began in a household where love was conditional. Her parents were constantly overwhelmed and emotionally unavailable. Both suffered from various forms of mental illness with a heaping portion of substance abuse. In this landscape, young Sophia quickly learned her needs were a burden.

When her psychological umbilical cord with her caregivers was cut by the sadness and grief of feeling unlovable and uncared for, she made an unconscious decision to focus on others' needs in the hope that her care and love would be reciprocated. She wasn't content with just being helpful; she needed to be indispensable. She became a parent to her parents.

This pattern intensified in adulthood. Sophia became a master of seduction in her ability to draw people in with her intense focus and seemingly boundless care. Her marriage to Jake was less a partnership and more of a hostage situation, with Sophia holding Jake's needs captive.

Sophia's primary ego addiction to flattery was always in overdrive. She didn't just compliment Jake; she bombarded him with praise, anticipating his needs before he even knew he had them. But she was quick to lash out when he didn't give her the adoration and validation she craved.

Financially, Sophia was a tornado of generosity. She spent lavishly on Jake, buying him expensive gifts and planning elaborate surprises. But heaven help him if he didn't show appropriate levels of gratitude. Then her secondary ego addiction to vengeance came raging forth, and she'd provoke wild fights to make him suffer.

After years of this emotional roller coaster, Jake, exhausted by Sophia's intense neediness and volatile outbursts, finally reached his limit. He left, leaving nothing but a note that read, "I can't breathe with you always trying to give me air."

When Jake left, Sophia's financial world imploded. She'd been so focused on anticipating Jake's needs that she neglected basic financial management. Their joint accounts were empty. Jake, tired of her financial fumbling, had been squirreling away money in a separate account.

The divorce proceedings were a financial bloodbath. Sophia, in her vengeance-fueled state, hired the most expensive lawyer she could find, charging it all to her high-interest credit cards. She fought for everything, including possession of Jake's beloved Labrador, not because she wanted it, but because she knew he did. Post-divorce, Sophia was drowning in debt.

Sophia's Dark Night of the Soul was a black hole of despair. Her worst fear had come true—she was alone, unneeded, and felt unloved. The sadness and grief she'd been running from her whole life caught up with her, tackling her with the force of a linebacker. Sophia's secondary ego addiction to vengeance reared its ugly head once again. She oscillated between plotting elaborate schemes to win Jake back and fantasizing about destroying his life. Her anger, no longer restrained, erupted like a long-dormant volcano.

In this pit of despair, Sophia finally faced her truth. She had to admit that her "selfless" giving had been anything but. Her supposed care of others was really just a manipulative form of control. She'd spent so long trying to hunt down love that she'd driven it away. Also, her intense focus on others' needs had left her own neglected and festering.

As she practiced her primary path of recovery, honesty, she stopped her people-pleasing obsession and began tending to her own needs. When she could be honest with others about what she really felt and thought, Sophia discovered her secondary path of recovery: joy. But finding joy wasn't about idle relaxation or passive acceptance. Sophia went after joy with the same intensity she'd once applied to caring for others. She threw herself into new hobbies for the sheer pleasure of learning. She started painting again, a once-burning passion, and learned to enjoy her own company in quiet periods of solitude.

The combination of honesty and joy led Sophia to her highest virtue: humility. She learned her true strength wasn't in being needed, but in being vulnerable. She discovered that real connection came not from hunting down others' needs, but from authentically sharing her own.

Financially, this transformation was revolutionary. Sophia redirected her intense focus toward understanding the world of money. She devoured personal finance books, attended a financial literacy course at her local community college, and joined an online community of other divorced women rebuilding their lives.

She attacked her debt with fervor and was determined to be self-reliant. Sophia took on three side hustles in addition to her day job—dog walking, freelance editing, and house-sitting. Every dollar she earned was a trophy proudly displayed in her rapidly growing savings account.

Three years after her divorce, Sophia's financial landscape was unrecognizable. Her debts were paid off, she had a robust emergency fund, and she was contributing to a retirement account.

As Sophia embraced humility, she began to heal her Sacred Wound of externalized sadness. She no longer needed to earn love. Instead, she found genuine connection by being authentically herself, flaws and all.

In her relationships, Sophia became truly beloved. Her intensity, once overwhelming, became a source of genuine compassion and care. She learned to love fiercely but freely, without the need to possess or control.

Sophia's journey from a child suppressing her needs to a woman embracing her authentic self was intense. But through this process, she discovered her Sacred Gift: Divine Love. This wasn't the suffocating, demanding love she'd known before. It was a love that burned bright but didn't consume, that could focus intensely without losing perspective. And it included loving herself enough to manage her money wisely.

CHAPTER ELEVEN

TYPE THREE—THE ACHIEVER (RACE CAR)

HOW TO STOP FLEXING ON SOCIAL MEDIA AND START FLEXING YOUR SAVINGS ACCOUNT

Type Threes are the Race Cars of the Enneagram—sleek, fast, and always competing for pole position. Want to get something done in record time? Just hand the task over to a Three and watch them slam the gas pedal to the floor. They'll change lanes, do 180-degree spins, and drive like their hair is on fire to get the job done. Hey, as long as they look good crossing that finish line, right? Gotta love those showboating tendencies.

These folks are all about impressing people with their accomplishments and putting on a flashy show. They'll figure out the criteria for success in any group or culture, then bend over backward to embody those ideals and make it all look easy. And they know how to market themselves better than a used-car salesman.

The Achiever's need for validation stems from a deep-seated fear of being utterly worthless, and on the inside, they're a hot mess of anxiety. Their psychological umbilical cord was cut by sadness (or shame) that they both internalized and externalized,

Type Three Ego Map: The Achiever or Race Car

ENLIGHTENMENT STRUCTURE	
MONEY MASTER	**THE BUILDER**
Sacred Gift (Holy Idea)	Divine Purpose
Greatest Hope (Basic Desire)	To feel completely valued
Greatest Virtue (Virtue)	Authenticity Modesty + Faith = Authenticity (cure for Deceit)
Secondary Recovery Virtue (Relaxation Point)	Faith (Primary Recovery Virtue for Type 6)
Primary Recovery Virtue	Modesty
Faux Virtue	Assertiveness
SHADOW STRUCTURE	
MONEY MONSTERS: AVOIDANT / ANXIOUS	**THE BURIER / THE BLINGER**
Ego Stress Response	Elusion Deceit + Evasion = Elusion (blocks Vanity)
Secondary Ego Addiction (Stress Point)	Evasion (Primary Ego Addiction for Type 9)
Primary Ego Addiction (Ego Fixation)	Vanity
Greatest Vice (Passion)	Deceit
Greatest Fear (Basic Fear)	Being worthless
Sacred Wound	Internalized & Externalized Sadness

(Read the chart from the bottom up.)

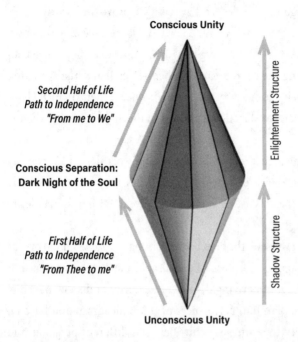

Conscious Unity

Second Half of Life
Path to Independence
"From me to We"

Enlightenment Structure

Conscious Separation:
Dark Night of the Soul

First Half of Life
Path to Independence
"From Thee to me"

Shadow Structure

Unconscious Unity

so they feel sadness and grief about how they perceive themselves *and* about how they think others perceive them. They're like a child performing in a recital, simultaneously ashamed of their own perceived inadequacy while dreading the judgment in the audience's eyes. As a result, there's this big, gaping void inside them that they're constantly trying to fill with shiny trophies and a carefully curated public image. Talk about high-maintenance!

I've witnessed an adult Three reduce kindergartners to tears during a friendly game of Chutes and Ladders because they couldn't stand the thought of losing. (Could that have been me?) And heaven forbid someone interrupts them while they're in the middle of an important task. "What do you mean I have to stop working and take the dog for a walk? Can't he hold it until tomorrow?"

These go-getters are desperately trying to prove their worth, often at the expense of their well-being. They'll work themselves to the bone, chasing that next promotion, big win, or any applause they can get, all while neglecting the deeper parts of themselves that actually matter. This vicious behavior pattern can wreak havoc on their financial lives if they don't learn to slow down and get in touch with their authentic selves.

To prevent their greatest fear of feeling worthless from coming true, they adopt their worst vice of deceit. While they aren't necessarily outright liars, the masks and personas they wear to impress people are a form of deception.

Have you ever seen the bian lian mask changers of Sichuan opera? They are virtuosic performers who can rapidly switch between elaborate masks in a mesmerizing display of dexterity and showmanship. Threes are the bian lian performers of the Enneagram and have an uncanny ability to seamlessly shift between different personas and identities, quickly adapting to the situation at hand.

But don't be fooled by the dazzling display—it's all an elaborate dance to dodge their sadness and grief. They're desperately seeking applause from any audience they can find, hoping the standing ovation will drown out the voice of their inner critic telling them they are worthless. This constant identity shuffle is so ingrained that it's like breathing. They're not even aware they're doing it most of the time.

To keep this show on the road, Threes unconsciously adopt their primary ego addiction to vanity. It's their go-to fix, giving them a hit of that sweet, sweet dopamine every time they puff up their own importance. Their life motto? "Look at ME!"—preferably in neon lights with a killer soundtrack.

But when you're always wearing a mask, it's easy to forget what your real face looks like. Threes are so busy trying to be whoever they think you want them to be, they lose sight of who they actually are. Talk about an identity crisis waiting to happen!

Perhaps Type Threes' most dangerous trait is their uncanny ability to deceive themselves first and foremost. It's like they've got an internal PR team spinning every story in their favor. This vain self-deception is what makes their outright lies so darn convincing—they've already sold themselves on the hype.

But wait, there's more! One of their worst traits is their tendency to treat people like human LEGO blocks—useful for building their skyscraper of success, but ultimately disposable. They've got a knack for seeing everyone as a potential stepping stone, ready to be used and discarded on their climb to the top.

The tragic irony? In their relentless pursuit of external validation, they often lose sight of the authentic connections that could bring real fulfillment. They're so busy trying to impress everyone that they forget to actually connect with anyone.

But hey, if they can harness that charisma for good and start seeing people as, well, people? Watch out—they might just change the world. And maybe, just maybe, they'll finally impress the one person they've been trying to win over all along: themselves.

My dear Type Three friends, I know the burden you carry is a heavy one. This persistent need to perform, to keep up appearances, to always be on the move—it is utterly exhausting. And I know the fear and insecurity that lurk beneath the surface, the terror of being exposed as unworthy, worthless, or lacking in some fundamental way.

The problem is that if you ever removed all the masks, you probably wouldn't even know who you are. Sadly, you rarely give yourself time away from work or endless projects to discover who you really are. No matter how impressive your résumé becomes, no matter how much praise you receive, there will always be that nagging voice whispering that it's not enough, that you are still somehow lacking because you aren't being validated for your True Self. It's an endless cycle of striving and self-doubt that can leave you feeling profoundly alone.

Sadly, in your struggle to keep up appearances and win the approval of others, you have learned to block out your own inner world, numbing yourself to the very feelings that make you human. You are adept at reading and responding to the emotions and values of those around you while your own authentic self remains shrouded in darkness. As a result, you have become a "human doing" rather than a human being.

Eventually, all that vanity and striving causes your Race Car to break down and crash. When you overextend yourself by pushing too hard, reaching beyond your abilities, or getting knocked sidewise by the random tragedies of life, you're confronted with failure and humiliation. The pain of failure, any failure, triggers your greatest fear that you are worthless. To compensate and avoid the sadness and shame you feel when failure lands in your lap, you instinctively switch to your secondary ego addiction, evasion. Evasion is the primary ego addiction of Type Nine, the Peacemaker or RV, and it's like borrowing an RV and being forced to take a break—but in a weird way.

Evasion combined with your worst vice of deceit creates your ego stress response of elusion, or extreme avoidance of problems. It pulls you into a pit stop, where you hide in the RV, eluding the humiliation of your failures and sense of worthlessness. Elusion also keeps your vanity temporarily at bay as you hide from the world and yourself while you recover. You might binge on television, video games, or social media, jump into a new project, or clean the house. Anything to escape. You might also blame others, take undeserved credit for something, or lie to dodge reality. Substance abuse can be a problem for Threes because it offers a quick way to elude everything.

In short, when practicing elusion, their new motto is *"Don't* look at me! Don't see me in my grief and failure."* Elusion isn't great, but it does keep the Three from creating more vanity-induced problems.[1]

The magic formula for this process is:

Deceit (worst vice/passion) + Evasion (secondary ego addiction/stress point) = Elusion (ego stress response)

So, if you're a Three, take a deep breath, put the car in neutral, and remember—your value isn't tied to your achievements or your accolades. You're a beautiful, irreplaceable human being and beloved child of the Divine, and that's the validation you really need. Only unconditional acceptance of yourself and the infinite love of the God of your understanding can fill the infinite hole of grief and sadness in your precious heart. Now, who wants to race me to the nearest therapist's office?

Money Monsters

The Burier: Money-Avoidant

Picture this: A Three standing on a tropical beach, phone in hand, posting #blessed on Instagram while their credit card company is sending them more red flags than a communist parade. But hey, as long as the neighbors think they're living the high life, who cares if they're one missed payment away from living in a cardboard box?

These folks have got the whole "stick your head in the sand and hope the money problems magically disappear" thing down to a science. Why bother dealing with that pesky thing called financial responsibility when you can focus on keeping up appearances?

Money is one of society's primary ways to measure worth, so when these Buriers take a look at their paltry portfolios or paychecks, it's like a sucker punch to their ego. It triggers all their fears of being worthless. After all, image is everything for a Three, and being poor is never a great public image.

The stress they feel around their finances is enough to push them into a permanent state of evasion. They're constantly trying to find new ways to elude the sadness and grief created by their financial troubles. And to shield themselves from this sadness, they've built a veritable fortress of avoidance. But, as we all know, the issues we refuse to confront only fester and grow until the Burier finds themselves six feet under, their financial life in shambles.

It's a real catch-22, isn't it? These Threes are so desperate to maintain their image of perfection that they bury their heads in the sand to hide from their grief and shame, only to watch their financial situation deteriorate even further. It's like a bad comedy skit.

Fun fact: The first line in chapter 1 of my first book, *From Monk to Money Manager*, is "I've always hated talking about money." Spoiler alert: I got over it, and you can too.

Traits of the Burier

The Workaholic Wunderkind: Buriers can have this nasty habit of putting their career on a pedestal and completely neglecting, well, everything else. Including their finances. The whole work-life balance thing? What's that?

In full disclosure, I'm writing this section at some ungodly hour while on vacation because I can't bring myself to unplug from work. But hey, at least I'm keeping up appearances, right? Clearly, I'm still a work in progress when it comes to finding that elusive personal-professional harmony.

As a hack, try scheduling "life appointments" with the same urgency as work meetings. Seriously, pencil in "touch grass" or "remember I have a family" right next to "crush souls in a board meeting." Your future self will thank you, probably while sipping a piña colada on an actual vacation.

Ostrich Impersonation: Admitting you're struggling financially is about as appealing as running naked through a mall food court. Eluding your problems might temporarily preserve your precious image of success, but at what cost? How long will you stick your head in the sand before you finally admit you need to change course and take appropriate action? Instead, set a timer for fifteen minutes of financial real talk with yourself daily. It's like ripping off a Band-Aid, but instead of hair, you're yanking out money delusions.

Status Symbol Insanity: Ooh, shiny new toy—have to have that! Buriers need to keep up that image of success, even if it means blowing their savings on status symbols they can't afford. How about a clear spending plan and budget instead? Before every purchase, ask yourself: "Will this impress my therapist?" If the answer is no, maybe reconsider. Try impressing yourself with a growing savings account instead. It's the ultimate status symbol—financial security.

The Off-Road Aversion: Not every competition is on an even track, and we don't all begin at the same starting line. Going off-road or taking a big risk can be hard for a Three when they aren't certain they can win, so they sometimes bow out of the race altogether and never cross the starting line. No career shifts or entrepreneurial ventures for this financial chicken. But as they say, "no risk, no reward." Time to get off the freeway, stop following traffic, and get a little more adventurous about your career and financial life. Start small. Maybe it's a low-risk investment or a side hustle. Remember, even Lewis and Clark started with a single step (probably into a puddle).

Comparison Concern Crisis: We can't forget the Three's obsession with constantly comparing our financial situation to everyone else. Because we just can't be content with our own journey. Nope, we Buriers have a nasty habit of measuring ourselves against our peers, family, and colleagues, or whoever pops up in our Instagram feed, which leads to feelings of inadequacy, depression, and inaction. As a cure, every time you catch yourself playing the comparison game, donate one dollar to charity. You'll either solve world hunger or break this habit. Win-win! Plus, it's a tax write-off. See? We can turn even our neuroses into a financial strategy!

The Blinger: Money-Anxious

More common among Type Threes is the Blinger, who uses their career, money, and luxuries as status symbols to pump up their ego. One of the most efficient, but unhealthy, ways for a Type Three to temporarily suppress their chronic feelings of worthlessness is to be esteemed in the eyes of others, and a quick, but expensive way to achieve social status is to have a lot of status symbols.

The Blinger conspicuously shows off their wealth through fancy cars, a big house, and any luxuries they can acquire. Having stuff others don't have makes the Blinger feel superior, temporarily concealing their deepest shame. These folks aren't trying to keep up with the Joneses; they want to crush it compared to the Joneses. It's like an endless game of financial one-upmanship, where the only sure winners are the credit card companies and corporate culture.

The Blinger is caught in both a spiritual and financial trap. While the Blinger looks rich, if you spend all your money on stuff, you'll always be broke—simple as that. And if you always compare your status symbols or wealth to others', someone will always beat you, and you'll be on a constant roller coaster of emotional highs and lows, destroying your wealth and happiness.

The irony is that true wealth has nothing to do with how much you make or status symbols and everything to do with prudent saving and investing. But admitting that would mean confronting the insecurities driving the Blinger's compulsive earning and spending habits.

Traits of the Blinger

The Vanity Trap: These Blingers will happily sacrifice their financial well-being, and their long-term security, upon the altar of admiration. They may not be successful, but they will sure look like it. Like children grasping at shiny baubles, they accumulate debt and live beyond their means, all to maintain a certain image or facade. Instead, try a thirty-day "Stealth Wealth" challenge. Dress down, wear an inexpensive watch, brown-bag your lunch. See who still likes you when you're not flashing the cash. Spoiler alert: Those are your real friends.

Monetary Milestone Mania: Threes often tie their self-worth to arbitrary financial goals. "I'll be happy when I make six figures," they say, only to move the goalposts to seven once they get there. It's like playing Whac-A-Mole with your self-esteem. Like financial mountaineers, they scale the peaks of success, only to find themselves gazing hungrily at the next lofty goal. For them, comparison is not just the thief of joy, but the very fuel that propels their restless existence.

They then find themselves trapped in an endless cycle of striving, of grasping, of never quite arriving. The more they strive and achieve, the more elusive satisfaction becomes because their identity is a construct built upon the shifting opinions of others. It's like trying to fill a black hole with Gucci bags—it's just never enough. As a solution, create a "Contentment Corner" in your home. Fill it with photos of your loved ones, mementos of cherished moments, and a giant mirror with "YOU ARE ENOUGH" written on it in Sharpie. Visit daily.

The I'll-Rest-When-I'm-Dead Delusion: Sleep? Vacations? Hobbies? That's for the weak. These Threes believe that every waking moment not spent earning or scheming is a moment wasted. They're running a race with no finish line. And what do they have to show for it? A bulging bank account, perhaps, but at the cost of neglected relationships, frayed mental health, and a nagging feeling that all their achievements ring hollow. Maybe try putting down the spreadsheets occasionally and going on a real date with your spouse or partner? And then schedule "Lazy Time" in your calendar. Treat it like a critical business meeting, because it is. Your assignment? Do absolutely nothing productive or related to technology for at least three hours. Warning: This may cause extreme discomfort and a potential identity crisis.

Financial Facade Fixation: These Blingers are masters of financial smoke and mirrors. They'll lease a luxury car they can't afford and throw lavish parties on maxed-out credit cards. Instead, start a "Real Rich vs. Fake Rich" journal. Every time you're tempted to buy something for appearances, write down what a truly wealthy person might do instead. Hint: It probably involves index funds and sensible shoes.

A Money Master—The Builder

Inevitably, the ego games of a Three create a crisis filled with sadness and humiliation that cannot be avoided. They push the gas pedal too hard, overextend themselves trying to look good, and crash hard into the guardrails of life, making complete idiots out of themselves.

When the Three's ego addictions to vanity and evasion, fueled by their worst vice of deceit, push them into a profound crisis of psychological separation and isolation, they enter the Dark Night of the Soul. For a Three, it's like being dropped into an infinite void of meaninglessness and despair. The game of life seems to have no value or purpose, reflecting their inner turmoil. In the Dark Night, they confront their greatest fear—feeling utterly worthless.

The problem is that until a Three breaks through to the other side of the Dark Night of the Soul, accomplishments and affirmations based on deceit and vanity are mostly worthless. All the striving, hard work, and efficiency the Three devoted to promoting themselves before the Dark Night reveal themselves as mostly empty self-aggrandizement. This epiphany may not be easy to articulate consciously, but a Three in the Dark Night feels their overwhelming grief and sense of failure, the pain of which threatens to destroy them.

The only way out of this seemingly infinite darkness is to break open, let go of their ego addictions, and embrace the virtue of modesty. Modesty is the Three's primary path of recovery and helps to cure their addiction to vanity, but it is born from an honest confrontation with their Sacred Wound and greatest fear. Once modesty becomes a daily part of their spiritual practice, the stress on their ego eases, and they can finally relax their defenses and ego games.

Modesty isn't about diminishing yourself, which for a Three can trigger even more feelings of worthlessness; it's about seeing and presenting yourself accurately. The solution for the Three is to find a balance between self-aggrandizement and self-loathing. Modesty requires an honest and forthright self-assessment of one's strengths and weaknesses, without fanfare or drama, and it stops the pendulum from swinging between narcissism and nihilism. It's about finding that happy medium between "I'm the greatest thing since Taylor Swift" and "I'm utterly worthless and should just crawl into a hole and die."

Because Threes are so terrified of failure, modesty allows them to admit openly when they make a mistake, without trying to hide it or shift the blame. They become more interested in becoming better individuals than in showcasing their accomplishments to impress others. Being modest doesn't mean lacking confidence or ambition; it simply implies a more genuine and authentic approach to their achievements. However, getting a Three to embrace modesty is a bit like asking a toddler to share their favorite toy—but hey, desperate times, right?

Along the way they need to be mindful of their faux virtue, which is assertiveness. This faux virtue isn't about expressing genuine needs or setting healthy boundaries; it's about dominating the spotlight and ensuring everyone knows just how fabulous they are. They're not so much asserting themselves as they are auditioning for the role of "Most Impressive Person in the Room." It's exhausting for everyone involved, including the Three, who is working overtime to maintain their image of success.

As the Three embraces modesty, they also start to develop more faith—their secondary path of recovery. For a healthy Type Three, faith isn't about believing in a particular doctrine or dogma but involves a shift in focus from external validation and achievement to a more profound trust in oneself and the world around them. It is faith and trust in the God of their understanding to take off all the masks and stand naked as their True Self, without vanity or deception. It takes a lot of trust in the universe for a Three to let their guard down and be vulnerable. But when they do, they learn to accept and love themselves for who they are, not just for their successes and accolades. Their worth is then no longer tied to external accomplishments but is inherent in their very being.

Instead of constantly striving for validation and recognition, the healthy Three learns to have faith in the natural unfolding of life and the journey toward self-discovery and growth. They have faith in the process, not just the outcomes of their efforts, and start to enjoy the journey rather than wait for the destination.

Faith is the primary path of recovery for Type Six (the Family Sedan), and when the Three leans into modesty, it is like their Race Car runs out of fuel, so they borrow a luxury Family Sedan from Type Six that is factory-loaded with faith. The Family Sedan runs beautifully on modesty, and in their new luxury ride, they have more room to pick up passengers with whom they can share the adventure of life. Besides, road trips are way more fun with friends.[2] Rather than constantly seeing people as objects to use on their way to the finish line, they become fiercely loyal to their friends, family, and their broader community.

A healthy Three then begins to embody their highest virtue that cures their deceit—authenticity.

The winning formula for a healthy Three is:

Modesty (primary recovery virtue) + Faith (secondary recovery virtue/relaxation point) = Authenticity (greatest virtue/virtue)

Authenticity is about Threes being genuine and aligning their actions and behaviors with their inner values and beliefs, not those of others. It's a shift away from seeking validation through external achievements and instead finding that validation from within. Only then do they discover that the vainglorious praise for their clever masks is empty and hollow.

Letting their authentic self shine brightly is what calls forth the true love and validation they've been so desperately seeking their entire lives. By revealing and living as their most authentic self, a Three finally fulfills their greatest hope: to feel completely valued for who they truly are.

At their highest level, a Three embodies their Sacred Gift of Divine Purpose. Divine Purpose is the understanding that the Three, and everyone else, has value, meaning, and a reason for being just as they are. They realize that everything belongs and everything has value, and they help others to see and experience that value as well. Embodying Divine Purpose is what makes life worth living for a Three and alleviates much of their self-created suffering. But only in stillness, silence, and solitude, in creative and rejuvenating not-doing, can they find their true center. They can then stop building monuments to their ego and use their resources and talent to work for the greater good, becoming the Builder.

The Builder is the Three who has moved from "me to We" and consciously embraces their interdependence rather than focusing solely on their independence. A healthy Three finally feels worthy and valuable because they see a Divine Purpose flowing through them and through all of existence, which helps to redeem the entire game of life in their eyes. They then embody the best traits of Type Three and authentically and loyally share the beauty of Divine Purpose with the world around them. The Builder is a true money master, using their resources not for empty vanity but for the glory of the Divine. Watch as they stop trying to climb mountains and instead move them!

Becoming a Money Master—The Builder

Please be sure to read (or review) the chapter 8 overview of these five steps before you get started here.

Acknowledge the pain from your Childhood Wounding.

I get it; facing your inner demons head-on isn't exactly a walk in the park. But as any good therapist will tell you, the only way out is through. That means you have to venture even deeper into your Dark Night to get to daylight.

Now, I've seen my fair share of Threes struggle with their money monsters over the years—folks who are so darn convinced that their self-worth is directly proportional to the size of their bank account or job title. And most importantly, I've seen it in myself.

Picture a little Three, starry-eyed and thirsting for validation, confined in a family where love was as mercurial as a weather vane in a tornado. Perhaps Mommy's and Daddy's affection came with a hefty price tag—constant achievement. Was it like being stuck on an endless hamster wheel of "look at me!" moments? "I got an A+!" "Watch me win this race!" But instead of genuine pride and unconditional love, you got a pat on the head and a "What's next?" Talk about a recipe for never feeling good enough.

In some homes, love was doled out like rewards in a twisted video game. Get good grades? Level up to parental affection! Fail a test? Sorry, kiddo, no love points for you today. It's emotional extortion, and you fell for it, hook, line, and sinker.

Then there were the homes where keeping up appearances was more important than nurturing a child's authentic self. "Don't cry, it makes us look bad." "Smile for the camera, we're a happy family!" Cue the internal shame spiral for daring to have actual human emotions.

And let's not forget the joy of constantly being measured against siblings, cousins, or the neighbor's perfect kid. For some, "Why can't you be more like your brother?" became the soundtrack of your childhood. There is nothing like feeling you are the family's disappointment to really cement that sadness and shame.

Some of us had parents who were physically present but emotionally AWOL. Our achievements were noticed, but our inner world? Might as well have been invisible. Cue the grief for having needs and feelings that weren't directly tied to success.

Remember, my fellow Threes, recognizing these patterns isn't about blaming our parents or wallowing in self-pity. It's about understanding the root of our drive to perform and our fear of being worthless. It's the first step in reprogramming our internal shame-o-meter and learning to value ourselves beyond our achievements.

To start identifying the roots of your issues, map out a trauma timeline of your life—the highs, the lows, the moments that really cut you to the core. Where did your anxiety first start bubbling up? What were the key events in childhood that shaped your obsession with external validation? What was it that made you feel ashamed of your authentic self and need to always wear masks for approval? Once you can pinpoint the origins of your Childhood Wounding, you're partway there. And don't be afraid to reach out for help—whether it's a trusted friend, a support group, or a qualified mental health professional, having that safety net can make all the difference.

Now, if you'll excuse me, I need to go call my therapist and hug a teddy bear. This trip down memory lane has left me craving a stiff drink and a participation trophy. But at least we're facing our demons together, right? Misery loves company, especially when that company understands the unique pain of being a human doing instead of a human being.

Stop reacting out of the sadness that created your money monsters.

Alright, my ambitious Type Three friends, it's time to face the music—and by music, I mean that nonstop internal soundtrack of "Eye of the Tiger" mixed with "I Will Survive" that's been pushing you to chase success like it's the last chopper out of Saigon.

To overcome the sadness and grief that birthed our money monsters, we need to embark on a daily practice of contemplation and compassion. Think of it as going to the gym, but for your psyche. Just like you wouldn't expect to win an Oscar after one acting class, don't expect to conquer your ego addictions overnight.

Contemplation for us Threes is about shining a spotlight on those ego addictions that are wreaking havoc in our lives. Set aside time each day for quiet reflection. I know, I know—sitting still and doing nothing productive sounds about as appealing as watching paint dry. But trust me, it's worth it.

One practice that might appeal to your achievement-oriented nature is creating a "vanity inventory." Get a large whiteboard, a stack of paper, or a spreadsheet, and start listing out all the ways you try to impress others or maintain your image of success through your money monsters. Then, next to each item, write down the reality of the situation. This exercise can help you see the gap between your carefully curated image and your authentic self, and maybe even find some humor in your impossible standards.

As you begin your practice, focus on your primary ego addiction: vanity. Get curious about it. What purpose has it served? How is it both helping and hindering you? Remember, this addiction developed as a survival strategy. It's not the enemy—it's more like an overprotective PR agent who hasn't realized you've outgrown your child-star phase.

Don't forget your secondary ego addiction to evasion either. Notice when it shows up and what triggers it. It's like your personal escape hatch—always ready when the pressure of maintaining your image gets too intense. Understanding both addictions will help you navigate stressful situations more skillfully.

Once you've identified these patterns, it's time to start cultivating your core virtues: modesty and faith. These are your primary and secondary paths of recovery that lead to your highest virtue of authenticity. Think of them as spiritual muscles you need to strengthen. How can you incorporate them into your daily life?

Consider starting and ending your day with this Authenticity Prayer:

*Eternal Truth, open my heart to your profound love and
heal the sadness that drives me. Empower me to embrace
modesty and walk in faith, secure in your all-encompassing
grace. Help me to surrender my addictions to vanity and
evasion so that I may authentically serve and love you
through those around me.*

The next crucial step is to cultivate self-compassion. Work on for-giving yourself for the coping mechanisms you developed to survive. You were just a kid trying to prove your worth in a world that didn't come with an instruction manual. Cut yourself some slack. The Blinger or Burier lurking inside you is just a manifestation of that scared and wounded child.

Try to extend this compassion to your caregivers. Understanding their Enneagram types can provide insight into their behaviors and motivations, making their inevitable mistakes more understandable. Maybe they also were Threes, passing down the legacy of performance and image.

Finally, focus on integrating modesty and faith into your routine. Start small and be consistent. Maybe it's acknowledging a mistake without trying to cover it up or resisting the urge to name-drop at your next social gathering. The path requires courage, persistence, and the ability to laugh at our own carefully constructed facades. Think of it like learning a new language—you'll make mistakes, but each attempt brings you closer to fluency in authenticity.

So, my fellow Threes, are you ready to get to work? Your future self—the one free from the tyranny of vanity and deceit, the one who's authentically successful—is waiting . . .

Learn to be less anxious or avoidant about money by confronting your money monsters.

Let's dive into how we can face our money monsters and become less anxious or avoidant about our finances.

For us Threes, our greatest fear is being worthless. That fear is the engine powering our Race Car, and it's been running on premium-grade sadness for far too long. It's time to trade in that gas-guzzler for something more sustainable.

Now, I know what some of you are thinking: *But Doug, my fear of worthlessness is what's made me successful!* Sure, my fear of spiders is what's made me an Olympic-level jumper. But at what cost, my friend? At what cost?

Here's the truth, fellow Threes: That ravenous wolf of anxiety or avoidance? It's really just our inner child, desperately trying to prove their worth through achievements and accolades. The more we attack it with shame or try to outrun it with our next big accomplishment, the louder it howls and the more damage it does. But when we approach it with understanding and compassion, we can begin to tame it.

So, how do we do this? Well, we need to take a page out of St. Francis's playbook. Remember the tale of the Wolf of Gubbio? Let's reimagine it with a Three twist:

Picture this: There's a town called Achievementville. They've got a serious problem with a wolf called "Never Enough." This wolf is terrorizing the townspeople, constantly pushing them to work harder, achieve more, look better. Sound familiar?

Enter St. Francis (that's you, by the way). Instead of trying to vanquish this wolf, you decide to have a chat with it. You approach it with compassion, understanding that its fierce energy comes from a place of fear and insecurity.

You say, "Hey there, Never Enough. I see you've been causing quite a ruckus. But I get it—you're just trying to protect me from feeling worthless. How about we make a deal? You stop pushing me so hard, and I promise to love and value you, regardless of what you achieve."

And here's the kicker: The wolf listens! It realizes it doesn't need to be so fierce anymore. You've shown it that true worth comes from within, not from external validation. Then maybe you and Never Enough go find a quiet spot under a shady tree to snuggle up and take a much-needed nap.

Now let's make this practical. It's time to get up close and personal with your money monsters. Don't just skim the surface here—we're talking deep-sea diving into your financial psyche. Create a "Money Monster to Money Master" transformation chart.

For a Blinger Three, it might look something like this:

Earning: Are you a workaholic, constantly chasing that next promotion or bonus? The countermove? Set boundaries at work and focus on what truly fulfills you, not just what looks impressive.

Saving: Do you struggle to save because you're always buying the latest status symbols? The countermove? Create a "Future Self" fund or IRA. Imagine your authentic, fulfilled future self and save for them.

Investing: Are you making risky investments to get rich quick and prove your worth? That's your "Blinger" on steroids. The countermove? Adopt a long-term, sustainable investment strategy that aligns with your values, not just potential bragging rights.

Giving: Do you avoid giving because you're afraid of having less, or do you only give when it makes you look good? The countermove? Practice anonymous giving. Feel the joy of generosity without the ego boost.

Now plaster this chart everywhere. Make it your phone background, stick it on your fridge, tattoo it on your forehead (okay, maybe not that last one). The point is, keep it visible.

Next, write a letter to money. Here's a starting point:

Dear Money,

   We've had a complicated relationship, haven't we? I've used you to prove my worth, to create an image of success. But I'm ready for something more authentic. I'm ready to value myself beyond what you can buy or what others think of me. I'm ready for a healthier relationship with you—one based on security, generosity, and true fulfillment.

Then, write a response from money. What might it say? Perhaps something like:

Dear Three,

   I've watched you chase me like I'm the answer to everything. But honey, I'm just a tool. Your worth isn't in your bank account or your job title. It's in your heart, your authenticity, your ability to connect with others. Use me wisely, but don't let me use you. You're already worthy, just as you are.

Remember, the goal isn't to silence your ambition or kill your drive. It's to understand the fear behind it, make peace with it, and ultimately transform it into something that serves your authentic self.

This journey isn't about becoming a different person. It's about becoming more authentically you. It's about realizing that your self-worth isn't tied to your net worth. It's about understanding that true success isn't just about what you achieve, but who you become in the process.

So, my fellow Threes, are you ready to face your wolf? To approach your financial fears not with a sword of ambition, but with an open heart of self-acceptance? It's time to transform those money monsters from fearsome foes into powerful allies on your journey to financial mastery.

Remember, you're not just chasing success anymore. You're redefining it. And that, my friends, is the ultimate achievement.

Build a strong financial life by earning, saving, and investing ethically.

If you are already rolling in the dough, congratulations! Your money monsters have served a useful purpose. You get a pat on the back, a gold star, and can leave for recess early. Jump ahead to the next step.

For the rest of you, it's time to tackle the Holy Trinity of Finance—earning, saving, and investing. Please see my first book, *From Monk to Money Manager*, for a more detailed list of tricks and tips. But if you are still struggling financially, start by looking hard at your skill set and finding work that aligns with your values and passions.

The good news is that you know how to hustle, so making money can come easily if you focus your attention, develop a marketable skill set, and monetize your talent. You might need more training or mentorship, but find some way to bring in more cash. Easier said than done, I know, but only you can solve this problem.

Where you likely struggle the most is in the areas of saving and investing. All that burying and blinging probably created some debt you'll need to tackle first, so make a plan and some hard sacrifices to get that debt under control!

To build up your savings, you have to stop spending money to impress others, chase status symbols, or pamper yourself. Instead, work to impress your future self, the one who will thank you for becoming financially fit.

And when it comes to investing, remember, it's not just about raking in the dough. It's about using your money as a force for good. Seek out those ethical investment opportunities and try not to destroy the future you are investing for. After all, what good is wealth if it comes at the expense of the planet and the people you love?

Use your money and your talents as tools to love and serve a suffering world.

Your unique superpower as a Three is seeing a goal and going after it with laser focus. You can build almost anything when you set your mind to it, including a strong financial future for yourself and those you love.

You're unstoppable when your objective stops being about you, and you can shift from thinking about "me to We." What is that passion project that feeds your soul and nourishes the world but not your ego? What life adventure would you be willing to go on because the journey alone was beautiful enough? Don't forget that all life eventually comes to a dead end, so try not to waste yours racing in circles on a track someone else built.

Your Sacred Gift is to embody Divine Purpose, which helps give the world meaning and direction and sees everything as worthy and valuable just as it is. You help point the world in the right direction and orient it toward true north, a world filled with more love and compassion. Each Enneagram type has a Sacred Gift, but yours is the one that can help to pull the rest of them together and point in one direction for the greater good, helping to build a better future for all.

You bring the sacred "why" to the world around you, and to quote Nietzsche once again, "If you have a *why* for life, you can get by with almost any *how*."[3] When you tame your money monsters and live your most authentic life as a Builder, you give the world around you a "why" to live and strive for. You'll finally see your sacred and irreplaceable role in the grand design and, through your example of authenticity, help others find clarity about their Divine Purpose in the grand blueprint of life as well. Your job is to lead the way with honesty and authenticity, showing how we all have a reason to live and a purpose that can only be fulfilled by being our authentic selves. What's more valuable and essential than that?

Tom's Story

Tom was raised in a family where emotions were treated like radioactive waste—handled with extreme caution and preferably buried deep underground. His parents viewed feelings as unnecessary baggage on the road to success. "Why are you crying? Winners don't cry. Now, stop being a baby and go practice your piano!" This environment cut Tom's psychological umbilical cord with a double-edged sword of sadness.

He internalized the message that because he had emotions, he was a loser. His parents' attitude also made him feel ashamed of how he thought others perceived him. He believed his value or worth was tied to his achievements. His own feelings and identity were irrelevant, even detrimental, to success.

This Sacred Wound of internalized and externalized sadness created Tom's greatest fear: being worthless. To cope, he developed his worst vice: deceit. Tom became a master of morphing into whatever the world wanted him to be to gain approval and competitive advantage.

Tom's primary ego addiction to vanity made his life look better than it was. He collected achievements like some people collect stamps and stepped on whoever was in his way. He also used money and status symbols to prop up his ego as a "Blinger," always driving a nice car and living in a beautiful house, no matter how much that stretched his budget.

Tom eventually found himself at the top of the corporate ladder, but the ladder was teetering on the edge of collapse from the exhaustion of keeping up appearances. The stress of running so hard and taking on so many responsibilities he wasn't competent to handle drove Tom to start drinking heavily to relieve his stress. His wife soon left him, tired of competing for attention with Tom's work and disgusted by his addictive behavior.

After this overdose of vanity, he switched to his secondary ego addiction: evasion. Tom avoided introspection. The combination of his worst vice (deceit) and secondary ego addiction (evasion) created elusion—a state where Tom refused to look at the mess he'd made because it triggered his grief and shame. He blamed everyone else for his problems and his failed marriage. When he started calling in sick from his heavy drinking, a performance review from hell exposed Tom's antics as a schemer, and he tumbled out of the sky.

In the darkest hour of his Dark Night of the Soul, Tom lost his job and then his friends, who realized Tom was more a résumé than a person. The sadness and grief he'd been running from his whole life finally caught up with him.

Tom realized he had a choice. He could keep running from his Shadow, or he could face it. He picked up the phone and called a therapist. It was time to get real—*really* real.

Through therapy, AA, and a lot of soul-searching, Tom began to practice his primary path of recovery: modesty. At first, it felt like trying to write a résumé without any achievements—awkward and terrifying. Slowly, however, he learned to value himself for who he was, not what he accomplished.

As Tom embraced modesty, he found himself naturally drawn to his secondary path of recovery: faith. Faith that the adventure of his life would be better if he dropped the vanity and the masks. Faith that he was worthy of love, regardless of his achievements. He started to trust that he was enough, just as he was.

The combination of modesty and faith led Tom to his highest virtue: authenticity. For the first time in his life, Tom showed the world his true face—emotions, flaws, and all. And guess what? The world didn't end. In fact, it got a whole lot more colorful, even through sobs and tears.

As his heart broke open, he surrendered to the God of his understanding and realized that vanity had kept his heart locked and prevented him from receiving the love and acceptance he so desperately desired. The sadness that had driven him for so long began to heal, replaced by a deep sense of self-acceptance.

With this newfound authenticity, Tom discovered his Sacred Gift: Divine Purpose. He realized that his purpose wasn't to build a tower of Babel to his ego but a stable platform for his authentic True Self to stand upon.

Tom's journey from vanity-driven achiever to authentic leader was a roller coaster, and at times he was pretty sure he'd left his stomach somewhere back at the ticket booth. But as Tom embraced his authentic self, he found a new career as a business coach, helping other high achievers find balance and purpose in their lives. His experiences became valuable tools in guiding others.

His clients loved him not for his polished facade but for his raw honesty and hard-earned wisdom. He was living proof that they could be successful without selling their souls, and that authenticity was the ultimate competitive advantage.

In one particularly poignant moment, Tom found himself giving a TED Talk. But instead of rattling off his achievements or "10 Hacks to Climb the Corporate Ladder," he told his story of failure, redemption, and the power of being real. As he stood on that red circular carpet, he realized he'd finally achieved the success he'd always wanted because he was using his gifts to make a real difference in the world and letting others see his True Self, warts and all.

Tom had finally become a true money master—the Builder. He wasn't just building wealth anymore; he was building a legacy of authenticity and purpose.

CHAPTER TWELVE

TYPE FOUR—THE INDIVIDUALIST (CUSTOM CAR)

HOW TO STOP AGONIZING OVER YOUR BANK STATEMENT AND START LIVING YOUR #GLORIOUSLIFE

Our dear Fours are like those exquisite, rare orchids you find in the deepest, most mysterious parts of the jungle. They're absolutely stunning, but oh boy, do they have some peculiar growing habits.

The closing stanza of Robert Frost's poem "The Road Not Taken" is an anthem for Type Fours:

> *I shall be telling this with a sigh*
> *Somewhere ages and ages hence:*
> *Two roads diverged in a wood, and I—*
> *I took the one less traveled by,*
> *And that has made all the difference.*[1]

But here's the catch: If you always take the path less trod, you might end up lost in the wilderness, wondering where you are and how to get back to civilization.

Type Four Ego Map: The Individualist or Custom Car

(Read the chart from the bottom up.)

ENLIGHTENMENT STRUCTURE	
MONEY MASTER	**THE FLAME**
Sacred Gift (Holy Idea)	Divine Glory
Greatest Hope (Basic Desire)	To feel their total uniqueness
Greatest Virtue (Virtue)	Equanimity Joy + Gratitude = Equanimity (cure for Envy)
Secondary Recovery Virtue (Relaxation Point)	Gratitude (Primary Recovery Virtue for Type 1)
Primary Recovery Virtue	Joy
Faux Virtue	Mindfulness
SHADOW STRUCTURE	
MONEY MONSTERS: AVOIDANT / ANXIOUS	**THE FLOP / THE FLINGER**
Ego Stress Response	Co-Dependence Envy + Flattery = Co-Dependence (blocks Melancholy)
Secondary Ego Addiction (Stress Point)	Flattery (Primary Ego Addiction for Type 2)
Primary Ego Addiction (Ego Fixation)	Melancholy
Greatest Vice (Passion)	Envy
Greatest Fear (Basic Fear)	Having no identity or significance
Sacred Wound	Internalized Sadness

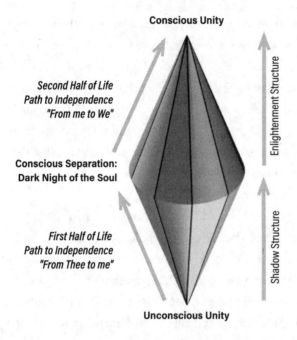

These folks have this uncanny ability to resist being put in any box. But much to their annoyance, there is a box for people who hate being put in a box—it's called being a Four. It's like they're allergic to convention, always striving to write their own rule book for life. As my wise Type Four brother once said, "It's hard to survive in the world when you try to invent all your own rules."

At their best, Fours are like unicorns prancing through fields of creativity who show the rest of us the magical beauty of life. Their empathy runs so deep, you'd think they have a direct hotline to everyone's heart.

But at their core, Fours often feel like they're missing some essential piece of themselves. Their Sacred Wound of internalized sadness (or shame) makes them think they're the only ones who don't have the "How to Be a Complete Human" manual. This feeling makes them afraid they have no unique identity, which then leads them down a path of envy, coveting everyone else's unique place in this world.

In response to all these intense feelings, Fours dive headfirst into their primary ego addiction to melancholy. This oddly soothing mindset hides a deeper pain and makes them feel exceptionally misunderstood. In their minds, their pain and suffering are more unique than what others experience, which is often true because they feel things more intensely. It's frequently said that Fours don't *have* feelings—they *are* their feelings.

When melancholy becomes too much, and they risk drowning in it, they become expert flatterers who look for someone to rescue or who will rescue them. When Type Four switches to their secondary ego addiction, flattery, they act more like an unhealthy Type Two. It's as if they've traded their broken-down Custom Car for an Ambulance and are blasting the siren at full volume to demand more attention than a Custom Car ever could. Their ego stress response is then codependency.[2]

The formula for this transformation looks like this:

Envy (greatest vice/passion) + Flattery (secondary ego addiction/ stress point) = Codependence (ego stress response)

This transformation moves them from withdrawing from the world in melancholy to fawning over others through flattery. It's a bit odd, but at least it gets them out of their shell, even if through an unhealthy attachment to others.

Fours also have an intense desire to find meaning and beauty in the world. That's what makes them such incredible artists and visionaries.

Fours' typical emotional roller coaster can lead to some interesting financial decisions in their quest for uniqueness. One minute, they're investing in obscure art; the next, they're swearing off materialism altogether. Their bank account often has difficulty keeping up with their volatile emotions.

They might switch from "I need this diamond-encrusted typewriter to express my true self!" to "I shall embrace poverty like a medieval monk!" faster than you can say "mood swing."

But here's the thing, my lovely Fours: Your intensity, your passion, your ability to see beauty in the strangest places—that's your superpower. You just need to channel it into building a life that's as stable as it is spectacular.

Your uniqueness isn't something to find—it's something you have *now*. You're not broken or incomplete; you're beautifully, wonderfully you. And that, my friends, is something to celebrate.

Money Monsters

The Flop: Money-Avoidant

Imagine a group of people who'd rather eat their own shoes than live inside a box of conventionality. Now try telling them they need to build wealth according to the rules of capitalism. It's like asking a cat to take a bath—theoretically possible but likely to end in hisses, scratches, and a whole lot of drama. In capitalist societies, building wealth means buying into the capitalistic system to some degree. At a minimum, this requires conformity to the rules of budgeting and bookkeeping.

Fours hate to follow conventions, which doesn't lead to financial discipline. Balancing a checkbook? That's for the mundane masses, darling. Fours are too busy writing sonnets about the existential crisis of their empty wallet. It's a misguided attempt to heal their Sacred

Wound through financial nonconformity and romanticizing financial struggle as part of their "unique" identity.

A money-avoidant Type Four is a fiscal disaster, so I call them the Flop. You can almost hear them face-planting on the pavement when discussing their finances. All the rules and conventions Type Fours disdain are useful when making a living, saving money, and building wealth. The routine discipline that helps generate lasting abundance often eludes them.

Traits of the Flop

The Tortured-Artist Archetype: They buy the romantic notion that true creativity thrives on financial struggle. They wear their empty bank account like a badge of artistic integrity, convinced that material success would somehow taint their creative soul. These folks believe that suffering is essential to the creative process. They may romanticize the idea of the "starving artist" and can quickly squander any accumulated assets, riding the roller coaster of inconsistent income. They'd rather wax poetic about the beauty of a sunset than sully their minds with thoughts of pedestrian matters such as budgets and interest rates. If this describes you, try reframing your art as a business. Set aside specific "starving artist" hours for brooding, then put on your business hat (maybe a beret?) and treat your art like the valuable commodity it is.

"I'm Not Worthy" Wailing: Fours often undercharge for their creative services or have difficulty setting appropriate prices for their work. They feel uncomfortable negotiating financial matters, which reflects their lack of self-worth. How about creating a "brag book" of your accomplishments and positive feedback? When it's time to negotiate, flip through it like it's your personal hype manual. Pretend you're haggling for a dear friend's work instead of your own. You'd fight tooth and nail for them, right? Do the same for yourself.

Budget-Induced Seizure Disorder: Flops often resist the structure, discipline, and consistency required for financial stability. They struggle with routine financial tasks like budgeting, saving, or long-term planning, viewing them as constraining to their artistic spirit or just too boring to be worth their time. Tip: Turn budgeting into an art project. Seriously. Make the most beautiful, creative budget spreadsheet the world has ever seen. Use colors, stickers, whatever floats your artistic boat. If your budgeting app were a canvas, what masterpiece would you create? Make financial planning your new medium.

Indulgent Impulses: When money-avoidant Fours spend money, they tend to make impulsive or emotionally driven financial decisions. They can easily overspend on experiences or items to fill an emotional void or express their unique identity. The indulgence may fill their soul hole for a moment, but on their credit card it can last a lifetime. Solution: Institute a one-week rule for any nonessential purchase. Write down what you want to buy and why. If after one week you still feel it's essential to your artistic soul, then maybe. Bonus points if you can turn the waiting period into a poem or interpretive dance about delayed gratification.

Rescuer Reliance: Flops tend to rely on others, such as family members, partners, or patrons, for financial support. They often struggle to achieve financial independence and autonomy, with an almost juvenile desire for a parental figure to acknowledge and care for them. "Mommy, Daddy, see how much I'm suffering? Please see me, acknowledge me, and save me!" As a hack, try starting a "Financial Independence" jar. Every time you want to call Mom and Dad (or your lover) for a bailout, put a dollar in the jar instead. Use that money to treat yourself to something that reminds you that you are grown-up and responsible. Maybe a nice fountain pen to craft those budgets?

Career Catharsis Careening: A Flop's career path can be as winding as Lombard Street, the windiest street in San Francisco, which only goes one way: downhill. Whenever they gain traction, these Fours change direction, never sticking with one discipline long enough to master a chosen field. They may even justify their lack of focus as an expression of their creativity. Instead, think of your career as the ultimate mixed-media project. Each new direction is just another layer or texture. But here's the trick: Don't allow yourself to try a new "medium" before you master at least one marketable skill from the one you're in. Build a portfolio that showcases your delightful complexity rather than your inability to commit, and then use it to create a profitable niche.

Instagram-Induced Inadequacy Disease: Flops often compare their creative output and career success to others unfavorably, leading to feelings of inadequacy, envy, and despair. Next time you find yourself drowning in a sea of "they're so much better than me," try this: Pick the person you're most jealous of and imagine what they'd envy about you. Would they kill for your ability to use seventeen shades of blue in a single painting? Would they sacrifice their vintage typewriter collection for your way with words? Write it down, embellish it, make it as dramatic and over-the-top as only a Four can. Pin it somewhere visible. *Voilà!* You've just turned your comparison into a self-compliment.

Even-My-Imposter-Syndrome-Feels-Fake Phobia: Deep down, the money-anxious Four may feel like a fraud unworthy of true success. These folks will overspend to compensate for their perceived inadequacy, hoping that the right tools, training, or experiences will finally fix them. Solution: Create an "I Am Enough" fund. Every time you're tempted to buy something to prove your worth, put that money aside instead. Use it for experiences that genuinely fuel your career, such as a class in entrepreneurship.

Magical Thinking: Some Flops believe if they invest enough time and money in their creative pursuits, success and financial stability will inevitably follow. They struggle to accept the realities of the marketplace, especially since there may not be a demand for what they want to supply. In marketplace endeavors, partner up with a business-minded friend or mentor. Have regular reality-check sessions where you bounce ideas off each other. Or hire a business coach. Their practicality combined with your creativity could be the secret to actual, sustainable success.

Feast-or-Famine Folly: A Flop's impulsive spending can lead to a boom-and-bust cycle, where periods of intense creative output and success are followed by financial scarcity and anxiety. This instability can take a toll on mental health and relationships over time. Instead, treat your finances like a long-term art installation. Set up automatic transfers to a savings account during your "feast" times. Call it your "Famine Prevention Fund."

As much as the money-anxious Four may believe that financial struggles are necessary, the truth is that financial stability and creative fulfillment are not mutually exclusive. In fact, having a solid financial foundation can provide the freedom and peace of mind to take creative risks and pursue passions with more intentionality.

As a former monk, I know firsthand the allure of renouncing worldly goods in the pursuit of spiritual enlightenment. But there's nothing inherently noble about financial struggle. In fact, constantly avoiding money issues can be a major block to living out your purpose and sharing your Sacred Gift with the world. Instead, use your natural creativity to build a more robust and authentic financial life.

The Flinger: Money-Anxious

When a Four is anxious about money, they grasp at it, wad it into tight balls, and then fling it as hard as they can at beauty, creativity, or individualism. They love money because it allows them to express themselves through any endeavor that feeds their soul or wards off their anxiety. Money becomes a medium for promoting their individuality and a misguided effort at healing their Sacred Wound of internalized sadness and grief. Unfortunately, Flingers tend to be self-absorbed, even decadent, in how they use their wealth, to the point of self-destruction through overwork, overconsumption, or both.

They may not have paid off their student loans yet, but a Flinger is likely to have a one-of-a-kind tapestry hanging in their living room or a priceless collection of vintage records. They won't settle for a good bottle of wine at a restaurant; it must be a great bottle, or there is no point in drinking anything. They can fling endless resources at whatever captivates them without hesitation. There is nothing wrong with pursuing your passion—just be prudent with your purchases.

One of my clients owns an accounting business and plays music as her hobby. She's spent more money on music equipment than I've spent on cars or clothes in my lifetime. There is almost no limit to how much money she'll spend on her form of creative expression, to the detriment of her retirement plan. Getting her off the make-money-to-spend-money treadmill has been a struggle, but over time, she's learned to tame her money monster and achieve financial independence.

Traits of the Flinger

The Green-Eyed-Monster Effect: Fours who obsess over wealth may constantly compare their financial status to others, especially those in their social or creative circles. They may feel intense envy and resentment toward those they perceive as more financially successful, leading to a toxic cycle of jealousy and self-loathing. They can feel compelled to accumulate more and more assets to demonstrate how amazing they are. Money symbolizes how special they feel about themselves, which puts them on an emotional roller coaster of superiority and inferiority, depending on who they are comparing themselves to. As Theodore Roosevelt aptly said, "Comparison is the thief of joy." Try starting an "Envy Alchemy" practice. Every time you feel that green-eyed monster rearing its ugly head, transmute that envy into acceptance. Write down exactly what you're envious of, then brainstorm three unique ways you could achieve something similar that's true to your authentic self.

Pretentious Peacocking: These Fours chase the next sartorial high, convinced that the perfect, unique outfit will make them feel genuinely seen and stand out. Or their home nest is a gallery of obscure, over-priced art pieces. Each one comes with a story: "This is an original print by an up-and-coming artist I discovered in a back-alley gallery in Berlin. You probably haven't heard of them." Instead, try being truly original and stop caring about what other people think.

Success Gives Me Hives' Hysteria: Even when money-anxious Fours have sufficient financial resources, they may struggle to enjoy or celebrate their abundance. They can feel undeserving of financial comfort or worry it will be short-lived due to their internalized sadness and lack of self-worth. Solution: Start a "Deserving Diary." Each day, write down one reason why you deserve financial comfort and stability. Did you create something beautiful? Were you kind to a stranger? Did you finally remember to water that long-suffering houseplant? Celebrate it all. Over time, you'll build a compendium of your worth that even your inner critic can't ignore.

Paralysis by Financial Analysis: Paradoxically, Flingers may also avoid or procrastinate regarding financial tasks. They may delay opening bills, filing taxes, or making important financial decisions due to the overwhelming anxiety they experience around money matters, even as they work hard to accumulate assets. Solution: Turn your financial tasks into a performance art piece. Set a timer for twenty minutes, put on your most dramatic playlist, and attack those bills like you're the star of a one-person show called "Fiscal Fury: The Reckoning." Make it so over-the-top that you can't help but laugh at yourself.

The Workaholic Woes: The wealth-obsessed Four may intensely pursue their work or creative pursuits, believing that if they work hard enough, they will finally achieve the financial success and recognition they desire. However, this relentless drive can lead to burnout, neglect of personal relationships, and a loss of joy in their creative process. Solution: Institute mandatory "Artistic Playdates" with yourself. Once a week, do something creative just for the sheer joy of it, with zero expectation of financial gain. Finger paint, write a silly limerick, choreograph a dance to your cat's meows. Reconnect with the part of you that creates for creation's sake.

The "Never Enough" Narrative: Despite their financial reality, money-anxious Fours may operate from a scarcity mentality. They may feel that there is never enough money to support their dreams and lifestyle. Chronic worry about their financial future fuels and justifies perpetual angst—even if their actual financial situation doesn't warrant such intense anxiety. For a fix, create an "Enough Is Enough" manifesto. Write down what "enough" looks like for you in vivid, poetic detail. How much money do you actually need to support your dreams? Put a number on it, then create a visual representation—a collage, a painting, an interpretive dance routine, whatever speaks to your soul. Place it somewhere visible. Every time you feel the "never enough" narrative creeping in, refer back to your manifesto. It's like creating a financial North Star for your wandering artist's soul.

Validation-Through-Valuation Disorder: Money-anxious Fours may tie their self-worth and identity to their financial status. They may seek validation or admiration from others based on their financial accomplishments or successes that make them stand out from the crowd. As a fix, create a "True Worth" portfolio. Fill it with things that represent your value beyond money—letters from friends, mementos of experiences you've cherished, photos of people whose lives you've touched. When you're tempted to equate your worth with your wallet, flip through this portfolio instead. It's like carrying around a portable self-esteem boost.

Ultimately, the path to financial serenity for the wealth-obsessed Four lies in recognizing that true abundance comes from within. It's about cultivating a sense of enoughness, gratitude, and purpose beyond the size of their bank account or the stuff their money can buy. By aligning their financial goals with their deepest values and desires, they can begin to use their wealth in a way that feels truly meaningful and fulfilling.

A Money Master—The Flame

I've had the privilege of working with many Fours over the years, and let me tell you, their journey to financial wholeness is a wild, beautiful, and sometimes gut-wrenching ride.

At the core of the Four's path is a deep yearning to know themselves, to peel back the layers of sadness and shame to find the sacred essence within. The journey of self-discovery can feel like wandering through a labyrinth full of twists, turns, and dead ends. But the prize at the center? A bone-deep sense of wholeness that allows Fours to radiate their gifts with authenticity and purpose.

For Fours, the path to money mastery is less about the specific financial strategies (although those are certainly important) and more about the inner work of coming home to oneself. It's about learning to alchemize the heavy lead of sadness and grief into the pure gold of self-love, to transmute the pain of feeling different into the power of embracing one's true uniqueness. In the second half of life, Fours tap into their eternal uniqueness that was always there, rather than a reactive uniqueness to the culture they live in. This requires breaking open and releasing the ego addictions holding them back.

And one of the most potent tools in the Four's arsenal? The cultivation of joy and gratitude. I know it sounds like the stuff of greeting cards, but for Fours, who are so attuned to the depths of the human experience, the practice of savoring the good can be utterly transformative.

I had a client, a Four, who started a gratitude journal to combat his tendency toward melancholy. Every night before bed, he would write down three things he was grateful for, no matter how small or seemingly insignificant. At first, it felt forced, even a little cheesy. But over time, something started to shift. He noticed little moments of beauty throughout the day—a kind word from a stranger, the way the light filtered through the trees, the taste of a perfectly ripe peach. And as he tuned in to the goodness around him, his relationship with himself started to soften. He became less critical, more compassionate, more willing to embrace the fullness of his being.

From that place of deepened self-acceptance, my client found the courage to make some bold moves in his financial life. He asked for a raise at work, started a side hustle teaching music, and built a budget. It wasn't always easy, and there were plenty of moments of doubt and fear along the way. But he could weather the storms and stay the course by remaining anchored in his gratitude practice.

Because Type Fours have a primary ego addiction to melancholy, it seems like they always live in the Dark Night of the Soul. Their ego addictions can make life difficult until they are finally willing to face their deepest pain forthrightly. When they can break open their ego in the Dark Night and face their Sacred Wound of internalized sadness with compassion, the light of love enters their life, and they begin to find joy in the miracle of all existence.

Joy is their primary path of recovery, and Fours might find joy in art, nature, deep conversations, music, cooking, or any other activity that allows them to connect with their inner selves without sadness, shame, or judgment. The more they can find joy in the mundane and ordinary aspects of life, the less stress their ego experiences, which relieves their melancholy.[3]

When their melancholy subsides through expressions of joy, they slowly open to their secondary path of recovery—gratitude.[4] For the Four, gratitude involves recognizing and celebrating the beauty in the distinctive aspects of their life. They learn to appreciate and express thanks to the people who understand and accept them for who they are and to feel genuinely grateful for their own experiences and accomplishments, no matter how difficult their life path has been.

Their secondary path of recovery of gratitude is the primary path of recovery for Type One (BMW), and when Fours learn to let gratitude into their world, it's like trading in their Custom Car for a smooth and luxurious BMW. Everything in their life starts to run better when they stop trying to stand apart and instead let life unfold gracefully. Plus, a Beemer has better shock absorption, which makes the road of life a lot less bumpy.[5]

Gratitude integrated with joy produces the highest virtue for Four—equanimity: the ability to find emotional balance, acceptance, and inner peace amid the intensity of their feelings and the ups and downs of life. Equanimity helps Fours navigate their emotional landscape with greater ease and resilience and let go of their envy. This calm composure allows the Four to become aware of their emotions without getting overwhelmed and accept their feelings as a natural part of their experience.

Their magic formula is:

Joy (primary recovery virtue) + Gratitude (secondary recovery virtue/relaxation point) = Equanimity (greatest virtue/virtue)

Most importantly, their highest virtue of equanimity brings to fulfillment their greatest hope: to find themselves. Fours spend most of their life buffeted by the turmoil of envy-induced emotions that course through them, savoring with odd delight the darker feelings and hurts that make them feel different and special. Only in the stillness of equanimity can they truly discover the magnificent beauty radiating from inside them as a precious child of the God of their understanding. They then actively participate in the rapturous glory they see flowing through all things, most especially inside themselves.

A trapdoor that Fours need to avoid falling through on their journey to money mastery is their faux virtue of mindfulness. Mindfulness practices are good for everyone, but Fours need to be careful not to abuse mindfulness as a way to hang on to past hurts and resentments or be too mindful of what everyone else is doing, exacerbating their envy.

When Fours can recognize their own inner beauty and talents, resting comfortably in their profoundly unique identity as an expression of the Divine, they achieve emotional balance while lighting up the world around them. From stillness grounded in gratitude and joy, their Sacred Wound finally heals, and their envy dissipates, revealing their Sacred Gift—Divine Glory. All of existence becomes redeemed in the eyes of a healthy Four when they can fully experience the Divine Glory surrounding and engulfing them.

When living from their True Self, Fours become a money master: the Flame. The Four then embodies the eternal flame of Divine radiance that shines forth from the darkness, lighting up the world with beauty and truth. With money in their pocket, the Flame knows how to bring the Divine Glory of God into the lives of others through their creative calling. What is more unique than that?

Ultimately, for Fours, becoming a money master is about learning to see themselves through the eyes of love and to recognize their inherent worth and value. It's about daring to bring their full, flawed, fabulous selves to the table in all areas of their life.

So to all the Fours out there, I invite you to take a deep breath and remember this: You are the Flame. You are the light that illuminates the shadows, the truth-teller that awakens the world to its own exquisite beauty. And as you tend to the sacred fire within, as you let yourself be nourished by joy and held by gratitude, you will find that the path to prosperity is not a destination, but a homecoming to your own radiant being.

Becoming a Money Master—The Flame

Please be sure to read (or review) chapter 8, which provides an overview of these five steps, before you get started here.

Acknowledge the pain from your Childhood Wounding.

Grab your favorite vintage cardigan and maybe a tissue or two; it's time to dive into those emotional depths you know so well—but this time with purpose. Your Childhood Wounds probably run deeper than a philosopher's late-night thoughts, but they're not as unique as your inner critic wants you to believe.

Remember those moments when you felt like an alien in your own family? It's as if everyone else got the script for "Normal Family Life" and you were handed the pages for "Brooding Outsider" instead. As a young Four, you likely experienced a profound sense of abandonment or neglect. Now, I'm not saying you were left in a wicker basket on someone's doorstep (though admit it, part of you thinks that would have been tragically romantic). Rather, you felt emotionally abandoned, even when surrounded by family.

Your emotional intensity was often misunderstood or dismissed. Remember all those times you were told to "just cheer up" or "stop being so sensitive"? Your deep feelings and innate sensitivity made you feel like a stranger in your own home.

Perhaps you experienced the loss of a parent or significant caregiver, either through death, divorce, or emotional unavailability. This early loss became the lens through which you viewed the world—a world of exquisite beauty and profound pain, with authentic connection always slightly out of reach.

These experiences cut your psychological umbilical cord with internalized sadness and grief. You learned to feel sad or ashamed of how you perceived yourself, developing a nagging sense that something was fundamentally missing or defective in your core identity. This sadness, grief, and shame became your constant companion, whispering that you'd never quite belong.

Internalized sadness became the fertile ground from which your fear of not having a unique identity grew. In response to feeling defective, you strived to be special, different, unique—anything but ordinary. It's like you thought, *If I can't be normal, I'll be extraordinary.* And let's face it, you've probably succeeded.

Your childhood likely involved a complex dance between longing for connection and fearing it. You yearned to be seen and understood, yet feared that truly being seen would confirm your worst fear—that you were indeed flawed beyond repair. In essence, your childhood was a poignant ballet of longing, misunderstanding, and the search for identity. It started with feeling different and often ended with you making that difference your defining characteristic. For many Fours, financial trauma is intertwined with this emotional alienation.

But remember, dear Four, this Childhood Wounding is only the opening chapter in a story that you get to continue writing. Your early pain isn't just tragic backstory; it's the fertile soil from which your unique perspective grows. After all, some of the world's most outstanding creative achievements have come from those who felt like they didn't quite fit in.

So here's to you, my beautifully complex Fours. May your uniqueness be your superpower, not your kryptonite. And may you find beauty not just in the depths of melancholy, but in the vibrant, messy spectrum of all your emotions. You're not just the black sheep of the family—you're the entire rainbow.

Now grab your detective hat and create a trauma timeline of your childhood. What messages did you internalize about your worth? When did you feel most misunderstood or unseen? Write it out, get curious, and most importantly, bring a hefty dose of compassion to the process. Be sure to look at your relationship with money and where your money anxiety or avoidance crept in.

Stop reacting out of the sadness that created your money monsters.

To overcome the sadness that birthed your money monsters, we need to embark on a daily practice of contemplation and compassion. Think of it as going to an emotion gym, but instead of lifting weights, you're lifting layers of melancholy. Just like you wouldn't expect to write a heart-wrenching sonnet after one poetry class, don't expect to conquer your ego addictions overnight.

Contemplation for you Fours is about shining a spotlight on your ego addictions of melancholy and flattery, not just brooding on past hurts but figuring out how these addictions are creating unnecessary pain in the present. Get curious about them. What purpose have they served? How have they shaped your unique identity? When do they show up, and what triggers them? Remember, these addictions developed as a survival strategy. They're not the enemy. Understanding both addictions will help you navigate emotionally charged situations more skillfully.

One practice that might appeal to your artistic nature is creating a "melancholy map." Get a large canvas or a stack of artisanal paper and start depicting all the ways your internalized sadness and grief manifests in your life. Use colors, symbols, words—whatever speaks to your soul. Then, next to each manifestation, create a contrasting image of gratitude and joy. This exercise can help you see the gap between your shame-based perceptions and a more balanced view of reality, and maybe even find some beauty in the contrast. Joy and gratitude are your primary and secondary paths of recovery that lead to your highest virtue of equanimity. Think of them as emotional art supplies you need to create a masterpiece of a life.

Consider starting and ending your day with this Equanimity Prayer:

> Divine Beauty, open my heart to your transformative love and
> heal the sadness that isolates me. Infuse me with the strength
> to cultivate joy and gratitude, rooted in your ever-present
> grace. Lead me away from my addictions to melancholy and
> flattery, so I may express my unique gifts with equanimity in
> glorious service to you through those around me.

Don't forget the crucial step of cultivating compassion for yourself and the people who raised you. And when you begin to integrate new habits into your routine, give yourself a lot of grace. In time, you might find that financial stability gives you even more freedom to express your unique vision. Now wouldn't that be a plot twist worth writing about?

Learn to be less anxious or avoidant about money by confronting your money monsters.

This next step is where you, the misunderstood protagonist of your own story, face your greatest challenge. Here's where we confront your financial Balrog, your monetary Voldemort—that nagging fear that you'll never be unique or special enough to truly succeed financially.

You can't vanquish this fear by dramatically throwing yourself into a pit of melancholy or by creating an elaborate, tortured persona. Trying to out-emotion your fear is like trying to douse a fire with absinthe. It only makes things more . . . interesting, but not necessarily better.

Instead, we need to take a page out of St. Francis's playbook. Let's reimagine the tale of the Wolf of Gubbio with a Four twist:

The little town of Gubbio has a serious wolf problem—we're talking a full-on furry nightmare. This wolf isn't just any old canine; it's a brooding, artistic type that howls haunting melodies at the moon at midnight and leaves abstract paw-print art all over town. The townspeople, being basic and mainstream, just don't get it and only want some sleep.

Enter St. Francis, the original empath. He hears about this lupine artist and thinks, *Hey, maybe we should try to understand this wolf instead of trying to make it conform to society's boring standards.* I know, crazy idea, right? But Francis was always weird.

So, Francis dances up to the wolf's den, flashing the Sign of Peace, with the townspeople taking bets on how long before Francis becomes a particularly tragic piece of performance art. Instead, the wolf slinks out to face him like a poet who just realized their latest work is actually a bit derivative.

Francis, in full therapist mode, starts chatting up the wolf. He's all, "Listen here, Artiste. You've been a real pain in the town's collective psyche. How about we find a way for you to express yourself without, you know, eating everyone's sheep?" His exact words are something like, "Brother Wolf, I see your pain, your longing to be understood. But I want to make peace between you and these fine folks. How about you promise to stop using them as unwilling participants in your art installations?"

And get this—the wolf nods! It's like a scene from an indie film, minus the obscure soundtrack.

Francis seals the deal, promising the wolf won't have to compromise its artistic integrity and will get an appreciative audience every night if it stops its reign of misunderstood terror. And wouldn't you know it? It works! The wolf becomes the town's poet laureate; the people start leaving out artisanal, locally sourced meats instead of running away screaming; and everyone lives authentically ever after.

Now picture your money monster as that misunderstood wolf. It's been terrorizing your financial village for years, leaving a trail of impulse purchases and unopened bank statements in its wake. Approach your wolf with compassion and understanding. Beating yourself up over past financial mistakes is about as effective as trying to pay your bills with beautiful, handwritten IOUs.

The wolf submitted to Francis because it finally felt understood. Your sadness and fear of being ordinary gives your money monsters power. When you face your financial fears with vulnerable courage and radical self-acceptance, they begin to lose their grip.

That ravenous wolf of financial anxiety or avoidance is really just the misunderstood, sensitive child within you howling for acceptance and validation. The more you attack it with shame or try to drown it in melancholy, the louder it howls and the more damage it does. But when you approach it with understanding and compassion, you can begin to tame it.

And here's where the magic happens: Once tamed, all that intense emotional energy that was causing havoc in your financial life can be integrated and harnessed for good. That's how you become a true money master. It's how you transform your Sacred Wound of sadness into your Sacred Gift of Divine Glory.

To make this transformation a practical reality, we're going to create a "Money Monster to Money Master" transformation chart that's worthy of a gallery exhibition.[6] Where do your Flop or Flinger tendencies show up in how you earn, save, invest, and give? Take a good, hard look at how these mindsets play out in each area. You might find some surprising contrasts.

For example, you might be a Flinger when it comes to earning, pouring your heart and soul into creative projects without much thought for their financial viability. But perhaps you're a Flop when it comes to saving, avoiding your bank statements like they're invitations to a mainstream pop concert. Or maybe you're anxious about earning a lot of money to stand out, but avoidant around giving because you fear not having enough for yourself.

Once you've mapped out these traits, pair each one with a corresponding action step to becoming a money master. These are the countermoves you want to make when your money monster starts to take control. Turn this into a visual masterpiece that captures the depth and complexity of your financial journey. Make it so hauntingly beautiful that you can't help but look at it every day.

Next, write a letter to money as if it were a complex character in the novel of your life. What would you say? How has your tumultuous relationship been? Be honest about your fears, your resentments, your expectations. Then, write a response from money to you. What might it say if it could speak?

Build a strong financial life by earning, saving, and investing ethically.

Let's dive into the Holy Trinity of Finance: earning, saving, and investing, Four style.

First up: earning. You Fours have a superpower here—your creativity and ability to see beauty where others don't. It's time to monetize that gift. Consider careers or side hustles that allow you to express your uniqueness. Maybe it's freelance writing, graphic design, or creating bespoke artisanal . . . well, anything. The world needs your singular vision!

Your weakness here? You might be tempted to dismiss financial success as "selling out" or resist doing anything that feels commercial. But remember, even Van Gogh had to sell a painting or two to buy more yellow paint. Reframe earning as a way to fund your artistic endeavors and personal growth.

Consider starting a business as an expression of your unique self. The entrepreneurial path can be as winding and interesting as you are.

Now, let's talk saving. I can hear your collective sigh from here. But instead of seeing saving as restrictive, view it as a way to fund your future dreams and creative pursuits. Your strength here is your ability to find beauty in simplicity. Use that to embrace minimalism (but make it aesthetic, of course).

Your weakness? Impulse purchases that speak to your soul but wreak havoc on your wallet. Before buying, ask yourself: "Will this still be meaningful to me in a month, or is it just filling an emotional void?"

Create a budget that feels like a poem rather than a spreadsheet. Categorize your expenses in ways that resonate with you. "Nourishing my body" sounds much better than "groceries," doesn't it? Use your artistic skills to make your budget visually appealing.

Finally, investing. This is where you build long-term wealth, and surprise, surprise—it's an area where your unique perspective can shine. Your strength here is your ability to spot trends before they're mainstream. Use that intuition to invest in companies or funds that align with your values and vision for the future.

Your weakness? You might be tempted to invest based on emotion rather than logic, or avoid investing altogether because it feels too "ordinary." Combat this by educating yourself about ethical investing. It's not just good for your conscience; it can be good for your wallet too. Imagine investing in companies that are making the world more beautiful, more sustainable, more . . . you.

Aim to invest at least 15 percent of your pre-tax income in a diversified portfolio that includes some "boring" index funds (think of them as the reliable bass line in your financial symphony) and some carefully chosen individual stocks or funds that resonate with your values (these are your soaring melody).

Remember to regularly review and adjust your financial masterpiece. Your life changes, your inspirations shift, and your money strategy should evolve with you.

Building a strong financial life isn't about conforming to societal expectations of success. It's about creating a life that allows you to fully express your unique self, to dive deep into your passions without the constant stress of financial instability. It's about having the resources to bring more beauty into the world.

Use your money and your talents as tools to love and serve a suffering world.

As a Four, you have a unique superpower: your ability to see beauty in the broken, to find meaning in the depths of human experience.

Now it's time to wield that power, along with your newfound financial wisdom, to illuminate the darkest corners of our world.

First, let's address your tendency to romanticize your suffering. Yes, the pain of the world can be profound, but your mission now is to alleviate it, not wallow in it. Your empathy is your strength; use it to truly understand the needs of others, not just dwell on your own.

Start by immersing yourself in causes that resonate with your soul. Get involved with a local art therapy program for troubled youth. Mentor aspiring entrepreneurs from underprivileged backgrounds. Your unique perspective could be the lifeline someone needs to find their own voice.

Remember, the world doesn't need another misunderstood artist bemoaning its state. It needs visionaries who can imagine a more beautiful future and have the guts to create it. Don't be the wealthy Four who funds yet another angsty indie film. Be the one who starts a community advocacy program that gives voice to the voiceless.

As you embark on this phase, consider how you can use your creative talents to make a tangible difference. Don't underestimate the power of your financial journey either. Your struggle with the Flop or Flinger money monsters has given you unique insights. Consider offering financial literacy workshops with a Four twist—"Budgeting for the Bohemian Soul" or "Investing: The Ultimate Act of Self-Expression." Your hard-won wisdom, delivered with your trademark depth and nuance, could be the perspective shift someone else needs.

As you grow in your ability to give, think about how you can create sustainable, beautiful change. Instead of just addressing symptoms, look for ways to transform the root causes of suffering. This might mean funding arts education in underserved schools, supporting mental health initiatives, or investing in eco-friendly businesses that make sustainability stylish.

Remember, your Sacred Gift as a Four is to unveil life's Divine Glory. You have the power to reveal the profound beauty and meaning in all of existence, even in its messiest, most painful moments. By becoming a money master, you're not just changing your own life—you're gaining the ability to help others see the inherent worth and beauty in themselves and the world around them.

Aria's Story

My fellow wordsmiths and literary dreamers, gather around for the tale of Aria, a Type Four whose journey from penniless poet to bestselling author would make even the most jaded literary agent weep into their craft coffee.

Aria's story begins in a childhood home where her straightlaced parents, while well-meaning, praised her siblings for their conventional achievements, but met Aria's late-night poetry sessions with concerned frowns and gentle suggestions to "maybe try accounting?" For them, there was a "right way" to dress, speak, and express oneself. When her parents divorced, their disdain turned to neglect as her interests were lost to theirs.

This created Aria's Sacred Wound of internalized sadness. She began to feel that her True Self was somehow defective, a narrative flaw in the family story. This sadness and grief burrowed deep within her, creating her greatest fear—that she had no unique identity, that she was just another forgettable character in the great novel of life.

To combat this fear, Aria developed her worst vice: envy. She looked at other kids with a mixture of longing and resentment, convinced that everyone else was special while she remained painfully ordinary. This envy became the fuel for her primary ego addiction to melancholy, using it to withdraw from the world and feel uniquely misunderstood.

As Aria entered adulthood, her financial life became a perfect reflection of her inner turmoil. She was the quintessential Flop, bouncing from one low-paying job to another, convinced that financial struggle was the mark of a true artist.

When her melancholy became too overwhelming, Aria would switch to her secondary ego addiction: flattery. She'd seek out mentors or fellow writers, showering them with praise and offers to edit, desperate for validation. This led to a series of unstable, codependent relationships.

The breaking point came when Aria found herself evicted from her tiny apartment. Her latest writing group disbanded due to creative differences (and her constant need for validation). She stood outside a used bookstore, a tattered notebook in one hand and her last five dollars in the other, feeling like a tragic heroine.

This was Aria's Dark Night of the Soul. The melancholy she had cultivated for so long no longer felt poetic—it felt like spiritual writer's block. Her uniqueness, which she had guarded so fiercely, now felt like a curse. She was miserable, broke, and alone.

Aria's transformation began in this moment of desolation. As she sat on a sidewalk bench outside the store, contemplating the artistic merits of becoming a living statue, she overheard a child excitedly telling a story to their parent. The joy in the child's voice, the pure delight in weaving a tale, pierced Aria's melancholy like a perfectly placed plot twist.

In that moment, Aria made a choice. Instead of sinking deeper into her familiar sadness and self-pity, she allowed herself to feel joy. It felt foreign, almost painful at first. But as she sat there, letting the child's storytelling wash over her, she realized that joy could be as unique and profound as melancholy.

Aria began to actively seek out joyful moments, no matter how small. She found them in clever turns of phrase overheard on the street, in the satisfaction of a well-constructed sentence, in the perfect metaphor that seemed to fall from the sky (when she could afford the coffee to sit and write).

As Aria practiced joy, she found herself naturally drawn to her secondary path of recovery: gratitude. She started to appreciate the beauty in her struggles, the resilience she had developed, the depth of experience that informed her writing. She began keeping a gratitude journal, filling it with observations that were uniquely Aria—poetic, quirky, and increasingly optimistic.

In time, and only fleetingly at first, the combination of joy and gratitude led Aria to her highest virtue: equanimity. She began to find balance, to see her emotions as characters in a story she could direct. This newfound equilibrium allowed her to approach her writing career and finances with a clear head for the first time.

Aria started small. She took a job at the bookstore, appreciating the access to literature as much as the steady paycheck. She began to see budgeting as a creative writing exercise rather than a mundane chore. She even found a unique angle for her skills, writing and editing blogs and newsletters for small businesses, combining her skills with a marketable niche.

As Aria's financial life stabilized, she realized that her uniqueness was not something to be desperately grasped but an innate quality that infused everything she wrote. She was distinctively herself, whether she was crafting a novel, balancing her books, or jotting down ideas for her next story.

Aria's financial success grew alongside her spiritual evolution. She published a series of novels—stories that touched readers deeply with their authentic exploration of the human experience—and became a successful author. A few years later, she started a small publishing house dedicated to amplifying voices that might otherwise go unheard.

Steadily, she began to fully embody her Sacred Gift of Divine Glory. She began to see the Divine beauty in everyone and everything, especially in the overlooked and mundane aspects of daily life. Her writing evolved, becoming a celebration of the glorious uniqueness inherent in all things, from the grand to the minute.

Now, as a true money master, the Flame, Aria uses her resources to bring more beauty and authenticity into the literary world. She funds writing programs in underprivileged schools, sponsors quirky literary festivals, and has even started a scholarship for young writers.

Aria's journey from Flop to Flame was a winding, sometimes backward, often sideways trek. But every word, every chapter, every plot twist of progress was uniquely, gloriously Aria.

CHAPTER THIRTEEN

TYPE FIVE—THE INVESTIGATOR (COMPACT CAR)

HOW TO STOP OVERTHINKING YOUR FINANCES AND START USING THAT DUSTY WALLET

Fives are the most cerebral and introverted of all types, with a rich inner life that is deeply curious about how the world works. These folks have strong personalities, but their gas tank for social interaction is about the size of a thimble, which is why I call them the Compact Car. They can't travel far in social circles without running out of gas.

Instead, they'd much rather analyze the world from a distance and are more traditionally called the Investigator or Observer, content to blend into the background and avoid being the center of attention. But don't let that minimalist exterior fool you—the rich inner life of a Five is anything but boring.

These are the true intellectual heavyweights, constantly gathering information, ideas, and resources in a desperate attempt to protect themselves from the cruel, unpredictable realities of life. At their worst, it's like they're hoarding nuts for the apocalypse, except the nuts are random trivia and the apocalypse is any social interaction requiring emotional vulnerability.

Type Five Ego Map: The Investigator or Compact Car

ENLIGHTENMENT STRUCTURE	
MONEY MASTER	**THE MIDAS**
Sacred Gift (Holy Idea)	Divine Truth
Greatest Hope (Basic Desire)	To know they are wholly capable and competent
Greatest Virtue (Virtue)	Non-Attachment Generosity + Mercy = Non-Attachment (cure for Avarice)
Secondary Recovery Virtue (Relaxation Point)	Mercy (Primary Recovery Virtue for Type 8)
Primary Recovery Virtue	Generosity
Faux Virtue	Gratitude
SHADOW STRUCTURE	
MONEY MONSTERS: AVOIDANT / ANXIOUS	**THE MOOT / THE MISER**
Ego Stress Response	Indulgence Avarice + Planning = Indulgence (blocks Stinginess)
Secondary Ego Addiction (Stress Point)	Planning (Primary Ego Addiction for Type 7)
Primary Ego Addiction (Ego Fixation)	Stinginess
Greatest Vice (Passion)	Avarice
Greatest Fear (Basic Fear)	Being helpless & incompetent
Sacred Wound	Internalized Fear

(Read the chart from the bottom up.)

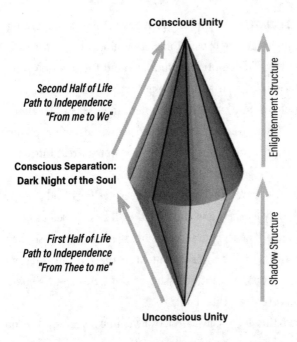

Conscious Unity

Second Half of Life
Path to Independence
"From me to We"

Enlightenment Structure

Conscious Separation:
Dark Night of the Soul

First Half of Life
Path to Independence
"From Thee to me"

Shadow Structure

Unconscious Unity

Fives tend to be accomplished truth-seekers, but they get worn out quickly from all that ceaseless data processing and need regular alone time to recharge. They also struggle to identify or even feel their own emotions and can have an even harder time managing the messy emotions of others. Just imagine Dr. Spock from *Star Trek*—reserved but able to analyze any situation with laser-sharp, dispassionate clarity.

If you want to connect with a Five, find some common areas of intellectual interest, because they're far more comfortable discussing ideas than intangible, mushy, and illogical feelings. When they're unhealthy, getting them to open up about their inner lives is like trying to pry open an oyster with your bare hands. They are like disembodied minds who thrive on knowing something you don't know.

The root of all this cerebral aloofness and stinginess with their emotions likely came from smothering or intrusive caregivers who lacked healthy boundaries in childhood. Whatever it was, something in that environment cut their psychological umbilical cord through fear and insecurity. The emotional world around them wasn't safe. They then internalized that fear, making them afraid of their perceived incompetence and inability to protect themselves. To guard their fragile psyches, young Fives learned to withdraw deep into their own minds, becoming suspicious of attempts at real intimacy or nurturing.

As a result, they carefully hoard their ideas, feelings, and energy, terrified that if they let their guard down, they'll be exposed as helpless and vulnerable. Their greatest fear is being incompetent, so they instinctively retreat from the world, content to analyze and "master" reality from a safe distance until they have it all figured out. Spoiler alert: None of us ever figure it all out.

To cope with this deep-seated anxiety, Fives unconsciously develop their worst vice: avarice. They've got to collect all the information, resources, and intellectual ammunition to keep that sense of helplessness at bay.

And heaven forbid a Five should ever confront this ugly avarice head-on—that would mean facing their greatest fear of being fundamentally flawed and inadequate. So instead, they adopt a primary ego addiction to stinginess, which provides all the self-soothing justification they need to keep hoarding their emotional, intellectual, and physical resources.

Ah, the joys of being a Five. It's no wonder these types often struggle to connect with others. But when they overdose on their primary ego addiction to stinginess, their Compact Car breaks down. In response, they shift to a secondary ego addiction: planning.

Planning is a quick but inelegant way to say that they are seeking immediate gratification as a temporary escape from their stinginess.

Gluttonous planning combined with avarice leads to radical indulgence, their ego stress response, which fleetingly breaks the addictive pattern of stinginess. Through indulgent behavior, Fives gain a respite from their usual pattern of holding back and hoarding resources—though often in unhealthy ways.

Their quirky formula is:

Avarice (greatest vice/passion) + Planning (secondary ego addiction/stress point) = Indulgence (ego stress response)

How a Five indulges their secondary addiction to planning can be weird and wild, like bingeing on sex, drugs, games, or bizarre fantasies. Although unhealthy in the long term, self-gratification releases the pressure built up by the reserved nature of the Five, preventing them from collapsing inward completely like a black hole when stressed.

Planning is the primary ego addiction of Type Seven (the Enthusiast or SUV), and it's like the Five temporarily trades in their Compact Car for a beat-up SUV so that they can take an off-road adventure and let a little spontaneity into their life. However, this indulgence can leave them broken and debased like the Prodigal Son if their debauchery runs amok.[1]

For example, one Type Five client held a respected position at an engineering firm but regularly traveled to other cities to seek bacchanalian parties where they could anonymously indulge their less noble desires.

Fives are sometimes known for having a fascination with the dark and macabre aspects of life, anything that is taboo. As Investigators, they get curious about things they are told not to look at.

When they finally learn to feel safe and secure, knowing they are a beloved piece of the Infinite Intelligence of the universe, all of that anxious grasping, that frantic hoarding of knowledge and resources, simply melts away, like morning mist before the rising sun.

It's a beautiful transformation to behold. These cerebral, emotionally stunted brainiacs go from being the most emotionally and intellectually tightfisted, miserly members of the Enneagram clan to freely giving of their time, talent, and treasure. Their stinginess morphs into this wonderful, expansive nonattachment—the ultimate hallmark of a healthy, actualized Five.

With this cerebral foundation established, let's examine how these patterns manifest in the Five's relationship with money.

Money Monsters

The Moot: Money-Avoidant

Money-avoidant Fives elevate their aversion to all things financial to an art form. These folks manage to transform their fear of helplessness and incompetence into a full-blown philosophical rejection of the very concept of money. Why bother with the petty concerns of the material world when you've got an entire inner landscape of intellectual curiosity to explore?

For these Fives, money is just about the most "moot" and irrelevant thing imaginable. After all, if you never need to deal with the stress and responsibility of trying to build a robust financial life, then you'll never have to confront your incompetence when it comes to managing money and interacting with the world. It's a foolproof plan!

But let's be real here: Moots may talk a big game about the irrelevance of material wealth, but deep down, they're as terrified of being helpless and incompetent as any other Five. They've just found a clever way to avoid confronting that fear head-on.

Moots have taken the Five's healthy financial frugality to the extreme. They're content to live a spartan, ascetic lifestyle as long as they never have to dirty their hands with the practical realities of earning, saving, and investing beyond the bare minimum.

Traits of the Moot

Masochistic Minimalism: Some Moots take the concept of "less is more" to such an extreme that their living spaces could make a monk's cell look like a five-star hotel suite. They pare down their material possessions to the bare essentials—a mattress on the floor, a few dog-eared academic texts, and a hot plate if they're feeling particularly bougie. Anything more than that is just clutter standing between them and their precious mental pursuits. If you are a Moot, challenge yourself to "upgrade" one item in your living space each month. Start small— maybe replace that sad, flat pillow with a comfy new one. Think of it as an experiment in how minor comforts affect your cognitive function. You might find that a slightly cozier environment actually enhances your mental pursuits.

Penny-Pinching Panic: These money avoiders are the miserly grandparents of the Enneagram, capable of stretching a single tea bag for a week. Instead, dear Moots, set up a "Mad Money" account. Allocate a small percentage of your income (even 1 percent will do) for guilt-free spending on nonessentials. Think of it as funding for field research into the world of material goods.

Ledger-Loathing Sickness: These folks would rather wrestle a rabid wolverine than sit down and deal with their financial paperwork and long-term planning. The mere thought of it makes their skin crawl. And heaven forbid they should ever consider outsourcing the drudgery to a financial advisor. That would be an unforgivable breach of their precious autonomy, not to mention a wasteful expense. Moots, for a practical solution, create a spreadsheet that turns financial management into a strategy game. Assign point values to savings goals and financial tasks. Treat it like a role-playing game where you're leveling up your "Financial Wizard" character. Before you know it, you'll be min-maxing your budget like a pro.

Affluence-Aversion Disorder: Moots couldn't care less about material wealth or social status. All that matters is honing their expertise in their chosen fields. Besides, driving a nice car might get them a date, and we can't have that, can we? To overcome affluence aversion, perhaps try reframing wealth as a knowledge-acquisition tool. Instead of viewing money as a path to vapid materialism, see it as a means to fund your intellectual pursuits. That nice car? It's a mobile research station. That designer bag? A stylish carrying case for your rare books.

Radical Risk-Rejection Reflex: Some Moots make your stereotypical octogenarian retiree look like a thrill-seeking adrenaline junkie. They wouldn't touch any sort of financial risk or investment with a ten-foot pole. The mere thought of losing even a penny of their hard-earned savings is enough to send them into a full-blown panic attack. They will stick to their tried-and-true savings accounts and CDs, thank you very much. No risky stocks or speculation for this crowd. As a solution, start with micro-investments. Use apps that round up your purchases and invest the spare change. It's low-risk and allows you to dip your toes into the investment world without feeling like you're betting the farm. Think of it as conducting a long-term experiment in financial growth.

Knowledge-Hoarding Hermeneutics: If you need to look up *hermeneutics*, you may not be a Five. These Moots won't waste time and energy pursuing something as pedestrian as financial gain when they could be expanding the frontiers of human knowledge. After all, money isn't a Platonic ideal, so why bother with it? What about applying your love of complex systems to finance? Dive into the fascinating world of economic theory or the psychology of money. Treat financial literacy as another field to master. After all, to understand money is to understand a fundamental aspect of human behavior and societal structure.

Defiant DIY Disorder: Money-avoidant Fives white-knuckle their way through their money woes and maintain their precious illusion of complete self-reliance. Instead, reframe seeking financial advice as "consulting an expert in the field." Just as you'd reference a respected authority in your area of expertise, view financial advisors as subject matter experts whose knowledge you can absorb and analyze. You're not surrendering autonomy; you're expanding your knowledge base.

The Miser: Money-Anxious

Misers are the Fives who are so gripped by the primal fear of not having enough to take care of themselves that they essentially transform their bank accounts into personal fortresses. These are the Ebenezer Scrooges of the Enneagram, the miserly misanthropes who will pinch a penny until it screams and begs for mercy.

These money-anxious fiscal hoarders don't just save for a rainy day—they stockpile funds like they're preparing for a biblical flood. They track every cent to ensure their self-sufficiency and protection from the slings and arrows of outrageous fortune. In the process, they fail to live fully. Forget about indulging in simple pleasures or anything that might make life more enjoyable. It's a tragic fate, really—these brilliant, cerebral Fives, so paralyzed by fear that they deprive themselves of life's most essential pleasures.

Misers labor under the delusion that money is the key to shielding themselves from all their fears and anxieties. If they can just amass enough wealth, then illness, injury, and even death might all be vanquished. Of course, no amount of money can permanently protect us from the fundamental realities of the human condition.

If only the anxious hoarders could learn to temper their avarice with a touch of generosity, to find the courage to step out from behind their financial fortress and truly engage with the world. Then they may discover that the path to true security lies not just in accumulating wealth but in cultivating meaningful connections and embracing the full spectrum of the human experience.

For example, Geoffrey Holt was a groundskeeper at a mobile home park who lived alone in a rundown trailer with little furniture and no computer, TV, or car. However, when he died in 2023, he left behind an estate worth $3.8 million. He was likely a Miser who anxiously saved money but had trouble spending any. At least Geoffrey Holt donated his fortune to his hometown of Hinsdale, New Hampshire (which is coincidently named after *Ebenezer* Hinsdale).

Traits of the Miser

"My Precious" Psychosis: Some Miser Fives are so paranoid by the thought of maybe, possibly, potentially not having enough resources that they become like Gollum from *Lord of the Rings*, preserving their "precious" portfolio. They will anxiously earn, save, and invest for their Precious but not for anything or anyone else, leaving them rich in cash and poor in life satisfaction. Instead, try creating a "Life Experience Fund." Allocate a small percentage of your resources to nonacademic experiences. Think of it as field research into the human condition. Who knows? That cooking class or salsa dancing lesson might just provide unexpected insights for your next theoretical breakthrough.

The Autonomy-Addicted Ascetic: These money-anxious folks resist depending on others, financially or otherwise, or having anyone depend on them. They might refuse to share financial information with their spouse out of fear of being controlled or appearing incompetent. As a hack, try to reframe interdependence as a complex system worthy of study. Start small—perhaps join a book club or rent space in a community garden. Observe how pooling resources (be it knowledge or tomatoes) can lead to greater outcomes. Consider it an experiment in symbiotic relationships. You're not losing autonomy; you're gaining data points on human interaction.

Hoarding Hysteria: Of course, all the Five's financial anxiety and obsessive resource-hoarding stems from that deep-seated fear of depletion, that primal terror of being incompetent. So these Misers hoard and hoard some more. To combat this tendency, set up a "Generosity Fund" alongside your regular savings. For every dollar you save for a rainy day, put a dime into this account. Use it exclusively to help others like your friends and family. Think of it as building a diversified social fund to complement your financial one. It's also called *tithing*.

Penny-Pinching Perfectionism: When it comes to their financial decision-making, these Misers take overthinking to a whole new level of neurotic indecision. They can spend hours, days even, meticulously researching every possible investment option or purchase decision, weighing the risks and benefits as if the very fabric of reality will unravel if they don't find the perfect way to allocate their resources. Instead, implement a decision-making framework with time limits. For purchases under $100, give yourself five minutes to decide. For $100 to $1,000, an hour. Over $1,000, a day. Treat it like a timed exam— you're training your brain to make efficient decisions under pressure. Remember, in finance, as in science, sometimes "good enough" data is more valuable than perfect data that comes too late.

Future Fiscal Fearmongering: While prudent financial planning and a strong emergency fund are essential, Misers have an unhealthy obsession with worst-case financial scenarios. They don't just worry about their future stability—they practically wallow in it, conjuring up vivid, apocalyptic visions of total destitution and ruin. For a fix, channel your vivid imagination into positive scenarios. For every doomsday scenario you conjure, force yourself to imagine an equally detailed positive outcome. Then, critically analyze both. You might find that your positive scenarios are just as likely (if not more so) than the negative ones. Treat it like peer-reviewing your own apocalyptic papers.

A Money Master—The Midas

It's a remarkable transformation when a Five finally breaks free from the stranglehold of their ego addictions. No longer content to stockpile their resources like a dragon clutching its gilded hoard, the healthy Five emerges as a veritable money master—a Midas who can transmute their former stinginess into pure, resplendent, nonattached generosity, and it isn't just about giving away money. Everything around them turns to gold.

As with all of us, the journey to becoming a money master starts with a harrowing Dark Night of the Soul, often several. For a Five, stinginess and planning inevitably create the pain and fear they are trying to avoid. In the Dark Night, a Five feels not just isolated (which is their comfort zone), but fundamentally incompetent to handle the life challenges crashing down around them. Most terrifyingly, they realize that all their careful withdrawal and preparation have actually left them more vulnerable, not less.

As difficult as these moments are, they can also catalyze the Fives' path to liberation. In order to find true mastery over their finances or any other aspect of life, Fives need to learn to break open and to let their inner world connect more meaningfully with the outside world. The key is their primary path of recovery—generosity.

Something remarkable happens when Fives learn to give generously of their time, feelings, talents, and yes, even some of their precious resources. Their stinginess starts to recede, and the stress on their ego begins to ease.

When a Five finally breaks open in the Dark Night of the Soul, it's like watching a fortress crumble—but in a good way. All that knowledge, all those resources they've been stockpiling like a doomsday prepper? They start spilling out into the world.

The shift begins when Fives realize that their fortress of knowledge and resources isn't protecting them—it's isolating them. They discover that genuine security comes not from hoarding but from creating networks of mutual support through sharing. They find that the world isn't trying to deplete them—it's trying to engage with them.

The one thing that can trip them up on this journey is their faux virtue of gratitude. In their quest to feel competent and self-sufficient, Fives can mistake their stinginess for genuine gratitude. This faux gratitude isn't about appreciation; it's about justifying their need to withdraw and keep everything for themselves. They're not so much grateful as they are terrified of depletion.

However, once they've embraced generosity as their primary path of recovery, their Compact Car starts to run out of fuel. It's just not fun to drive anymore. So what do they do? They go out and borrow a luxury Hummer from their friends in the Type Eight camp, and they adopt the Eight's primary path of recovery—mercy—as their own secondary path.[2]

Driving that big ol' Hummer helps the Five find their voice and assert their competency, sharing it with the world. And mercy, that's all about nonjudgment—of themselves and others. It allows Fives to be more vulnerable and open, to form deeper connections, and to accept that everyone has flaws, including themselves. They slowly learn they don't have to go it alone or be constantly competent. Life is much more fun when you don't have to be good at everything. Healthy play has nothing to do with competence but rather freedom, joy, and self-expression.

And when they combine generosity and mercy, that's when they unlock their highest virtue—nonattachment. No more clinging to their thoughts, their knowledge, or their possessions. It also means accepting their feelings as valid, being present with their emotional experiences, and expressing their emotions without judgment or fear. They become open to new perspectives, willing to unlearn and relearn. It also means finding a better balance between self-preservation and genuine connection, trusting that loving relationships can coexist with healthy personal boundaries. It's the true path to financial—and personal—liberation, free from avarice.

Their secret formula for success is:

Generosity (primary recovery virtue) + Mercy (secondary recovery virtue/relaxation point) = Nonattachment (greatest virtue/virtue)

Nonattachment heals the Five's Sacred Wound of internalized fear, bringing them into more harmonious unity with all of life rather than withdrawing from it. Armed with their impressive knowledge, they can use that competency more effectively to improve the world.

When the ego of the Type Five cracks open in the Dark Night of the Soul, it's like witnessing a supernova—they shower the cosmos with glitter and gold. All the information and wisdom (and yes, excess cash) they've been hoarding for decades starts to flow in reverse, going outwards, and it lights up the universe. Just remember that this is a process of continual growth, not a permanent state of perfection.

Nonattachment is what allows the Five to embody their Sacred Gift—Divine Truth. Their path to wholeness extends far beyond the mere accumulation of intellectual knowledge. It is a profound spiritual seeking, a quest for understanding that transcends the limitations of the material world.

In their quest, they find comfort and wonder in the great mysteries of existence. They see the Divine Truth that permeates all of life, that binds us together in the fundamental rhythm of the universe. These Fives know, at the deepest level, that everything has a purpose, a reason for being, and that everything belongs, especially them.

And as they radiate this Divine Truth, something miraculous happens—their heart becomes softened, their gaze expands to encompass both the brilliance and the messiness of the human experience. True wisdom is found not in absolutes but in the humble acceptance of ourselves and all of creation, with all its complexities and contradictions.

The healthy Five understands this essential truth. They do not shy away from the challenges and difficulties of life but rather meet them with abiding compassion—for themselves, for others, and for the world. This is the great gift they have to offer: not just the clear light of their intellectual mastery but the ability to share their knowledge with a warm heart that has learned to love generously and unconditionally.

In this way, the Enneagram Five becomes a living embodiment of the sacred. In their quest to transcend the material, they discover the wellspring of true purpose and meaning in how things really work. In sharing this Divine Truth, they inspire us all to look beyond the surface and find the wonder, belonging, and eternal truths at the heart of existence. Then they finally experience the fulfillment of their greatest hope: to know they are competent at the game of life.

Becoming a Money Master—The Midas

Please be sure to read (or review) chapter 8, which provides an overview of these five steps, before you get started here.

Acknowledge the pain from your Childhood Wounding.

I know the mere thought of delving into those old hurts and traumas probably has you wanting to retreat into your intellectual fortress and bury your nose in a book. Your rational mind is your primary defense system—it's kept you safe, made you competent, given you mastery over your chosen domains. But bear with me, my cerebral friends, because this is the foundation upon which you'll build your wealth and fulfillment.

Think of this exploration as creating a systematic database of your emotional patterns. Instead of running from the data because it's messy or threatens your defenses, approach it with your natural analytical prowess. Your childhood environment likely taught you that vulnerability equals weakness, that giving equals depletion, that engagement equals overwhelm. No wonder you developed such sophisticated methods of withdrawal and resource conservation.

Many Fives' psychological umbilical cord was severed by a profound sense of intrusion. Your childhood space—both physical and emotional—was likely under constant siege. Perhaps you had caregivers who were emotionally intense or demanding, who treated your boundaries like mere suggestions. Or maybe your inner world, your thoughts and feelings, were consistently overlooked or dismissed. It's as if you were living in a house without doors, where everyone felt entitled to your energy and attention. This constant intrusion led to your core fear: the terror of being overwhelmed, depleted, or proven incompetent. Your response? To withdraw into your mind, to hoard your resources, to build walls with knowledge and data. In financial terms, this often manifests as either complete avoidance of money matters or anxious overcollection of resources—both strategies designed to protect you from that original sense of overwhelm and incompetence.

Let's approach this analytically. Get out your whiteboard or spreadsheet and create a trauma timeline. Map out the key data points: When did you first learn to withdraw? What events taught you to hoard resources? What experiences shaped your relationship with money? Look for patterns, correlations, cause-and-effect relationships. This isn't just emotional archaeology—it's creating a foundational dataset for understanding your financial behaviors.

Remember, you don't have to do this alone, even though independence is your comfort zone. Think of working with a therapist or counselor as consulting an expert in an unfamiliar field. It's not weakness; it's intelligent resource allocation. You're not surrendering your competence by seeking help—you're expanding your knowledge base and skill set.

This process takes time, and that's okay. Apply your natural patience with complex systems to this inner work. The goal isn't to dismantle your defenses—it's to understand them so well that you can upgrade them from rigid walls into flexible, permeable boundaries that protect without isolating.

Remember, your analytical mind isn't the enemy here—it's one of your greatest tools for healing. We're just expanding its jurisdiction to include the emotional realm, including your relationship with money.

Stop reacting out of the fear that created your money monsters.

Let's approach this like a research study—with you as both scientist and subject. Your core fear of incompetence drives your financial decisions, so we need accurate data about how this manifests.

Start with daily contemplation, but frame it as data collection on your own behavior patterns. Set aside time each day for empirical observation of your financial reactions. What triggers your stinginess? What situations make you feel incompetent around money? When do you withdraw into research rather than take action? Let your journal become a research log tracking behavioral patterns and their correlations to financial decisions.

Your compulsive need to research and prepare before taking action isn't just perfectionism—it's a sophisticated defense mechanism against your core fear of incompetence. Notice how often you fall into the trap of thinking "just one more book" or "just a little more research" before making a decision. This isn't actually about gathering data—it's about avoiding the vulnerability of action where you might fail.

Focus particularly on your primary ego addiction to stinginess. Document when and how it manifests. What are the environmental triggers? What are the observable outcomes? Remember your secondary ego addiction to planning—when does it kick in? How does it lead to indulgence? Understanding these patterns is crucial for interrupting them.

Create a systematic observation log:

- Trigger events
- Initial reaction
- Defense mechanism employed
- Outcome
- Alternative responses that could have been more effective

Again, this isn't just journaling—it's building a database of your financial behavior patterns that you can analyze for insights and actionable conclusions.

Once you've identified these patterns, it's time to start cultivating your core virtues: generosity and mercy. These are your primary and secondary paths of recovery that lead to your highest virtue of nonattachment. Think of them as new skills you need to master. How can you incorporate them into your daily life?

I wrote the following Nonattachment Prayer for Enneagram Fives that you might use or modify. Perhaps try reciting it in the morning and evening and see if it helps.

Infinite Wisdom, open my heart to your enlightening love and dispel the fear that confines me. Instill in me the courage to be generous and merciful, trusting fully in your abundant grace. Help me release my addictions to stinginess and indulgent planning so that I may freely share my gifts in loving service to you through those around me.

The goal isn't to abandon your analytical nature—it's to expand its scope to include emotional and financial intelligence. You're not trying to become less cerebral; you're becoming more complete.

Learn to be less anxious or avoidant about money by confronting your money monsters.

Your money monster might look less like a snarling beast and more like a complex equation you can't solve. It's been keeping you stuck in the same financial ruts. Write a thoughtful letter to your money monster, telling it how it has negatively impacted your life. Then write a response letter back to yourself from your money monster. What might it say? What was it trying to protect you from, and what does it have to teach you?

Here's another trick you might try: Make a list of the Moot or Miser mindsets that get you in trouble the most and look at those each day in the morning and evening. Don't just leave them as broad generalizations. I want you to get really specific—describe those bad boys as they fit your unique situation. After all, what applies to one Five might be a total mismatch for another.

In fact, why not go even deeper? Take a long, hard look at how those unhealthy mindsets manifest in each of the key financial areas of earning, saving, investing, and giving. Maybe you've got some really anxious energy when it comes to earning and saving, but you're more of a mixed bag of avoidance and anxiety around investing. And when it comes to charitable giving—that might be a place of avoidance.

Once you've mapped out all those problematic money monsters, I want you to get your spreadsheet game on. Use that analytical prowess and pair each unhealthy mindset with the corresponding Midas mindset you want to cultivate instead.

Get creative with it. Why not try a money monster map or flow chart? That way, you can easily see where you're struggling and what countermoves to make when those beasts come crawling back. (For examples, see my website at douglynam.com.) Your challenge isn't to slay this beast but to understand it, break it down into manageable parts, and ultimately integrate it into your long-term financial strategy.

I know tackling all this emotional and mental stuff around money can be a real slog. But trust me, if anyone has the intellectual firepower to take on those money monsters and come out on top, it's you cerebral masterminds.

Build a strong financial life by earning, saving, and investing ethically.

Once you've laid that crucial emotional and spiritual foundation, we can start building your financial mastery. Who better to tackle those technical details than a bunch of data-loving intellectuals like yourselves? Just remember to keep that compassionate spirit alive, even as you delve into the nitty-gritty of earning, saving, and investing. If you're money-anxious and have already built your empire, skip ahead to the next step.

As a Five, you have tremendous interior resources to draw upon that can make earning money easier for you than for most. We live in an information-driven world, so your natural thirst for knowledge and understanding can be a real cash cow. How about taking that brilliant mind of yours and monetizing it? Provide the world with a skill or service it desperately needs. And if you've already got a good gig going, why not take things up a notch and become a bona fide expert in your chosen passion? The more specialized your talents, the more society will reward you. Use that cerebral superpower, my friends!

And as for the whole saving money thing? You Fives probably have that one locked down already. If not, start investigating a good budgeting and financial planning app. Your natural tendency toward minimalism can be a superpower. Before making a purchase, take a mindful moment to ask if it will truly add value to your life or just end up as clutter (physical or financial). Then build up that emergency fund—it's like a protective force field for your finances, allowing you to take calculated risks without fear.

You also have a natural advantage in the world of investing. One reason your money master is called the Midas (besides alliteration), is that your natural prowess in mastering intellectual pursuits means you start this race with a ten-lap lead. Think of Bill Gates, Warren Buffett, Mark Zuckerberg, or Ray Dalio, all Enneagram Fives who've risen to the top of the investing and entrepreneurial worlds. You just need to get over your Moot mindset, pull out those investing books, and get to work.

Your Achilles' heel, however, is giving. Once you amass some wealth, letting some of it go is likely a challenge. Your natural inclination toward avarice and stinginess is what holds you back the most from being a true money master. But you now have tools and strategies to help you work on those stumbling blocks.

Use your money and talents as tools to love and serve a suffering world.

This final step might seem at odds with your desire for independence and self-sufficiency. But this is where all your knowledge and financial savvy can create real, tangible impact in the world. The true purpose of this journey isn't just to accumulate wealth for wealth's sake. It's about using your financial resources to serve the greater good—of channeling your impressive intellect and expertise into making the world a better place. And I know you Fives are more than up to the task.

Your unique gift to the world is your ability to understand complex systems and share that knowledge. Think about how you can use this gift, backed by your financial resources, to address systemic issues in society. Maybe it's funding research into areas you're passionate about, or setting up educational programs that can help others achieve financial literacy.

Consider creating a structured giving plan that aligns with your values and interests. This isn't about random acts of charity; it's about strategically using your resources to create lasting change. Maybe you could set up a scholarship fund in your field of expertise, or support organizations that promote critical thinking and education.

Remember, giving back doesn't always mean giving money. Your time and knowledge can be just as valuable. Consider mentoring or teaching in your area of expertise. Your unique perspective and depth of understanding could be exactly what someone needs to break through their own barriers.

As you engage in this process, you might find that it actually deepens your own understanding and challenges you to grow in new ways. It's like the ultimate field study—you're not just theorizing about how to improve the world, you're actively participating in the experiment.

By becoming a money master, not only will you secure your own future, but you'll also gain the power to support and propagate the knowledge and values you hold dear—ensuring that your legacy continues to impact the world long after you're gone.

While others may perceive you as cold and aloof, we both know the tender, aching heart that lies within. That very sensitivity, that capacity for empathy, makes you uniquely suited to address the sorrows and struggles of our time. But too often, you have felt overwhelmed, compelled to withdraw into the sanctuary of your own mind.

Instead, can you bring that compassion forward, allowing it to be the guiding light that illuminates your path? The world desperately needs your Sacred Gift of Divine Truth—the profound wisdom born of your intuitive understanding of the web of interconnectedness that binds all of life.

With resources at your disposal, how will you choose to heal the cracks in that fragile tapestry? How will you leverage your wealth, knowledge, and very being to alleviate the suffering, sorrow, and sadness surrounding us? This is the sacred calling before you, and may you always have a quiet corner to retreat to when you need to recharge your batteries.

Evelyn's Story

Evelyn grew up in a run-down apartment complex with an emotionally volatile single father who worked two jobs. The chaos of their cramped living space drove Evelyn to seek refuge in the only quiet place she could find—her own mind. Books became her escape, the library her sanctuary. The vast, orderly universe of physics and astronomy offered a stark contrast to the unpredictable, messy reality of her daily life.

This childhood environment cut Evelyn's psychological umbilical cord through fear. She developed an overwhelming fear of being incompetent to meet life's challenges. To cope, she embraced her worst vice: avarice. For Evelyn, this manifested as an insatiable hunger for knowledge. If she could just learn enough, she'd finally feel safe and competent in a world that felt perpetually out of control.

As Evelyn grew, her primary ego addiction to stinginess took root. She also became a Moot, treating money as irrelevant and unnecessary. "Why bother with finances when there are galaxies to explore?" she'd rationalize.

Evelyn's brilliant mind propelled her through school and into a prestigious PhD program in astrophysics, but her empty bank account and massive student debt were black holes she dared not approach. When the stress of life overwhelmed her, Evelyn would periodically switch to her secondary ego addiction of planning, which for her was self-indulgent periods of excess drinking, smoking, and a little hard partying.

By her late thirties, Evelyn had made a name for herself in the scientific community, but her personal life was as barren as a distant moon. Then, life decided to test her.

It started with a persistent cough that wouldn't go away. After months of ignoring it, Evelyn finally saw a doctor. The diagnosis hit her like a supernova: stage 2 lung cancer. As Evelyn fought for her life, her finances crumbled further. Forced to take leave from her research position, the bills started piling up faster than space debris in low-Earth orbit. Her partner of five years, overwhelmed by the stress and unable to cope with Evelyn's emotional-withdrawal response to the crisis, left her.

In Evelyn's Dark Night of the Soul, knowledge failed to protect her from the harsh realities of life. For all her intellectual prowess, she was woefully incompetent when it came to managing real-world challenges. The fear she'd been running from all her life finally caught up with her.

Evelyn retreated into herself, obsessively researching alternative cancer treatments, planning elaborate health regimens, and ignoring the mounting bills. Her stinginess reached new heights as she hoarded every bit of energy and resources for her own survival, pushing away the few friends who tried to help.

One night, curled up on her bathroom floor after a particularly brutal round of chemo, Evelyn had an epiphany. She realized that all her knowledge would mean nothing if she couldn't use it to truly live. Evelyn faced a choice: continue hiding in her intellectual fortress or confront her demons—financial, emotional, and physical.

With trembling hands, she reached out—first to a cancer support group, then to a financial advisor. To her surprise, neither judged her. Instead, they helped her see her situation as just another system to understand, not unlike the cosmic systems she studied.

This perspective shift was the first step on Evelyn's journey to becoming the Midas. Slowly, she began to practice her primary path of recovery: generosity. She started small, sharing her story in support groups, offering her knowledge to help other patients understand their treatment options. As she gave freely of herself, the grip of fear began to loosen.

This opened the door to her secondary path of recovery: mercy. Evelyn learned to be gentle with herself, to forgive her past mistakes and limitations. She realized her worth wasn't tied to her knowledge, her bank account, or even her health status. She became kinder and more compassionate to others, able to welcome more love and light into her life. She started treating money with the respect it deserves and now sees it as an essential tool for her health and wellness.

As Evelyn combined generosity and mercy, she unlocked her highest virtue: nonattachment. She began to see that true security doesn't come from hoarding knowledge or emotions, but from engaging fully with the world, even with all its pain and uncertainty.

Evelyn's transformation accelerated as she built a community. She created a podcast that explains complex scientific concepts in relation to everyday life, including cancer and personal finance, and it became popular. Her unique ability to break down complex systems into understandable parts made her a sought-after speaker and writer.

As her cancer faded into remission, her rising popularity caught the eye of a tech company working on solutions for space travel. They hired her for a meaningful and lucrative position, and in time, she was able to pay off her medical and student loan debts. Years later, with money in the bank, Evelyn established a scholarship fund for under-privileged students interested in STEM fields. Money became a tool for her own well-being and the education of others. In this process, Evelyn fulfilled her greatest hope: to know she is competent not just in her field, but in navigating the practical and emotional aspects of life.

Finally, Evelyn embraced her Sacred Gift of Divine Truth. She now sees the interconnectedness of all things—including the role of money in the grand cosmic dance. Her financial journey became a metaphor for universal realities: the ebb and flow of resources; the importance of balance; and the power of vulnerability, connection, and letting go.

Evelyn, once the Moot, is now truly the Midas. Everything she touches turns to gold in the way she transforms knowledge into wisdom, scarcity into abundance, fear into understanding. She illumi-nates the path for others to find their own balance between the cosmic and the commonplace, the intellectual and the practical, the individual and the collective. She shows the world that true wealth lies not just in what we know or what we have, but in how we face life's challenges and share our gifts with others.

CHAPTER FOURTEEN

TYPE SIX—THE SKEPTIC (FAMILY SEDAN)

HOW TO STOP HIDING CASH IN YOUR MATTRESS AND START TRUSTING YOURSELF

Extraordinarily pragmatic, if a bit pessimistic, Sixes are sensible, reliable, and value safety above all else, hence my nickname for them as the Family Sedan of egos. They are always ready for the worst-case scenario, so you can always count on them to have jumper cables in their trunk and spare blankets, water, and emergency rations just in case something goes wrong on the highway of life. When the zombie apocalypse comes, it's good to have Type Six friends—they're fully prepped and have a space for you in their bunker.

Beneath that air of steadfast reliability lies a heart wracked by chronic anxiety, which is the source of their skepticism. These dear souls are forever looking to external authorities and established systems to provide them with the guidance and protection they feel they can't muster from within. A family, a church, a political party, a corporation—it doesn't matter, so long as it promises security. Yet it's a complex tap dance Sixes perform, for while they crave the stability of such structures and

Type Six Ego Map: The Skeptic or Family Sedan

(Read the chart from the bottom up.)

ENLIGHTENMENT STRUCTURE	
MONEY MASTER	**THE PIONEER**
Sacred Gift (Holy Idea)	Divine Trust
Greatest Hope (Basic Desire)	To know complete protection and guidance
Greatest Virtue (Virtue)	Courage Faith + Assertiveness = Courage (cure for Cowardice)
Secondary Recovery Virtue (Relaxation Point)	Assertiveness (Primary Recovery Virtue for Type 9)
Primary Recovery Virtue	Faith
Faux Virtue	Modesty
SHADOW STRUCTURE	
MONEY MONSTERS: AVOIDANT / ANXIOUS	**THE PARALYZED / THE PUPPET & PUGILIST**
Ego Stress Response	Self-Importance Cowardice + Vanity = Self-Importance (blocks Fear)
Secondary Ego Addiction (Stress Point)	Vanity (Primary Ego Addiction for Type 3)
Primary Ego Addiction (Ego Fixation)	Fear
Greatest Vice (Passion)	Cowardice
Greatest Fear (Basic Fear)	Being without protection or guidance
Sacred Wound	Internalized & Externalized Fear

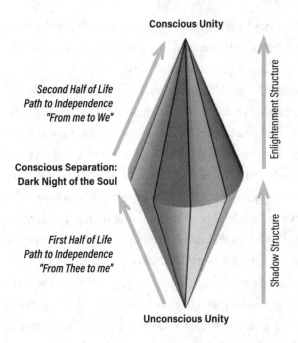

Conscious Unity

Second Half of Life
Path to Independence
"From me to We"

Enlightenment Structure

Conscious Separation:
Dark Night of the Soul

First Half of Life
Path to Independence
"From Thee to me"

Shadow Structure

Unconscious Unity

relationships, they are inherently mistrustful of others and recoil from the idea of being overwhelmed or subsumed by them.

The psychological umbilical cord for Sixes was severed by fear, which they directed internally and externally. This dual-edged fear stripped away their trust both in themselves and in others, so within the mind of the Six rages a cacophony of doubt—doubt in their own internal ability to protect themselves, and doubt in the abilities and motivations of all those around them. The roots of this anguish stretch back to the Six's tender childhood years when they felt threatened by the very environment meant to nurture and care for them. Their childhood environment wasn't always a safe haven, either being the source of a serious threat or failing to shield them adequately from one.

Is it any wonder, then, that the adult Six seeks out an authority figure, a support system, to fulfill the role their caregiving environment could not? Deep within, they harbor an abiding need for the security they were denied. And yet this need is tempered by a profound ambivalence—for how can they trust hands that once failed to catch them?

Unfortunately, the Six's distrust extends even to their own internal compass, the childhood guidance system that could not support or protect them in their time of greatest need. And so they search for a worldview, a community, a set of beliefs, which they hope will provide internal and external safeguards against the threat of abandonment and vulnerability.

Lacking a strong internal guidance system means they're also constantly looking for advice or validation. And it's not like they can even trust those opinions, because heaven knows they're never quite sure which one to listen to. Is it Aunt Mildred's siren song of financial conservatism? Or maybe Uncle Bill's hushed warnings about the coming economic apocalypse? The Six's head is like a tiny version of Congress, with each faction vying for control and all of them shouting at the top of their lungs.

Decision-making is so painfully complex for a Six that when they *do* finally make up their mind, they don't let go of their commitment without a robust fight. When a Six fully commits to a person, place, or idea, their loyalty becomes steadfast—because that commitment was hard-won, the fruit of anguished deliberation. Their fear of abandonment and being unprotected can make them cling desperately to relationships and loyalties, even when striking out on their own might prove the wiser course. Hence, their more common nickname is the Loyalist.

I once recommended that a Six client restructure an investment portfolio she'd inherited from her father and almost got a stapler thrown at my head. Admitting that the investment strategy was no longer sound meant challenging her father's decisions, creating an existential crisis. My opinion as a professional had little weight compared to her steadfast faith in her father's wisdom.

The Sacred Wound of internalized and externalized fear creates their greatest fear: being without protection or guidance. And their greatest fear creates their worst vice, which is cowardice. Don't get me wrong, these Sixes can be brave as all get out when it comes to physical confrontation. They'll happily fling themselves into a bar fight to defend a friend or give someone who crossed them a good old-fashioned what-for. But ask them to make a big, independent decision? Good luck with that. When unhealthy, their lack of self-confidence sucks all the courage right out of them.

To mask the pain of their cowardice and avoid seeing it for what it really is, they adopt a primary ego addiction to fear. Seeing threats everywhere justifies their anxiety, validating their cowardice as prudence. And you know what's really wild? These Sixes are actually remarkably calm and collected in a real crisis. Why? Because they were expecting it all along. "See, I told you so! My rampant paranoia was totally justified. Now quick, hand me my emergency rations and tinfoil hat before the world ends."

Keeping their threat-detection system at DEFCON 5 prevents them from disrupting the protective systems in which the Six has embedded themselves. And heaven forbid that their trust be seriously violated, forcing them to let go of their loyalty. That won't end well for anyone involved.

But when they overdose on their primary addiction to fear, these risk-averse, anxiety-ridden worrywarts can't even stand up for their basic needs, which ironically threatens their safety. How do they cope with all that stress? They reach for their secondary addiction—vanity.

When you mix a healthy dose of the Six's worst vice, cowardice, with a heaping helping of narcissistic vanity, you get a cocktail of pure, unfiltered self-importance as their ego stress response.

The formula looks like this:

Cowardice (greatest vice/passion) + Vanity (secondary ego addiction/stress point) = Self-Importance (ego stress response)

Suddenly, these folks are strutting around, chest puffed out, demanding that everyone pay attention to their oh-so-important opinions and decisions, putting themselves in charge. Never mind the fact that deep down, they're still a quivering mess of uncertainty and insecurity. The vanity is just enough to block out that pesky primary addiction to fear until the crisis has passed or their nervous system has a chance to rest.

It's a sight to behold. They trade down from a reliable Family Sedan to a bald-tired, rusty Race Car they borrow from Type Three, complete with mushy brakes. They drive it more like a deranged bumper car, but at least they're moving, right?[1]

These grandiose, self-important Sixes suddenly begin to manipulate everyone, promote themselves, or overwork. "Do this, do that, jump higher, you fools!" they demand, all while their inner voice is whimpering, *Please don't hurt me, please don't hurt me.* They can even become paranoid as they look for someone to blame for their problems. So the next time you encounter a Six in the throes of a vanity-fueled, self-important meltdown, just smile, nod, and slowly back away.

The path to wholeness for the Six lies in cultivating a profound faith not in external authorities but in themselves and the benevolence and competency that undergirds all of creation, including the deepest part of their soul. When the Six finds this, they find the true security that has eluded them. In that state of grace, their greatest weakness—their consuming cowardice—transforms into their greatest strength of unbridled courage.

When healthy, Sixes are extremely brave and have tremendous grit, becoming pioneers in their chosen pursuits. They rest in the mystical trust expressed by Julian of Norwich that "all shall be well, and all shall be well, and all manner of things shall be well."[2]

Money Monsters

The Paralyzed: Money-Avoidant

Money-avoidant Sixes are the financial equivalent of a deer caught in the headlights. These sweet souls are all about security and stability, so you'd expect them to be great with money. But when it comes to actually doing something with that hard-earned cash? Complete paralysis sets in.

The combined ego addiction of cowardice and desire for a secure future is a recipe for some serious financial freeze-up. These folks are so terrified of making the wrong move that they do absolutely nothing, pick the most conservative investments possible, or repeatedly shift their strategy while never committing to any real action.

I once worked with a Six who spent *two and a half years* agonizing over which investment advisor to hire. Meanwhile, their hard-earned cash was just sitting there, slowly losing its purchasing power during a period of peak inflation in a bull market. *Any* investment choice would have been better than doing nothing.

Traits of the Paralyzed

Radical Risk Aversion: When it comes to investments, ventures, or any decision that even remotely smells of uncertainty, the risk-averse Six recoils. They'll research every possible option but never choose, paralyzed by the fear of making the wrong choice and suffering devastating losses. They believe their money is safest hidden in a metaphorical mattress. But in economics, no risk means no return. As a practical tip, start small. Think of it as dipping your toes in the kiddie pool before diving into the ocean. Begin with a total market index fund. It's like financial training wheels—not exciting, but it'll get you moving without fear of a face-plant.

Lemming Syndrome: The lemming is a Six who would rather outsource all their financial responsibilities to a spouse, friend, or family member than have to deal with the burden themselves. They convince themselves that by handing over the reins and following someone else's lead, like a lemming, they're alleviating their stress. In fact, by abdicating personal responsibility, they're setting themselves up for potential disaster. To conquer this problem, start by taking ownership of one small aspect of your finances—maybe it's tracking your daily expenses or paying one specific bill. It's like learning to make your own bed before tackling the whole house. Baby steps, but they're *your* baby steps.

Doubters' Delusion: Is that investment firm legit? Can that financial planner be trusted? The doubting Six is perpetually plagued by a deep-seated mistrust of any and all institutions or authority figures in the world of personal finance. They view the entire system as a rigged game. Fiduciaries were invented to help solve this problem. I get it, trust is hard, but instead of mistrusting everyone, become your own expert. Take a basic financial literacy course. It's like learning to change your own oil—you might not become a mechanic, but at least you'll know if someone's trying to sell you snake oil.

Panicked Procrastination: The complexities of budgeting, bill-paying, and general money management can reduce the money-avoidant Six to an anxiety-ridden mess. They procrastinate on financial tasks, avoid opening statements, and generally bury their heads in the sand until the problem becomes a full-blown crisis. Like a diet or exercise routine, caring for your financial life needs to be a daily or weekly practice done in small increments. Breaking things down into smaller, bite-size decisions helps to reduce the feeling of being overwhelmed. Set aside a few hours each week to attend to your finances, and stick to a routine.

Independence Inertia: Out of fear, some would sooner chew off their own arm than admit they need help, even as they flounder and struggle to keep their head above water. Instead, channel that stubborn streak into learning, not isolating. Reach out for help.

Analysis Paralysis: Cowardice can cause a Six to analyze every financial decision within an inch of its life rather than actually decide. When this happens, it's time to embrace the "good enough" philosophy. Set a deadline for each financial decision. When the timer dings, make your best guess and move on. Remember, a "B" in financial management still beats an "F" for frozen in fear.

The Puppet and the Pugilist: Money-Anxious

Type Sixes with money anxiety display a unique dual nature in their financial behavior:

As Puppets: They compliantly follow financial advice or cling to secure paychecks, desperately seeking guidance and protection from trusted authorities. You won't find much creative thinking when Type Six is in Puppet mode. If they follow prudent financial advice, however, they can build a strong, if uninspiring, financial future. Unfortunately, their loyalty to friends and family makes them vulnerable to manipulation and poor financial advice.

As Pugilists: When their trust is violated or security threatened, they transform into aggressive defenders of their financial territory. They start throwing financial punches with the desperate fury of a cornered boxer. Once, when I sent a routine email containing a minor typo, a new Type Six client immediately pulled their account. Their trust, once broken, is nearly impossible to regain.

This Jekyll and Hyde dynamic stems from their core fear of being without support or guidance. The transformation between these two states can be triggered by even minor financial threats or betrayals.

At the most foundational level, these Sixes think that having lots of resources and financial security will provide the protection and support they desperately desire. While this is not entirely incorrect, their anxiety about money often derails them from reaching their objective of financial abundance or having a full and meaningful life.

Traits of the Puppet/Pugilist

Research Mania: Some money-anxious Sixes will spend hours upon hours poring over spreadsheets, scouring the internet, and seeking reassurance from anyone who'll listen, all in a desperate attempt to eliminate any risk from their financial decisions. "But what if I choose the wrong investment?!" they'll wail, as they curl up in the fetal position, muttering something about diversification. Instead, set a research timer. Give yourself a solid hour to dive into those spreadsheets, then force yourself to surface for air. Remember, perfect information doesn't exist, so aim for well-informed instead of omniscient.

Loyalty-Bound Losses: These Sixes often sacrifice their own financial well-being out of an excessive loyalty to employers, family, or coworkers. They'll stay in underpaying jobs for years because they "owe it to the team," turn down better opportunities to avoid "betraying" their current workplace, or sacrifice their own retirement savings to help family members with money troubles. Their financial life becomes a puppet to everyone else's needs, enduring financial abuse out of misplaced loyalty. I once had a Six client who passed up a promotion because she felt guilty about abandoning her department, even though she was living paycheck to paycheck. As a solution, reframe that work ethic. Instead of martyring your financial future on the altar of loyalty, channel that dedication into building your own security first. Remember: You can't be truly loyal to others if you're one emergency away from financial collapse.

Apocalypse Anticipation: Like their money-avoidant counterparts, these folks are utterly convinced that their financial world is one step away from total collapse. "What if I lose my job?! What if my house burns down?! What if the entire global economy implodes?!" they'll shriek, as they frantically stockpile canned goods and gold bullion. Being prepared is important, but you have got to draw the line somewhere. Instead of prepping for financial doomsday, channel that energy into creating a robust emergency fund. Aim to have enough to cover three to six months of expenses. Once you hit that target, celebrate by eating one of those canned goods you've been hoarding. Congrats! You're prepared, not paranoid.

Temper-Tantrum Time Bombs: The moment anything goes slightly wrong with their finances, these Sixes throw a fit. It could be a spouse overshooting their budget, a mistake on the electric bill, or getting a side of fries when they paid for a salad upgrade. Whatever went sideways is a reason to bloody someone's nose. Every time you're tempted to blow your top over a financial hiccup, hug someone or compliment them instead. You're channeling that energy into something more productive than yelling at the bank teller.

Chump Churning: These anxious Sixes become perfect puppets for the financial media machine. Instead of sticking to a balanced, long-term investment strategy, they let their fear drive them to dance to whatever tune cable news is playing that day. "The market's up? Better buy! The market's down? Sell everything!" They'll move in and out of positions based on the latest "expert" prediction or dramatic headline, becoming a marionette controlled by talking heads and clickbait articles. Remember folks, financial news networks need constant drama to keep viewers glued to their screens, and brokers make money every time you trade—whether that trade helps or hurts you. Instead, implement the "Hands Off" rule. Every time you're tempted to make a reactionary trade based on the latest financial "breaking news," you have to do twenty push-ups first. By the time you're done, the urge will have passed, and you'll have killer arms. Win-win! The market rewards patience, not panic.

Security-at-All-Costs Complacency: Their quest for financial security often undermines their actual security. These Sixes will stay in toxic jobs, maintain draining investments, or hoard cash unproductively—all in the name of safety. Remember: True security comes from adaptability, not rigidity.

Pundit Puppetry: Much like Lemming Syndrome, Pundit Puppetry is the obsessive need to find pundits to help them make decisions. While seeking out trusted financial advice is typically a good move, obsessively following pundits can be a problem if they are not carefully vetted or have ulterior motives. Remember, TV and social media are entertainment designed to prey on your fears and manipulate your emotions, with something to sell you along the way. As a hack, for every financial guru you follow, you must also follow a comedian. Balance those doom-and-gloom forecasts with some laughs.

A Money Master—The Pioneer

When a Six's ego addictions to fear and vanity send them spiraling into the Dark Night of the Soul, it hits them particularly hard because it strips away their entire support system. Imagine a Family Sedan with all its safety features suddenly disabled—no airbags, no seat belts, no antilock brakes. Their carefully constructed network of security measures crumbles, leaving them face-to-face with their greatest fear: being without support or guidance.

The only way out of the Dark Night for the Six is to find their primary path of recovery: faith. Now, I'm not talking about religious dogma here—this is about cultivating a deep trust in their own inner compass and the benevolence of the universe, even in the face of suffering. By placing trust in something greater than themselves and developing their inner resources, they find the courage to face difficult challenges and take risks on their own.

As they turn inward and tap into that wellspring of faith, the Six can start to relax their grip on their ego defenses. The stress on their anxious psyche begins to ease, and that opens the door to their secondary path of recovery: assertiveness. Assertiveness is the primary path of recovery for Type Nine (the RV), and it's like the Six trades in their safety-loaded Family Sedan for a luxurious RV from Type Nine, allowing them to stretch out and relax. Most importantly, they finally find themselves more at peace with the world.

Although they look like a healthy Nine when practicing their secondary path of recovery of assertiveness, they still drive the RV like a Six and will loyally bring all their friends along for a fun ride as they move from independence to interdependence.[3]

Healthy assertiveness for a Six isn't about dominating others—it's about finding the courage to stand up for their needs, express their views without self-important vanity, and be true to themselves, even when fear tries to hold them back.

The trap for a Six on this journey is their faux virtue of modesty. In their quest for security and certainty, they can mistake their self-doubt for genuine modesty. They'll downplay their abilities and achievements with the vigor of a politician denying a scandal, all while secretly hoping someone will reassure them of their worth. This faux modesty isn't about being humble; it's about preemptively protecting themselves from potential criticism, failure, or taking responsibility for their decisions.

When Sixes blend their real virtues of faith and assertiveness, they unlock their highest virtue: courage. No longer paralyzed by their chronic fear and doubt, they transform into loyal, fearless leaders, the true pioneers of the Enneagram. They remind us all that sometimes, the bravest thing we can do is simply to keep on driving, no matter how dark the night may be.

Their magic formula to true security is:

Faith (primary recovery virtue) + Assertiveness (secondary recovery virtue/relaxation point) = Courage (greatest virtue/virtue)

As Nelson Mandela so eloquently said, "Courage is not the absence of fear, but the triumph over it."[4] And that's exactly what the money-savvy Six achieves. Armed with trust in themselves and the universe, they can face any financial challenge head-on, their assertiveness steering them confidently down the road to wealth and abundance.

By embodying this courage, the Six's greatest hope—to know they are protected and guided—finally becomes a reality. No longer needing to rely on external authorities or support systems, they cultivate a deep sense of inner autonomy. They learn to trust their instincts, make their own choices, and embrace uncertainty as a natural part of life's journey.

This, my friends, is the Sacred Gift of the courageous Six: Divine Trust. It's a radical acceptance of the essential goodness of reality, a recognition that they are interconnected with an eternal, loving support system that guides and protects all of creation. With this mindset, they become true money masters—the Pioneers, leading the way for others to follow. Their very presence instills trust and faith in those around them.

In short, the Pioneer is a paradox of sorts—a worrier who's found the courage to take the reins, a doubter who's learned to trust their inner compass, and a cautious soul who's willing to take a leap of faith. They're the financial equivalent of a superhero, using their powers of analysis, loyalty, and resilience to build a life of abundance and fulfillment.

Becoming a Money Master—The Pioneer

Please be sure to read (or review) the chapter 8 overview of these five steps before you get started here.

Acknowledge the pain from your Childhood Wounding.

For the Skeptic or Family Sedan of the Enneagram, confronting the Childhood Wounds at the root of their money monsters can feel like staring down a pack of ravenous wolves. Sixes are hyper-attuned to any potential threats to their security and sense of belonging, so diving into those old emotional hurts is enough to make their hands shake with anxiety.

But, my dear Sixes, your path to becoming a true money master begins right here—with the willingness to acknowledge the pain of your past and how it has shaped your relationship with wealth and abundance. Those money woes you've grappled with as an adult? They're inextricably linked to the core wounds that formed when your psychological umbilical cord was severed, leaving you feeling isolated, unprotected, and afraid.

Many Sixes grow up in households where their caregivers were unreliable or emotionally unavailable. Growing up in a chaotic, unstable, or volatile home with a lot of conflict, financial insecurity, or family dysfunction can also leave Sixes feeling perpetually on edge, never sure what to expect from day to day.

Others were raised in families or communities with an overabundance of strict rules, regulations, and authority figures. This can leave them feeling smothered, mistrustful of those in power, and uncertain about their own ability to make decisions.

Some Sixes are deeply wounded from a profound betrayal of trust, whether it's from a parent leaving the family, a friend abandoning them, or a mentor letting them down. Perhaps there was sexual abuse or a radical violation of their faith in others. Perhaps a lack of adequate emotional support, validation, and encouragement created deep-seated doubts about their own capabilities and worth.

Whatever it was, those formative experiences cast a long shadow over their financial lives, fueling the ego addiction to fear that keeps them anxious, avoidant, or just uncertain.

I know the mere thought of unearthing your old traumas makes you want to curl up in a ball and hide. But take a deep breath, my anxious friend, and let's get to work. Grab a big whiteboard, a stack of paper, or a spreadsheet and start mapping out your trauma timeline— all those pivotal moments, both big and small, that have shaped your wary relationship with yourself and money.

Look for the patterns, the recurring themes, the core wounds that keep driving you back into that familiar seat of fear and vanity. It may take time, and it certainly won't be easy, but this is the crucial first step on your journey to becoming a money master. And remember, you don't have to navigate these dark waters alone. Reach out to a trusted therapist, counselor, or even a supportive community group. These allies can help you face your inner demons with the courage that is your birthright as a Six.

Because make no mistake, Skeptic—once you've stared down the darkness of your past and emerged with a newfound sense of self-trust, that's when the real transformation begins.

Stop reacting out of the fear that created your money monsters.

The key to taming your money monsters is approaching your fears with radical self-compassion. Remember, you were just a scared, wounded child, doing the absolute best you could to survive in a world that often felt hostile and unpredictable. In many ways, that anxious, ever-vigilant part of you is still very much alive, desperately seeking the safety and guidance it was denied long ago.

So be gentle with yourself, my friend. Taming these beasts isn't about attacking or punishing them—it's about meeting them with the same reverent courage that St. Francis displayed when he confronted the Wolf of Gubbio. These are not enemies to be vanquished, but frightened parts of yourself that long to be soothed and integrated.

What spiritual practices from your tradition might help support you on this journey? Could a daily meditation or contemplative prayer routine provide the grounding you need to face the world without feeling so easily overwhelmed? And how can you cultivate forgiveness—for yourself and for those who wounded you—so that you might live with greater faith, assertiveness, and courage?

Try this short Courage Prayer I've composed, reciting it morning and evening as a way to anchor yourself in the virtues that will empower your transformation:

> *Steadfast Protector, open my heart to your unwavering love*
> *and calm the fear that haunts me. Fortify my faith and*
> *embolden my assertiveness, grounded in your unshakable*
> *grace. Guide me to relinquish my addiction to fear and vanity,*
> *so I may courageously use my gifts in loving service to you.*

The journey may be arduous, but the reward is a financial life rooted in confidence, not crippling anxiety. So take a deep breath, my anxious friend, and prepare to meet your money monsters with the very qualities that make you a Six—loyalty, discernment, and an unshakable commitment to courageously finding your way, no matter how uncertain the road ahead may seem.

Learn to be less anxious or avoidant about money by confronting your money monsters.

One key exercise I recommend is to really get granular with those Paralyzed or Puppet/Pugilist mindsets that tend to trip you up the most. Don't just leave them as vague generalizations—no, I want you to explore those money monsters in a way that speaks directly to your life circumstances. How do they apply to the different categories of *your* earning, saving, investing, and giving behaviors? Chances are, you'll find some stark contrasts.

Perhaps you're all in when it comes to the disciplined saving habits needed to build up that emergency fund, but the mere thought of venturing into the stock market has you breaking out in hives. You might find yourself Paralyzed by indecision when it comes to investing, terrified that you'll make the wrong choice and jeopardize your family's security, but a Puppet when it comes to earning money and avoiding stepping into your true earning potential. Or perhaps you aggressively lash out as a Pugilist at anyone who dares to threaten your carefully constructed budget.

Once you've identified those problematic money monsters in granular detail, I want you to get your analytical superpowers firing on all cylinders. Pair each of those unhealthy mindsets with the corresponding Pioneer virtue you want to cultivate instead. Why not go the extra mile and create a visual money monster map or flow chart? That way, you can easily reference it whenever those beasts come crawling back, ready to derail your progress.

Heck, take it a step further and turn the whole thing into a poster—plaster it on your wall or your bathroom mirror. Immerse yourself in the antidotes to those anxious, mistrustful tendencies, so that slowly but surely, the faithful Pioneer within you can emerge.

Take a deep breath, summon your courage, and get ready to transform those money monsters into loyal, trustworthy allies.

Build a strong financial future through earning, saving, and investing ethically.

When it comes to padding your pockets, you Sixes have some serious superpowers. That unwavering loyalty, dogged tenacity, and good old-fashioned elbow grease? Pure gold, my friends. Employers will trip over themselves to get their hands on dependable, hardworking Loyalists like you who are always there to shoulder the heavy lifting.

And let's not forget that innate problem-solving prowess of yours. As natural-born troubleshooters, you've got an uncanny knack for sniffing out pain points that people are desperate to fix and will pay handsomely to solve. So why not put that analytical mind of yours to work? What innovative, risk-mitigating solutions can you dream up that'll have clients and customers banging down your door?

Sure, you might need to do a little more training to round out your skills, but don't let that hold you back. Think big, my cautious companions: What untapped needs exist in your community or industry that you can swoop in and monetize? With your research prowess keeping you ahead of the curve, your earning potential is through the roof.

When it comes to the saving game—that's where you Sixes truly shine. That cautious, disciplined nature of yours? That is literally money in the bank when it comes to building a rock-solid nest egg. At your best, you have budgeting, emergency savings, and retirement funding down to a science. Your knack for contingency planning puts the other types' budgeting skills to shame. Medical bills, job loss, inflation, you name it—at your best, you're always one step ahead, ready to weather any financial storm.

Unlike some of your more impulsive Enneagram brethren, you Sixes don't tend to get tripped up by those little frivolous purchases that can derail a savings plan. Nope, your innate prudence keeps you laser-focused on the long game.

The key is to truly harness that Loyalist loyalty—but this time, direct it toward your future self and loved ones. What can you do today to ensure ironclad financial security and peace of mind down the road? With your analytical prowess, I know you can crunch the numbers and devise the perfect strategy.

Now, when it comes to investing, Sixes have a leg up—you are no stranger to mastering complexities and problem-solving, which is a superpower in the financial arena. So why not put that prowess to work? Dive in, become a financial literacy ninja, and let those trouble-shooting skills shine. Sure, you might always lean toward more conservative, wealth-preservation strategies, but there's nothing wrong with taking the slow and steady approach.

Remember the old fable of the Tortoise and the Hare? Well, Sixes are the textbook tortoises of the financial world. Don't feel the need to keep up with the flashy investment gurus or try to replicate their road maps. Stick to what feels right, trust your instincts, and keep plodding forward bravely—because slow and steady will likely win this race.

The key is to not let that paralysis by analysis get the best of you. Sure, it's great to do your due diligence, but at a certain point, you've gotta pull the trigger. Channel that courage and dive into the world of investing with the same zeal you bring to every other challenge.

Use your money and talents as tools to love and serve a suffering world.

For cautious Sixes, letting go of your hard-earned resources can be a mental hurdle. But buried beneath that natural tendency to hold on tight is an equally strong sense of community and civic duty. And as you start amassing that wealth, I bet you'll find a deep wellspring of fulfillment in directing those resources toward the causes and institutions you're most passionate about.

You likely have an innate drive for fairness and empathy for the underdog. Let that guide you when it comes to strategic giving. I can just see you meticulously researching nonprofits, making sure your donations are making the maximum impact on the issues that matter most to you. That discernment and due diligence gives you a keen eye for sniffing out the most effective and trustworthy charitable organizations.

Once you've committed to a cause, you Skeptics become the steadfast advocates and supporters that charities dream of. Your giving isn't some sporadic, feel-good gesture; it's a long-term, consistent investment in creating lasting change. But it's not just the financial support, is it? You are the kind who also roll up your sleeves and get your hands dirty. That grassroots engagement gives you an intimate understanding of the real-world challenges these charities face, informing your giving strategies in a profound way.

Your analytical mind might even identify those pesky systemic issues underlying social and environmental woes, and start directing resources toward advocacy, policy reform, and other efforts to address root causes. Talk about making a seismic impact!

And as you gain that expertise in navigating the philanthropic world, I have a sneaking suspicion you'll be eager to share your knowledge and experience. Picture it—the Sixes, serving as trusted advisors, guiding others on effective charitable giving. Now that's the kind of legacy-building I can get behind.

The Sixes' unique blend of discernment, loyalty, risk-management savvy, community orientation, hands-on engagement, and systems-level thinking make you all-stars when it comes to philanthropic giving. As a Pioneer, you have the power to leave an indelible mark, guiding others and catalyzing transformative solutions for a hurting world.

Zoe's Story

Zoe's story begins in a household where unpredictability was the only predictable thing. Dad lost his job more often than most people lose their car keys, while Mom's mood swings gave Zoe emotional whiplash.

This tumultuous environment cut Zoe's psychological umbilical cord with a double-edged sword of fear. She internalized the message that the world was a chaotic, unreliable place that she couldn't protect herself from, and externalized it by seeing threats lurking around every corner.

From this wound, Zoe's greatest fear roared to life: being without support or guidance. This fear constantly pushed her to seek safety and security in any group. She was like a remora fish, desperately attaching herself to any "shark" that seemed strong enough to protect her.

To keep her greatest fear at bay, Zoe developed her worst vice: cowardice. This cowardice translated her fear of abandonment into a constant state of anxiety and indecision. She could overthink a decision with the dedication of a conspiracy theorist parsing grainy footage, always finding a reason to doubt herself and seek guidance from others.

Fueling this entire system was Zoe's primary ego addiction: fear, which manifested in her life as industrial-strength anxiety. Zoe used it to justify her constant need for reassurance and security. This combination of fear and cowardice led to Zoe's money-anxious Paralyzed behavior. She'd rather walk on hot coals than make a financial decision without consulting her entire social network, horoscope, and Magic 8 Ball.

Zoe would find increasingly elaborate ways to justify her financial paralysis, weaving a web of rationalizations more complex than the tax code. "I'm just being prudent," she'd declare, while her untouched savings account gathered dust and lost value to inflation.

Zoe was so scared of making the wrong move that she made no moves at all. Her retirement plan was limited to buying lottery tickets (but only when her horoscope said it was a lucky day). As for her career, she was stuck in a dead-end nonprofit job that she loyally clung to because her boss was a friend, and she really liked her coworkers.

When fear led Zoe into a stress spiral, she unconsciously switched to her secondary ego addiction: vanity. Suddenly, our anxious, indecisive Zoe transformed into a know-it-all, frantically busying herself with an endless to-do list.

Tragedy struck when her nonprofit went under and had to close. Her friends scattered in the wind searching for new jobs, many of them moving away for better opportunities. In this moment of crisis, with a future as financially secure as a sandcastle at high tide, Zoe crashed headlong into her financial Dark Night of the Soul. She was forced to confront the ugly truth: Her relentless pursuit of security and risk avoidance had left her financially adrift.

In the depths of her Dark Night, Zoe finally broke open. She realized that her fear wasn't protecting her; it was paralyzing her. Her desperate search for support and guidance had actually left her more vulnerable than ever. She'd built a financial fortress out of other people's opinions, and it was crumbling around her.

In this moment of crisis, Zoe found the courage to practice her primary path of recovery: faith in her own inner strength and resilience. She was like a chronically seasick person who decides to become a deep-sea diver. She started small—first reading a few books on financial planning, then making minor financial decisions without polling her Facebook friends. As Zoe embraced faith, she found herself naturally drawn to her secondary path of recovery: assertiveness. She began to see that her constant deferral to others was just a fancy mask for her fear. With assertiveness, she could stand up for her own financial needs and make decisions without needing a committee vote.

The combination of faith and assertiveness led Zoe to her highest virtue: courage. She began to see that seeking constant reassurance wasn't bringing her security; it was bringing her stagnation. Courage meant facing her financial reality head-on, making decisions even when they were scary, and trusting in her own judgment.

As Zoe embraced courage, she began to heal her Sacred Wound of fear. She realized that while the world could be unpredictable, she had the inner resources to handle whatever came her way. Her greatest hope—to know she is guided and supported—began to manifest not through external security, but through inner strength and resilience.

Zoe's transformation from the Paralyzed to the Pioneer was like watching a wolf dog who thought it was a nervous chihuahua find its real bark. She built an emergency fund and even started planning for retirement. Slowly, she turned her fear into financial security.

But the real magic happened when Zoe fully embraced her Sacred Gift: Divine Trust. She realized that true security wasn't about constant vigilance and worst-case-scenario planning, but about trusting in her own abilities and the fundamental goodness of life. She started using her natural talent for spotting potential problems to help her community prepare for real emergencies, transforming her anxious hypervigilance into a valuable skill. She applied for and got a higher-paying job working for a humanitarian relief organization, leveling up her career.

Zoe's financial journey became a testament to her newfound courage. She found a balance between prudent planning and bold action, between seeking advice and trusting her gut. And the best part? She did it all without losing her Zoe-ness—she was still careful, still security-minded, but now with a backbone of steel, a solid income, and a well-diversified portfolio.

CHAPTER FIFTEEN

TYPE SEVEN—THE ENTHUSIAST (SUV)

HOW TO QUIT YOUR FOMO HABIT AND EMBRACE THE JOY OF FINANCIAL STABILITY

Picture this: a souped-up SUV, engine roaring, tires caked with mud from its last adventure, peeling out of a gas station in search of the next exhilarating off-road experience. That's your typical Seven in a nutshell—the ultimate all-terrain vehicle of the ego world. Often called the Enthusiast, Sevens are creative, curious, and joyful. The world is their playground, and they're always eager for the next exhilarating ride.

But beneath their mud-splattered exterior lies a complex psychological engine. Sevens had their psychological umbilical cord cut by fear, which they promptly externalized. They're afraid the world won't provide the resources or nourishment they need, leaving them stuck in pain or deprivation.

Their fear of pain or privation creates their worst vice of gluttony, but we're not just talking about an extra helping of dessert here. Sevens are gluttons for life itself—experiences, opportunities, adventures. Their metaphorical plate isn't just full; it's overflowing onto the table, the floor, and probably the

Type Seven Ego Map: The Enthusiast or SUV

(Read the chart from the bottom up.)

ENLIGHTENMENT STRUCTURE	
MONEY MASTER	**THE GROUNDED**
Sacred Gift (Holy Idea)	Divine Fulfillment
Greatest Hope (Basic Desire)	To know complete satisfaction
Greatest Virtue (Virtue)	Contentment Mindfulness + Generosity = Contentment (cure for Gluttony)
Secondary Recovery Virtue (Relaxation Point)	Generosity (Primary Recovery Virtue for Type 5)
Primary Recovery Virtue	Mindfulness
Faux Virtue	Mercy

SHADOW STRUCTURE	
MONEY MONSTERS: AVOIDANT / ANXIOUS	**THE GORGER / THE GRABBER**
Ego Stress Response	Frustration Gluttony + Resentment = Frustration (blocks Planning)
Secondary Ego Addiction (Stress Point)	Resentment (Primary Ego Addiction for Type 1)
Primary Ego Addiction (Ego Fixation)	Planning
Greatest Vice (Passion)	Gluttony
Greatest Fear (Basic Fear)	Being trapped in pain or privation
Sacred Wound	Externalized Fear

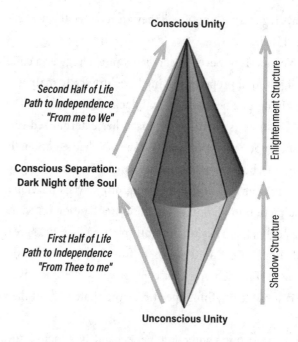

Conscious Unity

*Second Half of Life
Path to Independence
"From me to We"*

**Conscious Separation:
Dark Night of the Soul**

*First Half of Life
Path to Independence
"From Thee to me"*

Enlightenment Structure

Shadow Structure

Unconscious Unity

neighbor's yard too. The irony? In their desperate attempt to avoid pain, they often end up creating more of it. It's like trying to outrun your shadow—the faster you go, the faster it follows.

This fear of pain, especially the pain lurking in their own psyche, is what drives Sevens to go anywhere and do anything to escape the present moment. Want to see a Seven squirm? Trap them in a room with nothing to do. It's like watching a Range Rover stuck in neutral— all that horsepower with nowhere to go.

As kids, many Sevens likely experienced inconsistent or inadequate nourishment—physical, emotional, or both. Now they're trying to fill that seemingly bottomless pit of need, always striving for more experiences to keep the possibility of pain or deprivation at bay and suffering from a constant need for stimulation. It's like their gas gauge is broken, always registering empty, and they are terrified the next gas station will be closed.

For example, one Type Seven friend had a rare allergy as a child and couldn't digest food properly, leaving her chronically malnourished and in pain despite her parents' and doctors' best efforts. The trauma from that time is what likely caused her externalized fear of the world and Type Seven personality. (She also had emotionally inconsistent parents, but let's not blame the parents for everything.)

To mask their fear and justify their gluttony, Sevens develop a primary ego addiction to planning. Planning is a fixation on whatever is coming next in life. They're constantly plotting their next great escape, getting high on the anticipation of future pleasures. FOMO (fear of missing out) is their constant companion, sometimes making it hard to commit to anything specific, as they hate to limit their options.

But when this planning addiction inevitably drives them into a ditch through overindulgence and being overextended, they switch to their secondary ego addiction: resentment. That's when they borrow a beat-up BMW from Type One and adopt the One's primary addiction to resentment as their secondary ego addiction. Resentment combines with their worst vice of gluttony to create extreme frustration or "gluttonous resentment." This is a deep frustration with themselves, others, or future plans, becoming hypercritical and perfectionistic. Frustration is their ego stress response, an emotional guardrail that temporarily blocks their manic distraction-seeking and forces them into the painful present moment or to reflect on mistakes in the past.[1]

The equation looks like this:

Gluttony (greatest vice/passion) + Resentment (secondary ego addiction/stress point) = Frustration (ego stress response)

Watching a Seven wallow in frustration is a pitiful sight, like seeing a bright balloon suddenly deflate. But it serves a purpose: reining them in just enough to prevent their balloon from popping and avert total collapse. With luck, this phase is short-lived—providing a brief respite for them to catch their breath before they're back in their SUV, tearing off toward the next horizon.

For a Seven, there's always another adventure just around the corner. Their theme song could well be U2's "I Still Haven't Found What I'm Looking For."[2] Because no matter how much they experience, that deep-seated fear of privation keeps them constantly searching for more.

When healthy, they finally realize that the source of true fulfillment is never outside themselves but comes from healing their Sacred Wound and reconnecting with their eternal essence. As in the famous passage from St. Augustine's *Confessions*, "Because you have made us for Yourself, our hearts are restless till they find their rest in Thee."[3]

Money Monsters

The Gorger: Money-Avoidant

The money-avoidant Seven treats their bank account like it's a leaky bucket in a rainstorm. No matter how much they pour in, it all just trickles away, leaving them with nothing but a puddle of regret and a collection of shiny, useless trinkets. The Gorger is not just keeping up with the Joneses; they're trying to lap them on the hedonic treadmill. New gadget? Gotta have it. Exotic vacation? Sign them up!

This isn't your garden-variety retail therapy. This is full-blown financial self-medication. The Gorger uses their wallet like a time machine, desperately trying to escape the present moment and all the pesky feelings that come with it. Unfortunately, the dopamine hits they get from each purchase are shorter than a goldfish's memory. They're already eyeing the next model before the new car smell has even faded.

The Gorger's motto? "Treat yo'self!"—every day, in every way, until the credit card company starts sending carrier pigeons with overdue notices. FOMO isn't just a feeling for these Sevens; it's a way of life. They're so scared of missing out on the next big thing, they miss out on little things like financial security and peace of mind. The future? That's a problem for Future Seven. Present Seven is too busy buying tickets to Burning Man.

In essence, the Gorger is the Prodigal Son of the Enneagram, living it up in the far country until they've blown through their inheritance faster than you can say "bankruptcy." But hey, at least they've got great stories to tell . . . if only they could afford the bar tab to share them.

Traits of the Gorger

Delayed-Gratification Deficiency: Sevens treat delayed gratification like it's a communicable disease. They'd rather max out their credit cards than wait for payday. Budgeting? That's for people who don't know how to live in the moment. As a solution, create a "Future Fun Fund." Every time you resist an impulse purchase, put that money in a special account. It's like you're saving up for a mega-adventure instead of just delaying gratification. You're not missing out; you're leveling up! Hint: One important Future Fun Fund to have is an IRA or 401(k) for that mega-adventure called financial independence.

Escape-Artist Ailment: These Gorgers use their wallets like teleportation devices, ready to zap them away from any uncomfortable emotion. Feeling blue? Time for some retail therapy. Is anxiety creeping in? Quick, let's go out to eat! Instead, start an "Emotion Exploration" journal. When you feel the urge to book that impromptu trip to

Timbuktu, write down what you're feeling and explore why instead. It's like emotional skydiving but without the costly plane ticket.

FOMO Fever: Sevens are so scared of missing out on fun experiences that they're missing out on this little thing called financial stability. As a profound spiritual practice, embrace JOMO (Joy of Missing Out). See how good it feels to stay home and say no to a few opportunities. Not all of them, but just dial it back a bit and see if your life can go from a fever pitch to a normal temperature.

Planning Phobia: Ask a Gorger about their five-year financial plan, and watch them break out in hives. They need a financial planner who's part accountant, part therapist, and part zookeeper. As a cure, turn financial planning into a game. Create a "Money Master" avatar and level up your financial skills. Each time you stick to your budget or save money, give your avatar cooler accessories and advance them up a game ladder that sticks to your fridge. Put an exciting goal at the top of your fridge and mindfully celebrate when you reach it.

Responsibility Rejection: Gorgers treat bills and commitments like they're radioactive. They need a hazmat suit just to open their bank statements. Maybe if we rebranded budgeting as an extreme sport, they'd be more into it. Try renaming your bills as "Adult Achievement Unlocked" notifications. Each time you pay a bill on time, wear a silly hat for an hour and give yourself a ridiculous title like "Supreme Overlord of Electricity" or "Duchess of Water Conservation." It's adulting made fun.

Commitment Issues: Sevens are about as committed to their financial goals as a pet lizard is to its human. They're always looking for the next shiny thing, convinced that the grass (and the bank balance) is greener on the other side. Make your goals sexy by starting a "Financial Fling of the Month" club. Each month, commit to a new short-term financial goal. It's like speed dating but for your money. You might just find a long-term financial relationship you want to stick with.

Experience Junkie: Who needs a savings account when you can have memories? Gorgers collect experiences like they're Pokémon cards—got to catch them all! Instead of throwing money at every opportunity, challenge yourself to create "Zero-Dollar Adventures." Yes, fun can be free. Get creative with free local events, nature hikes, or home-based experiences like game nights.

Boundary Bugs: A Seven's financial boundaries are as solid as a wet paper bag. They loan or give away money to friends and family without proper due diligence. "Sure, I'll buy drinks for the whole bar!" If you struggle with healthy financial boundaries, create a mental "Money Moat" around your finances. Before making any financial decision, imagine you have to cross a moat filled with money-eating piranhas. Would you still do it? If not, maybe it's not worth the risk to your financial castle.

The Grabber: Money-Anxious

Money-anxious Sevens are like financial alchemists, forever trying to turn their pocket change into gold bars. They've combined the Seven's gluttony with the greed of a cartoon villain, creating a Hollywood climax of financial chaos.

The Grabber isn't content with just chasing experiences; they're chasing dollar signs. They want *all* the money, convinced that if they can just stuff their mattress full enough, they'll finally feel satisfied. Spoiler alert: They won't.

These Sevens are the get-rich-quick scheme's best customers. They're more likely to bet on a three-legged horse than invest in a stable mutual fund. Crypto? They're all in. Day trading? It's their new hobby. They're not just chasing the Next Big Thing; they're sprinting after it like it's the ice cream truck of their childhood dreams.

The real kicker? Sometimes, by sheer dumb luck, they win. And when they do, they strut, preen, and tell everyone within earshot about their financial genius. Meanwhile, they conveniently forget to mention all the times their schemes went up in smoke.

Take poor Tom, for example. He was a former client who got bitten by the crypto bug. He withdrew his retirement savings and dove headlong into the crypto world. Tom's retirement savings vanished when the crypto market crashed and the Chinese company holding his digital wallet closed down overnight, taking his money with them.

The moral of the story? The Grabber's FOMO is so intense that they often miss out on the biggest thing of all—a secure financial future. They're so busy trying to grab the golden ring that they don't notice they're on a Slip 'N Slide to bankruptcy.

Remember, Grabbers, in the world of finance, if it sounds too good to be true, it probably is. And if someone promises you can get rich quickly, the only one getting rich quickly is them—at your expense!

Traits of the Grabber

The "I'll Be Happy When..." Syndrome: These folks are always chasing the next financial milestone, convinced that's when they'll finally feel secure and be content. How about creating a "Happy Now" journal instead? Each day, write down one way your current financial situation allows you to do something that makes you happy and that you're grateful for. It's like creating a highlight reel of your financial present, not just dreaming about the sequel.

Financial Constraint Aversion: Money-anxious Sevens treat budgets as fun-sucking vampires, and will often work hard to have enough money so they don't need to worry about a detailed budget. As a trick, rebrand your budget as a "Fun Funds Allocation Strategy." It's not about limitations; it's about mindfully maximizing your joy per dollar. Create categories like "Spontaneous Shenanigans" and "Calculated Capers" to make budgeting feel like plotting a heist . . . but legal.

Persistent Scarcity Mindset: Despite often having more dough than a bakery, these rare Sevens operate like they're always one paycheck away from living in a cardboard box. This leads to a financial life that's part Scrooge McDuck, part shopaholic—a truly bizarre combination. Try starting a "Money Monsoon" jar or digital account. Every time you catch yourself worrying about money, put a dollar or more in. Use the accumulated funds for a random act of kindness. You're literally turning anxiety into generosity.

High Risk Tolerance: Grabbers approach the financial world like it's an extreme sport. Safe, steady investments? *Boooring.* They'd rather bet their life savings on a hot tip from their Uber driver about a cryptocurrency named after an obscure meme. Instead, channel your inner adrenaline junkie into "Investment Parkour." Create a balanced portfolio that includes some higher-risk options but also a range of moderate and conservative choices. It's like building your own financial obstacle course—thrilling, but with safety nets.

Financial Overoptimism: These Sevens consistently overestimate returns and underestimate risks, creating financial projections that belong more in a fantasy novel than on a spreadsheet. Create a "Choose Your Own Adventure" story for your bank account. For every optimistic financial projection you make, also imagine a pessimistic outcome. Then choose your path.

Financial Identity Crisis: For these Sevens, self-worth and net worth are more closely linked than identical twins. On a good day in the market, they're on top of the world. On a bad day, it's like someone canceled Christmas and their birthday simultaneously. As a solution, create a "Money Mood" chart for your fridge and track how your mood correlates with financial events. You might get tired of that game quickly enough to make changes. It's like being your own financial therapist, minus the couch.

Analysis-Paralysis Ailment: Despite their typically impulsive nature, these Sevens can get stuck in research mode faster than a computer freezing on Windows 95. They'll spend weeks analyzing investment opportunities, only to make a split-second decision based on a gut feeling or a particularly persuasive Instagram ad. Instead, implement the "3–2–1 Rule." Research for 3 or more days, consult 2 trusted sources, then make 1 decision. It's like a countdown to financial blast-off, but with less chance of exploding on the launchpad.

Keeping Up with the Joneses (. . . and the Smiths . . . and the Kardashians) Cancer: Grabber Sevens aren't just trying to keep up; they're trying to lap the competition. As an alternative, start the "Reverse Jones Effect." Challenge yourself to find the most creative ways to save money or make your current possessions awesome. It's like being a financial MacGyver—the less you spend, the cooler you are. Besides, no one really cares enough to watch what you're doing anyway.

Remember, Grabbers, money can't buy happiness, but it can buy therapy—which might be a good investment at this point.

A Money Master—The Grounded

When the Seven's gluttonous pursuits—from food, travel, and substances to the latest get-rich-quick scheme—finally catch up with them, they crash into the Dark Night of the Soul.

It's as if they've been on a sugar high for years, and suddenly the crash hits them all at once. They're forced to confront the inner emptiness they've been running from, and let me tell you, it's not a pretty sight. They wake up to a pile of bills, broken relationships, and possibly serious addictions.

But if they can muster the courage to face their fears, they can break open their ego and let some light in. It's like cracking open a piñata—messy, but full of surprises.

The key? Mindfulness. For a Seven, this is about as appealing as watching paint dry. But it's their primary path of recovery and ticket to freedom. They must learn to savor the present moment instead of always chasing the next thrill. It requires mindful consumption, not gluttonous consumption, of the opportunities and experiences surrounding them in the here and now. They must slow their roll and be enamored with the present moment's beauty, goodness, and fullness.

A solid daily meditation practice is their best resource for becoming more emotionally and financially fit. Embracing mindfulness is the cure for their addiction to planning and eases the stress on their ego. With less stress and fewer ego problems to defend against, their secondary path of recovery opens up: generosity.

Imagine a Seven learning to give instead of always taking from life. Practicing generosity allows the Seven to give of themselves rather than trying to get fulfillment from outward sources, which is a key step to overcoming their gluttony. It's like they've traded in their gas-guzzling SUV for a quiet, efficient Compact Car borrowed from Type Five. Suddenly, they're content to observe life and just enjoy the moment as it is rather than always racing ahead to a future that never arrives.[4]

When mindfulness and generosity combine, they produce the Seven's highest virtue: contentment.

Their magic formula to living happily ever after is:

Mindfulness (primary recovery virtue) + Generosity (secondary recovery virtue/relaxation point) = Contentment (greatest virtue/virtue)

This contentment is transformative. When Sevens learn to face their emotions rather than running from them, they start building deeper relationships rather than skimming the surface of life. This introspection leads to a deeper understanding of themselves and gets their lives off autopilot, awakening them to their True Self.

Contentment requires embracing vulnerability and facing life's challenges without constant stimulation or escapism. When the Seven stops running away from their inner life and the turmoil that resides there, they start making huge strides in personal and financial growth.

However, they need to watch out for the faux virtue of mercy. Misplaced mercy toward their worst tendencies is their spiritual trap-door. In their quest for endless stimulation and escape from pain, Sevens can mistake their avoidance of discomfort for self-compassion. They'll forgive and forget faster than you can say "consequences," because holding on to anything negative might harsh their buzz. This faux mercy isn't about true forgiveness; it's about maintaining their own freedom from pain and boredom. They're not so much merciful as they are auditioning for the role of "Most Likely to Ghost Their Own Problems."

As they cultivate contentment, however, something extraordinary occurs. Their Sacred Wound doesn't just start to heal; it transforms into their Sacred Gift—Divine Fulfillment. When Sevens embody Divine Fulfillment, they suddenly see the world through new eyes. The messy game of life that once drove them to distraction? It starts making sense when they realize that true happiness isn't found in the next adventure or the latest gadget, but in that quiet place within where the sacred resides. It's as if they've been searching for the meaning of life in a nonstop global scavenger hunt, only to discover it was in their pocket the whole time.

By dropping their ego addictions, facing their Shadow, and following their path to wholeness, Sevens discover an infinite fullness inside themselves as a magnificent expression of the God of their understanding. They find contentment and inner peace—the true goal of all their external searching. When that happens, they finally fulfill their greatest hope: to know complete fulfillment.

Most importantly, Sevens have an epiphany that would make Oprah proud: *They realize they're here to bring fulfillment to others.* And let me tell you, watching a Seven shift from chasing fulfillment to embodying it is like seeing a tornado turn into a gentle, life-giving rain. It's still exciting, but in a way that nourishes rather than uproots everything in its path.

In this state, Sevens become truly grounded money masters. They're no longer trying to fill an infinite hole with finite experiences. Instead, they're content to "Be Here Now," finding joy in the present moment and using their resources wisely for those they love and the world around them.

The Seven's journey to becoming a money master is about discovering the wealth of contentment within and sharing that Divine Fulfillment with the world. Who knew that sitting still could be the greatest adventure of all?

Becoming a Money Master—The Grounded

Please be sure to read (or review) the chapter 8 overview of these five steps before you get started here.

Acknowledge the pain from your Childhood Wounding.

Facing your Childhood Wounds may seem daunting, but it's a crucial journey for you. Your tendency to seek constant stimulation and avoid pain isn't just a personality quirk—it's rooted in early childhood experiences that shaped your view of the world.

Many Sevens report growing up in environments where their emotional needs were overlooked or dismissed. This wasn't necessarily due to malice, but perhaps because your caregivers were overwhelmed, distracted, or simply ill-equipped to provide the nurturing you needed. As a result, you learned to turn to external sources for comfort and excitement.

The emotional neglect you experienced might have been subtle. Perhaps when you were sad or scared, instead of receiving comfort and understanding, you were given distractions—toys, treats, or activities. While well-intentioned, this approach taught you to avoid negative emotions rather than process them.

Others might have experienced trauma or loss that shattered their sense of safety and abundance. It's as if life handed them a box labeled "Carefree Childhood" but inside was just a bunch of packing peanuts and a note saying "LOL, just kidding."

The fear that the world wouldn't provide for your emotional or physical needs is what cut your psychological umbilical cord. This fear became externalized, manifesting as an endless quest for stimulation and a reluctance to sit with difficult emotions or situations. It's as if you were served a steady diet of disappointment sandwiches with a side of letdown fries, so your young psyche decided, "Well, if the world doesn't provide, I'll just have to build my own all-you-can-eat buffet."

The common thread? These experiences left little Sevens feeling like the world was an unreliable, sometimes painful place that couldn't be counted on to meet their needs. So, they externalized their fear, projecting it onto the world around them rather than recognizing it within themselves.

This externalized fear manifests as a constant anxiety that there won't be enough—enough fun, enough options, enough distractions to keep the pain at bay. It's like they're perpetually preparing for an apocalypse of boredom and limitation.

The result? A turbocharged escape artist, always on the run from pain and always chasing the next hit of excitement. They're not running away from monsters under the bed; they're running away from the monster of unmet needs and unfulfilled desires that lives in their own psyche.

But by constantly fleeing from fear, Sevens often run headlong into the very experiences they're trying to avoid.

As you create your trauma timeline, look for instances where you felt unsupported during tough times, or when your feelings were minimized in childhood. Perhaps there were moments of inconsistent nurturing, where care was present one day and absent the next, leaving you unsure and anxious.

Remember, this process isn't about blaming anyone. It's about understanding the roots of your patterns. Recognizing these wounds can be painful, but it's also the first step toward healing and finding true fulfillment—not just momentary excitement.

This process of self-discovery will take some time. It's emotionally taxing work, so be patient with yourself.

Stop reacting out of the fear that created your money monsters.

This journey requires daily effort, but don't worry—we can make it as exciting as possible. You'll need to master two skills: contemplation and compassion.

Contemplation for Sevens starts by being mindful of how your ego addiction to planning negatively impacts your daily life. It's about managing that fear of pain and privation that fuels your constant need for stimulation. Creating a daily meditation practice can help, and there are some pretty cool meditation apps out there that might pique your interest.

I get it—sitting still might feel like torture for you. So, let's get creative. Maybe your contemplative practice is a mindful hike in nature, or a solo dance party where you really tune into your body and emotions. The key is finding a practice that calls to your adventurous spirit but allows for quiet reflection.

One practice that might appeal to your creative side is using a large whiteboard or piece of paper to brainstorm all your ideas and problems of the day. Dump everything out of your head, then play connect-the-dots to see what patterns emerge. How is your addiction to planning and your fear of missing out contributing to your issues? After this mental decluttering, try sitting quietly for ten to twenty minutes. I know it sounds challenging, but think of it as training for your next big adventure.

During this quiet time, focus on your primary ego addiction to planning. Get curious about it. What good things has it helped you achieve? Where did it come from? What fears is it trying to protect you from? Most importantly, how does it create unnecessary suffering for you and those you love, especially around money?

Then, reflect on your secondary ego addiction to resentment and the frustration it produces. When does it show up? What triggers it? What problems is it trying to solve, however imperfectly?

Once you can see these patterns, it's time to focus on your primary and secondary virtues: mindfulness and generosity. How can you deploy these throughout your day to stop reacting out of fear? Maybe you could create a daily mantra or prayer that incorporates these virtues, such as this Contentment Prayer:

Eternal Presence, open my heart to your fulfilling love and ease the restlessness within my heart. Strengthen my capacity for mindfulness and generosity, anchored in your boundless grace. Help me release my addictions to planning and resentment so that I may be content to serve you through those around me in the present moment.

Remember, Sevens, a spiritual practice is crucial for your mental health. Without one, it is easy to fall into a cycle of constant distraction and miss out on the deeper fulfillment you're seeking.

Regular sessions with a therapist can also be incredibly helpful in exploring your Childhood Wounds. If that's not accessible, look into free counseling services offered by various religious or community organizations. The goal is to find a safe space to unpack your past experiences.

Don't forget the crucial step of cultivating compassion for yourself and the people who raised you. And when you begin to integrate new habits into your routine, give yourself a lot of grace. Mindfulness might feel uncomfortable at first, like trying to sit still during an adrenaline rush. But by reducing your reliance on constant planning and distraction, you'll start to find a richer, more fulfilling life experience.

Learn to be less anxious or avoidant about money by confronting your money monsters.

Alright, my adventurous Sevens, it's time for the ultimate quest—taming your money monsters! I know you'd rather be planning your next exotic vacation or trying out a new restaurant. But trust me, this is an adventure worth taking.

Behind your money avoidance and anxiety lies your greatest fear—the fear of pain and privation. It's like a wild animal inside you, always pushing you to seek the next thrill or distraction. But here's the thing: You can't outrun this beast. The more you try to escape it, the more power it gains over you.

Instead, imagine you're the protagonist in an epic tale (because let's face it, you love a good story). Your mission? To befriend the wild beast within. It's like that classic tale of St. Francis and the Wolf of Gubbio, but with a Seven twist.

Picture this: In the bustling town of Sevenville, a restless spirit keeps all the inhabitants constantly on the move. This spirit, let's call it the FOMO Fox, has everyone chasing after the next big thing, never able to sit still or enjoy what they have. This drives the townspeople crazy and leaves them exhausted. Sound familiar?

Now, along comes our hero (that's you!) who decides to face this FOMO Fox (your wounded inner child) head-on. But instead of trying to trap it or chase it away, you approach it with curiosity and compassion. You realize that this fox isn't trying to cause harm—it's just scared of being in pain or alone.

As you get closer, you notice the fox's tail between its legs. And you realize the fox is not a fearsome beast at all, but a frightened creature seeking comfort and security. You speak to it gently: "Hey there, FOMO Fox. I see you're trying to protect me from pain. But you know what? We're missing out on the beauty of the present moment."

The fox looks up at you, surprised by your understanding. You continue, "How about we make a deal? I'll promise to love you unconditionally. In return, can you help me stay in the present moment and help me face my difficult emotions? Maybe take a rest, and let's just snuggle with each other for a while."

From that day on, you and your inner FOMO Fox work together. You learn to enjoy the present moment while still planning exciting futures in a grounded way. You find that true fulfillment comes not from constant novelty, but from deep engagement with life as it is.

Remember, Sevens, the FOMO Fox inside you is just a scared child seeking comfort. The more you try to outrun it with endless plans and distractions, the louder it howls. But when you face it with courage and compassion, you can transform that restless energy into your greatest strength.

By taming your FOMO Fox, you're not giving up on adventure—you're opening yourself to the greatest adventure of all: discovering the richness of the present moment and the depth of your own being. This is how your Sacred Wound of fear transforms into your Sacred Gift of Divine Fulfillment.

To make this transformation a practical reality with your money, we're going to get up close and personal with your Gorger and Grabber mindsets. Don't just skim the surface here—take a deep-sea dive into your financial psyche. How do these money monsters show up in your earning, saving, and investing? Take a good, hard look at how these mindsets play out in each area. You might find some surprising contrasts.

For example, you might find yourself in constant Gorger mode when it comes to experiences—always spending on the next big thrill. But when it comes to investing, you're more of a Grabber, anxiously chasing the next big jackpot. Or perhaps as a Seven, you're a master at earning and networking, but saving? That's about as appealing as a vacation in a library.

Now, here's where it gets fun. Once you've mapped out your money monster traits in each category of earning, saving, and investing, it's time to pair each trait with its corresponding countermove. Why not turn this into a visual masterpiece? Create a "Money Monster to Money Master" transformation chart.[5] Make it colorful, make it bold—heck, make it so eye-catching that you can't help but look at it every day.

Go wild with this! Plaster it on your walls, make it your phone background, stick it on your fridge. Surround yourself with these reminders of your journey from financial chaos to money mastery, complete with practical action steps.

Remember, this isn't about dampening your natural enthusiasm—it's about channeling it into financial fulfillment. We're not trying to turn you into a boring budget bot but into a financially savvy superstar.

Build a strong financial life by earning, saving, and investing ethically.

Now let's talk about building a financial future that's as exciting as your wildest adventures. If you are money-anxious and already have your yacht, congrats! Skip class and go to the next step. For the rest of you, when it comes to padding those pockets, you've got some serious superpowers up your sleeve that need harnessing.

That quick mind of yours that's always racing to the next adventure? Channel it into scenario-planning for your financial future. That boundless enthusiasm and ability to see possibilities where others see obstacles? Pure gold, my friends. Employers will be falling over themselves to harness your innovative energy if you channel it right. You're the idea generators, the out-of-the-box thinkers who can breathe life into stagnant projects and inspire entire teams.

And let's not forget that natural charm and adaptability. As social butterflies and quick learners, you've got an uncanny knack for networking and spotting exciting opportunities. So why not put that versatile mind to work? What groundbreaking, never-been-done-before ideas can you dream up that'll have the world buzzing?

Think big, my adventurous friends—what untapped experiences or services can you create that people didn't even know they needed? With your finger always on the pulse of what's new and exciting, your earning potential is as limitless as your imagination.

Just remember to stay grounded and be on the lookout for when that "ooh, shiny!" distraction starts to kick in, ready to knock you off course. Channel that Seven zest for life, focus your energy, and show the world what a financial powerhouse a motivated Seven can be. The only limit is your attention span—so get out there and turn those ideas into cold, hard cash.

Saving might not be your natural strong suit, but hear me out.

Think of it as planning for future adventures. That optimistic nature you have? It can be a secret weapon in building a rock-solid nest egg. Instead of seeing budgeting as restrictive, reframe it as a way to fund even bigger and better experiences down the road.

Unlike some of your more cautious Enneagram cousins, you Sevens have a gift for finding joy in any adventure. The trick is to apply that same enthusiasm to your financial adventure into abundance. With your imagination, I bet you can dream up a saving strategy that's anything but boring. And what epic adventures can you plan for your retirement?

When it comes to investing, you Sevens have a unique advantage—your optimism and future casting can be a superpower in the financial world. So why not put that foresight to work? Dive into the exciting world of finance, become a trend-spotting guru, and let that Seven intuition shine. Your natural affinity for risk might lead you to more adventurous investment strategies, and that's okay! Just remember to balance it with some steadier options.

Think of investing like planning the ultimate road trip. You need a mix of thrilling sights and reliable pit stops. Don't feel pressured to stick to the boring, well-trodden path. Chart your own course, trust your instincts, and keep moving forward with that signature Seven enthusiasm—because the most exciting journeys often lead to the biggest rewards.

The key is not to let FOMO derail you. Sure, it's great to keep your options open, but at a certain point, you've got to commit to a direction. Channel that Seven courage and dive into the world of investing with the same gusto you bring to every new experience. The financial promised land awaits the Sevens who are willing to embrace the adventure of long-term planning.

Use your money and talents as tools to love and serve a suffering world.

For you Sevens, philanthropy doesn't have to be a dull obligation—it can be your greatest thrill yet. Your natural zest for life, coupled with your ability to spot exciting possibilities, makes you uniquely suited to shake up the world of giving. Instead of just writing checks, you have the power to create transformative experiences that address real-world issues while satisfying your craving for novelty and impact.

Picture yourself funding housing and clean-water projects in remote areas, or wildlife conservation initiatives that take you to exotic locations. Your quick mind and forecasting abilities could lead you to support cutting-edge solutions to systemic issues. You could be the catalyst for groundbreaking approaches to age-old problems.

And don't forget about harnessing your natural storytelling abilities. You could fund and participate in creating compelling narratives about social issues through documentaries, podcasts, or interactive digital stories. Your enthusiasm could inspire others to take action, creating a ripple effect of positive change.

Your unique blend of enthusiasm, creativity, adaptability, big-picture thinking, and hands-on engagement will make you a superstar in the world of charitable giving. As a grounded Seven, you have the power to inject excitement and innovation into philanthropy, inspiring others and catalyzing transformative solutions for a world in need.

Your wealth isn't just a ticket to personal experiences—it's a tool to create experiences that change lives. You can create a legacy of joy, innovation, and positive change by aligning your resources with your natural gifts.

The world is waiting for your unique brand of philanthropy. So what are you waiting for? Get out there and start changing the world, one exciting project at a time. After all, who said saving the world can't be the ultimate adrenaline rush?

Grace's Story

Grace's childhood was like a Choose Your Own Adventure book where someone had ripped out half the pages. Her parents were well-meaning but wildly inconsistent, treating raising kids like a part-time job. One day, it was all hugs and ice cream; the next, it was missed dinners and broken promises. Little Grace learned quickly that if she wanted joy in her life, she'd have to generate it herself.

This emotional Tilt-A-Whirl sliced through Grace's psychological umbilical cord faster than you can say "attachment issues." The world became a potential-pain buffet, and Grace was determined to skip the main course of suffering and go straight to the dessert of distraction.

Fast-forward to adult Grace, a bona fide Gorger of experiences and spirits (the liquid kind). Her greatest fear? Being trapped in pain or boredom. Her solution? Keep the party train rolling, baby! Grace's worst vice, gluttony, wasn't just about food (though she never met a late-night drive-thru she didn't like). It was a gluttony of everything—thrills, booze, you name it.

Grace's primary ego addiction, planning, was on overdrive. She wasn't just living for the weekend; she was planning for every weekend until the end of time. Money? That was just fuel for her nonstop party mobile.

But here's where our tale takes a turn darker than a black hole's basement. Grace's drinking, once her trusty sidekick in the fight against boredom, became the villain of her story. She started showing up to work smelling like a brewery's lost and found, her planning addiction now focused solely on when and where she'd get her next drink.

One fateful Monday, Grace stumbled into work three sheets to the wind and proceeded to projectile vomit onto her boss's shoes during a client meeting. Faster than you can say "you're fired," Grace found herself unemployed, uninsured, and thoroughly unraveled.

Suddenly, Grace was face-to-face with her deepest fear: deprivation. She was trapped, not by external circumstances, but by the very web of chaos she'd spun. Welcome to the Dark Night of the Soul, population: one very hungover Seven.

In this darkness, Grace's planning addiction went haywire. She bounced between grandiose schemes to "get back on top" and paralyzing panic about the future. When the planning finally short-circuited, she switched to her secondary ego addiction, resentment, which, combined with gluttony, created frustration. She was angry with everyone and everything—the economy, her parents, her ex-boss with the vomit-magnet shoes. And, in a more honest moment, she was frustrated and angry with herself.

But in the depths of this darkness, something unexpected happened: Grace broke open. It wasn't pretty—imagine an emotional piñata filled with years of unprocessed feelings and stale beer—but it was necessary. In this raw, vulnerable state, Grace finally entered AA and began to face the fear she'd been running from her whole life.

And then, like a lotus growing from the mud, Grace began to practice her primary recovery virtue: mindfulness. She started small, just five minutes a day of sitting with her thoughts without planning her next escape. It was like trying to meditate in a tornado, but slowly, she began to find peace in the present moment.

As her mindfulness muscle grew, Grace found herself naturally leaning into her secondary recovery virtue: generosity. After a long stint in rehab and recovery, she started sponsoring other addicts, finding joy in helping others without expecting anything in return. It was like discovering a new kind of high—one that filled her up instead of leaving her empty.

The combo of mindfulness and generosity unlocked Grace's highest virtue: contentment. She began to find satisfaction in the here and now, no longer constantly chasing the next drink or thrill. Her greatest hope—to feel fulfilled—began to manifest itself, not through external adventures or liquid courage but through an inner journey of self-discovery.

As Grace's contentment grew, her Sacred Wound of externalized fear began to heal. The world no longer seemed like a constant threat. Instead, she saw abundance all around her—in recovery meetings, in new sober friendships, in the simple joy of a clearheaded morning.

Finally, Grace was ready to embrace her Sacred Gift: Divine Fulfillment. She realized that true fulfillment wasn't about accumulating experiences or emptying bottles, but about being fully present in each moment and sharing her joy with others. She became a substance abuse counselor, using her hard-won wisdom to help other thrill-seekers find balance and sobriety.

Most importantly, she now had a good job and began rebuilding her finances from the rubble.

Grace, once the Gorger, had become truly Grounded. Her finances stabilized as she learned to find excitement in saving and investing as much as in spending. She still loved adventure, but now she planned and budgeted for it, finding as much joy in the anticipation as in the experience itself.

And so, like the Prodigal Son, Grace returned home—not to her childhood house, but to her True Self. She had squandered her resources on wild living, hit rock bottom, and found her way back to a life richer than she could have imagined.

Now, if you'll excuse me, I have a sudden urge to check my sobriety coin collection . . .

CHAPTER SIXTEEN

TYPE EIGHT—THE CHALLENGER (HUMMER)

HOW TO STOP BULLDOZING OTHERS AND BUILD A MAGNANIMOUS EMPIRE

Imagine an ego built like a fortress on wheels, capable of plowing through life's toughest terrain without flinching. This is Type Eight of the Enneagram—the Challenger, or as I fondly call them, the Hummer of ego consciousness. These individuals are powerhouses of strength and self-confidence. With an unwavering sense of justice, they're not afraid to use that Hummer as a battering ram. They are straightforward and hardworking, and their superpower is having super amounts of energy.

But beneath that rugged exterior lies a complex inner world shaped by early childhood experiences that cut their psychological umbilical cord in a particularly painful way. For Eights, this severance came through a profound sense of betrayal or rejection, leaving them feeling unprotected and vulnerable in a world they perceived as hostile. This shattering experience stripped away their innocence and trust, replacing it with a burning anger that became externalized—pushed outward against a world that had hurt them so deeply.

Type Eight Ego Map: The Challenger or Hummer

(Read the chart from the bottom up.)

ENLIGHTENMENT STRUCTURE

MONEY MASTER	THE DYNAMO
Sacred Gift (Holy Idea)	Divine Justice
Greatest Hope (Basic Desire)	To experience complete freedom from harm and control
Greatest Virtue (Virtue)	Innocence Mercy + Honesty = Innocence (cure for Lust)
Secondary Recovery Virtue (Relaxation Point)	Honesty (Primary Recovery Virtue for Type 2)
Primary Recovery Virtue	Mercy
Faux Virtue	Joy

SHADOW STRUCTURE

MONEY MONSTERS: AVOIDANT / ANXIOUS	THE DETONATOR / THE DOMINATOR
Ego Stress Response	Rigid Withdrawal Lust + Stinginess = Rigid Withdrawal (blocks Vengeance)
Secondary Ego Addiction (Stress Point)	Stinginess (Primary Ego Addiction for Type 5)
Primary Ego Addiction (Ego Fixation)	Vengeance
Greatest Vice (Passion)	Lust
Greatest Fear (Basic Fear)	Being harmed or controlled
Sacred Wound	Externalized Anger

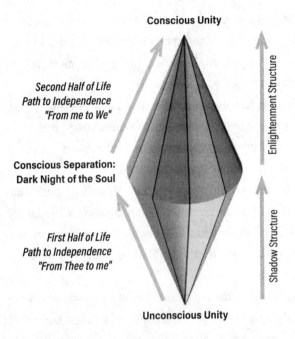

Conscious Unity

Second Half of Life
Path to Independence
"From me to We"

Enlightenment Structure

Conscious Separation:
Dark Night of the Soul

First Half of Life
Path to Independence
"From Thee to me"

Shadow Structure

Unconscious Unity

This externalized anger became the Eight's Sacred Wound, the raw, tender spot from which their entire personality structure grew. It's as if they took that anger and used it to forge an impenetrable buffer zone around themselves, determined never to be hurt or controlled again. This wound created their greatest fear: being harmed or controlled by others.

To cope with this fear, Eights adopt their worst vice—lust. But it isn't just about sex or seeking thrills; it's a lust for intensity. It's about constantly challenging the world, pushing against every boundary and limitation, asserting their autonomy at every turn. It's their way of saying, "I am here, I am strong, and I will not be overcome."

To mask the pain that this constant intensity can create, Eights develop a primary ego addiction to vengeance. This isn't about petty revenge; it's about pushing back against any perceived threat, maintaining their sense of control in a world that once made them feel powerless. It's like they're constantly revving the engine of their Hummer, ready to charge at any obstacle. Their guiding motto is "The best defense is a good offense."

With so much externalized anger, they can easily overdo it, leading to personal and professional problems. With a strong hedonistic streak and a love of intense feelings, they also tend to overdo food, sex, or anything that brings them satisfaction.

Not even Hummers can run over every obstacle or push aside every barrier. When Eights overdose on their addiction to vengeance, creating a five-car pileup, or when they face a situation that genuinely intimidates them, they switch gears to their secondary ego addiction: stinginess.

The combination of their lust for intensity and stinginess creates a state of rigid withdrawal—a temporary blockade against their usual vengeful tendencies. It's like they've traded in their Hummer for a beat-up Compact Car they borrowed from Type Five, driving cautiously and conservatively until they feel safe enough to return to their natural state.[1] They become miserly with their emotions and opinions, retreating into a protective shell. It's their ego stress response, and it's a bit like watching the Hulk try to fold himself into a Smart Car—hilarious but also kind of impressive.

The formula for this ego stress response is:

Lust (greatest vice/passion) + Stinginess (secondary ego addiction/ stress point) = Rigid Withdrawal (ego stress response)

Understanding this complex inner landscape is crucial to comprehending how Eights navigate the world, including their approach to finances and power. Their journey to wholeness involves learning to soften their hard exterior and reveal the tender innocence and capacity for mercy beneath their armor. It's also about learning that true strength doesn't mean running over everything in your path. Sometimes, it's having the courage to be vulnerable and realizing that the most important and useful vehicle on the road isn't the one with the biggest engine, but the one that knows when to give others a lift.

When they mature into their healthiest version, Hummers become dynamic champions of mercy and justice.

Money Monsters

The Detonator: Money-Avoidant

Money avoidance in Type Eight presents a unique paradox. Eights typically don't shy away from money itself, but rather from financially prudent boundaries and limitations. The Detonator approaches fiscal constraints with all the subtlety of a wrecking ball, often "detonating" budgetary limits when their lust for intensity or desire for revenge overtakes common sense.

This type of Eight doesn't want money limitations to control them. Unfortunately, this attitude often leads to reckless spending to control their immediate circumstances, to the detriment of their long-term financial health. They might grab the check at a meal out with friends just to show them who's boss, even when their bank account is running on empty.

My former client Brenda detonated her life savings pursuing lawsuits against anyone she felt had wronged her, often with little chance of success. Even in cases where she was justified, her desire for vindication led to imprudent financial decisions. The pyrrhic victories she occasionally achieved never covered the mountain of legal bills she

TAMING YOUR MONEY MONSTER

accumulated, leaving her financially depleted in her later years. When unchecked by reality, the pursuit of justice (or revenge) can lead to personal economic disaster.

At their worst, Detonator Eights struggle with taking responsibility for their financial troubles. Admitting fault feels like a blow to their ego. Instead, they may externalize blame, creating a cacophony of accusations that make everyone around them miserable. This behavior often stems from a sense of entitlement, a belief that they deserve things they haven't earned—as if life owed them a refund for past hardships.

The hard truth for Detonators is difficult to swallow: If you believe all your money problems are someone else's fault, you're likely missing a large piece of the puzzle. It's like blaming the iceberg for the *Titanic*'s poor navigation.

For these Eights, the path to financial health begins with self-reflection and accountability. They need to recognize that true power comes from mastering the art of strategic restraint. With conscious effort, Detonator Eights can channel their formidable energy into financial strength rather than self-sabotage.

Traits of the Detonator

Financial Brinkmanship: Detonators often push their finances to the edge, pushing the boundaries of financial prudence to the limit. They're the Evel Knievel of finance, always trying to jump the Grand Canyon of debt with a motorcycle made of maxed-out credit cards. How about finding ways to blow up that debt instead? What about creating a *Kill Bill* challenge, where you focus on killing one debt every month? Find a way to celebrate when you destroy one opponent, then move on to your next victim. Keep going until you kill them all.

Rebellious Spending: To assert independence, they may engage in impulsive or excessive spending, especially when advised against it. It's as if budgets are challenges to be conquered rather than helpful guardrails. Instead, turn budgeting into a game of strategy. Create a "Rebel's Guide to Wealth" where you outsmart the system by saving and investing more than you spend. It's not about following rules—it's about beating them at their own game.

Vulnerability Aversion: Detonators often dodge financial discussions or transparency, perceiving them as potential weaknesses. They're like financial lone wolves, resistant to seeking help even when it's clearly needed. How about reframing financial discussions as power moves? Knowledge is power, right? So diving into your finances isn't showing weakness—it's arming yourself for financial freedom.

Short-Term Focus: These Eights tend to prioritize immediate gratification of their copious desires over long-term planning. They're more likely to buy a sports car impulsively than contribute to a retirement fund. Why worry about retirement when you can live like a rock star today? As a hack, challenge yourself to delay gratification like it's an extreme sport. Set a goal to outlast your impulses for increasingly longer periods. Start small—maybe wait a day before a purchase, then a week. Before you know it, you'll be a long-term planning ninja rather than a hedonic wimp.

Risk Glorification: Detonators can glorify financial risks, viewing conservative money management as boring or weak. They're the financial equivalent of adrenaline junkies. As an alternative, treat conservative investing like you're infiltrating enemy territory. It's not boring—it's a covert operation to stealthily build your financial empire right under everyone's noses.

Avoidance Through Aggression: When confronted about their spending habits, these Eights transform into financial Hulks. *"EIGHT SMASH PUNY BUDGET!!!"* They don't just avoid the issue; they redecorate the room with overturned furniture to distract from their overdrawn accounts. Channel that aggression into aggressive saving. Instead of intimidating others, intimidate your debt. Smash those bills until they shrink in fear (and in balance).

Financial Amnesia: Some Detonators might subconsciously forget about bills or financial obligations as a form of avoidance. It's not that they can't remember—it's that they don't want to, and they don't care how you feel about it. How about turning bill-paying into a conquest sport? Create a "Wall of Vanquished Expenses" where you display paid bills like trophies. It's celebrating your victories over financial obligations.

Chrematophobia: Chrematophobia is an irrational fear of money that can make it difficult for someone to spend money or pay their bills. One former client, a money-avoidant Type Eight, had her power and utilities cut off temporarily because she hadn't paid her bills for several months, even though she had a multimillion-dollar trust fund. While any type can have chrematophobia, I've seen it more often in Eights. Their lust for intensity works against them when money-avoidant because it becomes a *passionate* avoidance of money. Try exposure therapy by facing your fear of money in easy, small steps. Break tasks down to the smallest step you are willing to do right now, and only do that. Maybe just check your balance once a week. Gradually build up to more complex financial tasks. Start slow but don't back down.

Identity Defiance: They might avoid financial success to defy expectations or rebel against a financially focused upbringing. It's like financial self-sabotage as a form of identity assertion. "You want me to be financially responsible? Well, watch me set fire to this pile of cash!" How about redefining financial success on your own terms? Maybe for you, it's not about a big house in the suburbs but funding a butt-kicking nonprofit that fights for a cause you believe in. Make your financial empire as distinctive and powerful as you are.

Financial Planning Aversion: Detonators tend to treat financial planning like a particularly tedious chore. These Eights often possess a big-picture mindset, which is great for visionary thinking but less ideal for managing the nitty-gritty of day-to-day finances. They'd rather delegate these tasks to others or, more often, simply overlook them entirely. I once had a Detonator client who, when asked about his retirement plan, confidently stated, "I'll figure it out when I get there." It's as if they believe financial stability is something that just happens, like puberty or male-pattern baldness. Again, approach financial planning like you're plotting world domination. It's not tedious paperwork—it's your battle plan for conquering your financial future. Plus, imagine the look on everyone's faces when you reveal your master plan for early retirement.

The Dominator: Money-Anxious

The money-anxious Eight turns every financial interaction into a power play. They wield wealth like a weapon, using it to sculpt the world—and the people in it—to their liking.

For the Dominator, money isn't just a means of exchange; it's an extension of their formidable will. They use it to control, to punish, and to reward, much like a stern deity dispensing judgment from on high. Every dollar spent, every gift given, comes with strings attached—strings that can quickly turn into chains.

This approach to finances stems from the Eight's deep-seated fear of being controlled or harmed. By dominating others financially, they believe they're protecting themselves. It's a financial fortress they've built, but one that often becomes a prison—not just for those around them, but for the Dominators themselves.

The Dominator often fails to realize that their financial stronghold isn't as impenetrable as they think. The people in their lives, tired of being manipulated, begin to play the game right back. They learn to navigate the Dominator's moods, to present the facade of compliance while secretly resenting every moment. It's a Machiavellian dance of dollars and cents, where affection is currency, and every interaction is a transaction.

Consider the case of a wealthy former client of mine. He used his financial power to puppeteer his daughter's life, doling out necessities like college tuition and even basic comforts in exchange for strict adherence to his values and whims. The result? A daughter who became an expert in surface-level compliance while nurturing a deep-seated resentment. She played the game, biding her time until she could inherit his wealth and finally live life on her own terms. He may have controlled his daughter's actions, but he lost her heart in the process.

While the Dominator may think they're creating a world of order and respect, they're actually fostering a breeding ground for resentment, deceit, and eventual abandonment. When their wealth or power wanes, they often find they've surrounded themselves not with loved ones but with fair-weather friends who swiftly vanish.

The tragic irony is that in their quest for control and security, the Dominator often creates the very situation they fear most—a world where they can't trust anyone, where every relationship is transactional, and where true intimacy is as rare as a depreciation-proof car.

The path forward for the Dominator is challenging but vital. It involves recognizing that true power doesn't come from controlling others but from fostering genuine connections. It's about understanding that money can be a tool for growth and mutual benefit. The Dominator must learn to loosen their grip on the financial reins, to trust others, and to find security in interdependence rather than iron-fisted control.

Only then can they transform from a feared tyrant to a respected leader, from someone who uses money to constrain to someone who uses it to empower. It's a journey from financial domination to true abundance.

Traits of the Dominator

Power-Through-Prosperity Tunnel Vision: These Eights treat their bank account like a scoreboard in the game of life. Every dollar is another point proving their dominance. Instead of measuring your worth by your net worth, create a "Life Impact Scorecard." Track how many people you've helped, battles you've won for the underdog, and positive changes you've catalyzed. You're not just accumulating wealth; you're building an empire of influence for good.

Control-Freak Economics: These Eights micromanage their finances with the intensity of a general planning D-Day. Every penny must fall in line or face court-martial. Try delegating some financial tasks to trusted advisors. Think of it as building your financial special forces team—each member with their own mission, all serving your greater strategic vision.

Philanthropic Puppeteering: When Dominators do engage in charitable giving, it can be with strings attached. They may use their generosity as a means of control, expecting recognition or compliance in return for their "benevolence." Try anonymous giving instead. Be a financial superhero without the cape and glory. Plus, it's a challenge: Can you do good without getting credit? Bet you can't!

Financial Paranoia: Dominators often see financial threats where none exist. They may be constantly on guard against perceived attempts to take advantage of them financially, leading to a pervasive sense of mistrust in their relationships. Healthy diligence is good, but like anything taken too far, it can become problematic.

Try this: Start small with a "Trust Fund" (and no, I don't mean the kind Paris Hilton has). Set aside a small amount of money—let's say 1 percent of your income or another fixed amount—specifically for trusting others. Use it to lend money to a friend, help out a family member, or invest in a start-up. I want you to mentally write off this money. Consider it gone. If it comes back with interest, great! If not, well, you were prepared for that. The point isn't the money—it's the practice of trust. It's like trust weight lifting. Start with small weights (amounts), and gradually increase them as you build your trust muscles.

Aggressive Investing: Dominators can be surprisingly aggressive investors. They may view the financial market as another arena to conquer, often taking high-stakes risks in their quest for financial dominance. Risk and reward are correlated, so sometimes that works out, but sometimes it really doesn't. As a suggestion, divide your portfolio into "Conquest" and "Kingdom" funds. Satisfy your need for financial domination with the Conquest fund, while building long-term stability with the Kingdom fund. It's not playing it safe; it's diversifying your attack strategy.

Emotional Shielding: These Eights often use their financial success as a shield against emotional vulnerability. Why deal with messy feelings when you can solve problems by throwing money at them? Challenge yourself to solve one personal problem each month without using money. This time it's like *emotional* weight lifting—uncomfortable at first, but you'll be flexing those feeling muscles in no time.

Financial Ultimatum Addiction: Dominators may frequently resort to financial ultimatums in their relationships. "My way or the highway" becomes "My way or no pay," using money as leverage to get their way. Before making demands, ask yourself: "What would a benevolent dictator do?" Find ways to exercise power while strengthening alliances, not destroying them. Remember, true power comes from having people want to follow you, not fear you.

Catastrophic Thinking: Despite their outward bravado, Dominators can engage in worst-case-scenario thinking about their finances. They may be haunted by fears of sudden financial ruin, driving them to ever-greater attempts at control. Having a "Financial Doomsday Plan" is always a good idea, but once you've outlined how you'd handle worst-case scenarios—like a recession, job loss, or market crash—you can stop worrying and start conquering. It's not pessimism; it's strategic preparedness.

Financial-Fortress Alienation: Dominators view wealth as armor against life's uncertainties. They're not just saving for a rainy day; they're stockpiling for Armageddon. This constant state of financial vigilance can lead to missed opportunities for growth and connection with the people they love. Instead of building an impenetrable money bunker, create a "Financial Adventure Fund." Every month, allocate a small percentage of your savings to experiences that build connections. It's not letting your guard down; it's tactical relationship-building.

Competitive Spending: For these Eights, every purchase is a power move. They need the biggest house, the flashiest car, the most impressive everything—not for enjoyment, but to assert dominance. Channel that competitive spirit into a "Personal Best" challenge instead. Compete against your past self in savings goals or investment returns. You're not keeping up with the Joneses; you're crushing your own records.

Financial Martyrdom: These Dominators wear their financial stress like battle scars, demanding respect for their sacrifices while complaining about how hard they work. How about accepting that your workaholism is really all about you? Try this: For every hour you spend building your empire, spend at least ten minutes enjoying what you've built. Power without pleasure is just self-imposed prison.

The path forward for Dominators involves recognizing that true security comes not from domination but from connection. It's about understanding that money is a tool for living, not a weapon for control. As they learn to loosen their iron grip on their finances and the people around them, they may find that the real wealth in life comes from trust, vulnerability, and genuine relationships—things that, ironically, their money anxiety has been pushing away all along.

A Money Master—The Dynamo

The Eight's path to enlightenment begins, like all of us, in the Dark Night of the Soul, and is the equivalent of a head-on collision with reality. It's here, when things have fallen apart, that they can finally see how their lust for intensity and thirst for vengeance have created suffering for themselves and those they love. Our Eight slowly begins to realize their Hummer of an ego has been causing more pileups than progress, and they're sitting in the wreckage, surrounded by the debris of broken relationships and missed opportunities.

I've seen Eights who've turned their entire lives into a demolition derby, some even landing in jail because they couldn't put the brakes on their revenge-fueled road rage. Jail is a nightmare for everyone, but for an Eight, whose greatest fear is being controlled or dominated, it's especially hellish.

But here's where it gets interesting. If they choose to break open rather than break down, they start to see how their ego addictions have manifested their greatest fear. It's like they've been running from a monster, only to realize they're the one who has been wearing the monster costume all along. In their quest to be free from harm and control, they've created circumstances that put them in pain and leave them powerless.

This is when they can truly begin to practice their primary path of recovery: mercy. They learn to be merciful toward themselves and the world and don't need to push back against every limitation or always be in control.

As they start to embrace compassion and acceptance, something magical happens. Their ego stress begins to dissolve. Suddenly, they don't feel the need to turn every interaction into a UFC match, and they learn that no one "wins" in life because it was never a competitive sport but a game of cooperation. They finally realize that it's their constant challenging and pushing against others that forces people to push back, which triggers the Eight's fear and stress.

However, they need to be mindful of their faux virtue: joy. When an Eight is especially joyful, it usually means they are overindulging in their worst vice: lust. This faux joy looks suspiciously like chaos and is more like the fun of a divorce party in a smash room than the calm that authentic joy brings.

When an Eight breaks open in the Dark Night of the Soul, it's as if they trade in their vengeance-fueled Hummer for a tricked-out Ambulance borrowed from Type Two.[2] This transformation is nothing short of revolutionary. The Hummer, once an unstoppable force and intimidating presence, now gives way to a vehicle designed for a different kind of strength—one that heals rather than conquers.

This new ego vehicle runs incredibly well on mercy, a fuel that seemed scarce in the Eight's previous journey. But this mercy isn't weakness. It's a new form of strength, one that requires even more courage than their previous displays of power. It takes true bravery to lay down arms and offer help instead.

The battering ram of confrontation becomes a gurney, ready to lift up those who have fallen. The armor plating that once deflected attacks now houses supplies to mend wounds.

The Eight, accustomed to charging ahead, finds themselves navigating the streets of life with a new purpose. They're still first on the scene and taking the lead in any crisis, but instead of dominating the situation, they're there to provide critical support. Their intensity, once used to overpower, now energizes their ability to protect and nurture.

Behind the wheel of an Ambulance, they also begin to adopt honesty as their secondary path of recovery, mirroring Type Two's primary path of recovery. Honesty for the Eight isn't about not lying; it's about being authentically vulnerable. It's honesty about what they truly feel and allowing themselves to show their warm, tender, gooey center without fear of being perceived as weak. They can be honest about their feelings, fears, and anxieties without feeling like they're handing over their kryptonite to potential enemies.

This shift requires more courage than any battle they've ever fought. They're not just being honest with others; they're being honest with themselves, perhaps for the first time. They're acknowledging that beneath their fierce exterior lies a world of complex emotions, fears, and yes, even anxieties.

Now, here's where the real alchemy happens. When an Eight combines mercy and honesty, you get the Eight's highest virtue: innocence. We're not talking about naive, Bambi-in-the-forest innocence here. This is a state of openness and freedom that celebrates the innate goodness of reality. It's like they've taken off their armor and realized the world isn't out to get them after all.

The secret to their success is:

Mercy (primary recovery virtue) + Honesty (secondary recovery virtue/relaxation point) = Innocence (greatest virtue/virtue)

This innocence allows Eights to access their gentler side without feeling like they're going soft. They can see the world through compassionate, forgiving eyes without losing their strength. It's not that harm will never come to them, but they're no longer controlled by the fear of it and can finally drop their lust for intensity that pushes the world around and away.

When they surrender their fears and take off their armor, they actually fulfill their greatest hope: to experience complete freedom from harm or control. By connecting with their True Self, they find a spiritual freedom that transcends all material constraints. It's like finding out the key to your jail cell was in your pocket all along.

As they embody this innocence, Eights unlock their Sacred Gift: Divine Justice. No longer are they seeking justice for their bruised egos or how the Eight thinks the world should be run; now they're championing the cause of others with love and innocence, accepting that the God of their understanding has a plan far greater than the one-person warpath of an Eight. They become powerful allies for the vulnerable, using their strength to stand up for those who can't speak for themselves.

Divine Justice is merciful, and balances strength with empathy, assertiveness with understanding. Healthy Eights operate with integrity and transparency, using their lust for justice to fuel positive change rather than perpetuate conflict. As Gandhi wisely said, "An eye for an eye makes the whole world blind." Rather than poking people's eyes out, the Dynamo starts handing out eye patches and taking away the pointy sticks used to poke more out. They become filled with passionate intensity for selfless acts of love and service.

As a Type Eight, Dr. Martin Luther King Jr. brought Divine Justice through the civil rights movement. He wasn't just a spiritual leader; he was a money master who understood that Divine Justice needs significant financing, and he wielded money as a force for good. Some people think that Mother Teresa of Calcutta was also an Eight, and look at how much money she funneled through her charities!

The more money an Eight can bring to the table, the larger their arena for positive action becomes. Now that's what I call a return on investment!

Becoming a Money Master—The Dynamo

Please be sure to read (or review) the chapter 8 overview of these five steps before you get started here.

Acknowledge the pain from your Childhood Wounding.

For you Eights, facing these wounds might feel like removing your armor in the middle of a war zone. Your childhood likely taught you that vulnerability equals weakness, and weakness gets you hurt. But here's the plot twist: Confronting this pain is the most courageous thing you can do. It's not about being weak; it's about being strong enough to face your inner demons.

Remember, you didn't become a fortress overnight. Those walls you've built, that intensity you wield like a weapon—they're the result of early betrayals, moments when you felt powerless or controlled. Maybe you had to grow up too fast, becoming the protector when you should have been protected. Or perhaps you learned that the only way to survive was to be tougher, louder, more dominant than everyone else.

Eights often emerge from childhoods marked by adversity, where they learned early on that the world can be a harsh and unforgiving place. Their Sacred Wound of externalized anger typically stems from experiences of betrayal, powerlessness, or the need to grow up too fast.

Picture a young Eight, perhaps in a chaotic or unsafe environment. Maybe there was physical or emotional abuse, or perhaps they were thrust into the role of protector for younger siblings or even a parent. These children often feel they can't rely on adults to keep them safe, so they take on that responsibility themselves.

Some Eights might have experienced a profound betrayal by a trusted authority figure. Imagine a child whose parent abandoned the family, or whose teacher humiliated or abused them. These experiences can shatter a young Eight's trust in others and instill a deep-seated belief that they can only rely on themselves.

In other cases, Eights might have grown up in environments where vulnerability was seen as weakness. Maybe they were told to "toughen up" whenever they showed emotion, or perhaps they witnessed a parent being victimized and vowed never to be in that position themselves.

Economic instability can also play a role. An Eight who grew up in poverty might have experienced the powerlessness that comes with financial insecurity, driving them to seek control through accumulating wealth and resources.

The common thread in all these scenarios is a child who feels fundamentally unsafe in the world and decides to make themselves big and strong to combat that feeling. They externalize their anger as a protective shield, pushing against a world they perceive as hostile.

It's crucial to understand that this anger isn't just rage—it's a life force, a fierce determination to protect themselves and those they care about. The young Eight learns to puff themselves up, to become larger than life, to intimidate before they can be intimidated.

This is how their Sacred Wound of externalized anger is born. The Eight pushes their anger outward, against the boundaries of the world, in an attempt to carve out a safe space for themselves. They learn to rely on their own strength and willpower, often at the cost of vulnerability and trust.

But here's the beautiful twist in the Eight's story: This very wound, when acknowledged and healed, becomes the source of their greatest strength. Their capacity for protection, their unwavering support for the underdog, their ability to move mountains—all of these admirable qualities are rooted in that original wound.

So, to my powerful Eight friends, I say this: Your anger, your force, your intensity—these are not things to be ashamed of. They are the crucible in which your strength was forged. The key is learning to wield that power with wisdom and compassion, to protect without dominating, to be strong without losing touch with your gentle core.

Remember, the goal isn't to eliminate your intensity, but to channel it productively. When you do, you'll find that your financial life—and indeed, your whole life—becomes not a battlefield, but a platform for making a real, positive impact in the world. And isn't that what your younger self was trying to do all along?

Creating a trauma timeline can be particularly powerful for you Eights. Get a huge whiteboard or spreadsheet and map out the moments when you first armored up, when you decided that control was the only way to feel safe. Pay special attention to your relationship with money. Did you equate it with power? Protection? The ability to never be vulnerable again? Or is money something you fear might control you?

This process isn't about wallowing in past hurts. It's about understanding the source of your strength, and yes, your pain. It's about recognizing that the very things that made you a survivor might now be holding you back from truly thriving.

Finding allies for this journey might be challenging. Your instinct is to go it alone, to never show weakness. But even the mightiest warrior needs a squad. Look for a therapist who isn't intimidated by your intensity and who can match your directness with equal force. Seek out mentors who've walked this path and come out stronger. Build a support network that respects your strength while helping you explore your vulnerabilities.

Remember, acknowledging these wounds isn't about becoming soft. It's about becoming whole. It's about turning that incredible force of will that's gotten you this far toward healing and growth. You've conquered so much in your life. Now it's time to conquer your past, not by defeating it, but by embracing it, understanding it, and using it to fuel your journey to becoming not just a money master, but a master of your own story.

This is your hero's journey. And like every great hero, the first step is acknowledging the call to adventure. Are you ready to answer it?

Stop reacting out of the anger that created your money monsters.

It's time to tackle your anger issues. Your journey to mastery requires two skills that might initially feel like kryptonite: contemplation and compassion. But trust me, these are your secret weapons.

Contemplation for an Eight isn't about sitting cross-legged, chanting, "*Ommmm.*" It's about strategic analysis of your inner battleground. Try this: Set up a massive whiteboard in your war room (aka home office or bedroom) and map out your anger issues. Where did your need for control actually leave you powerless? When did your vengeance backfire? This isn't navel-gazing; it's a tactical assessment.

Yeah, I know. Vengeance and intensity, that desire to push back against others, feels good. It's like a shot of adrenaline straight to the heart. But let's be real: It's also leaving you isolated, constantly on guard, and probably with a string of burned bridges in your wake. Your journey starts with recognizing how your primary ego addiction—vengeance—is impacting your life.

TAMING YOUR MONEY MONSTER

The key is to find a way to quiet that constant need for power and control, even if just for a few minutes a day. It's not weakness; it's regrouping.

Now, let's talk compassion. I know, it sounds soft. But here's the truth: Compassion is strength. It takes more power to show mercy than to seek vengeance. Start by being compassionately curious about your primary ego addiction to vengeance. How has it served you? What fears is it trying to protect you from? How is it creating unnecessary collateral damage in your life? Remember, you didn't choose to be wounded; you adapted to survive. Now it's time to adapt again, not to just survive, but to thrive.

Then, examine your secondary ego addiction—stinginess. When does it show up? What triggers it? How is it actually leaving you with less, not more? How is it blocking you from being vulnerable and showing the world your True Self?

Your challenge is to integrate mercy (your primary path of recovery) and honesty (your secondary path) into your daily life to reveal your loving innocence. They'll help you stop reacting out of anger and instead respond with patient and purposeful power.

Consider starting and ending your day with this Innocence Prayer:

Divine Protector, open my heart to your powerful love and temper the anger that drives me. Endow me with radical mercy and tender honesty, secure in your unyielding grace. Help me to surrender my addictions to vengeance and stinginess so I may innocently love and serve you through those around me.

Remember, Eight, this journey isn't about becoming less powerful. It's about becoming more purposeful with your power. It's about transforming from a wrecking ball into a precision instrument of compassionate, merciful force for positive change. Your intensity, your passion, your strength—these are gifts. The challenge is to wield them with the finesse of a master swordsman in service to the world.

Learn to be less anxious or avoidant about money by confronting your money monsters.

Now, I know what you're thinking. *Confront my money monsters? Ha! I eat monsters for breakfast!* And while I appreciate your bravado, my fierce friend, this isn't a battle you can win with sheer force. Trust me, I've seen Eights try to strong-arm their finances into submission. It isn't pretty.

Instead, let's take a page from St. Francis's playbook. You remember the guy who tamed the Wolf of Gubbio? Here's the CliffsNotes version:

St. Francis walks up to this big, bad wolf that's been terrorizing a town. Instead of going in guns blazing (which, let's be honest, is your usual MO), he approaches with peace and understanding. And guess what? The wolf chills out. Turns out, it was just hungry and scared.

Your money monsters—whether the Detonator (avoidant) or the Dominator (anxious)—are just like that wolf. They're not evil. They're not out to get you. They're just scared and trying to protect you in their own misguided way.

So, here's what I want you to do, my powerful Eight: Approach your money fears with curiosity and compassion. Start by getting real with yourself. What are you really afraid of when it comes to money? Is it the fear of being controlled? Of not having enough power? Of being vulnerable? Write it all down. No holds barred. You're not sharing this with anyone, so let it all hang out.

Next, create your "Money Monster to Money Master" chart.[3] But make it an Eight-style chart. Instead of fluffy categories, use battle terms. "Financial Ambush Points" for where your money monsters trip you up. "Strategic Countermoves" for your master strategies. Make it bold, make it in-your-face. Heck, use red pen if you want—I know you Eights love your power colors.

Now, here's where it gets interesting. For each "Ambush Point," I want you to dig deep and ask yourself: "What is this behavior really trying to protect me from?" Remember, your money monsters, whether they're making you avoid your finances or dominate them, are just trying to keep you safe in their own twisted way.

For example, if you're a Detonator who avoids dealing with money because it feels like a constraint, ask yourself: "Am I really protecting my freedom, or am I just scared of feeling controlled?" If you're a Dominator who's anxiously micromanaging every cent, ask yourself: "Am I really in control, or am I just terrified of being vulnerable?"

Here's a challenge for you, mighty Eight: Write a letter to money. Yeah, you heard me right. Pretend money is a person you're in a relationship with. What would you say? How has your relationship been? Be honest about your fears, your resentments, your expectations. Don't hold back—I know you won't.

Then write a response from money to you. What might it say if it could speak? This isn't about making money the bad guy. It's about understanding the relationship from both sides. It's like couples therapy, but for you and your bank account.

Remember, the goal isn't to destroy your money monsters. It's to understand them, to integrate them, to transform them into allies. Your fierce energy, your power, your intensity—these are all incredible assets when it comes to managing money. But only if you're using them consciously, not reactively.

Build a strong financial life by earning, saving, and investing ethically.

If you're money-anxious and have built your empire, skip ahead to the next step. For the rest of you, this phase isn't just about accumulating wealth; it's about creating a bastion of security that allows you to protect and provide for those you care about. Let's dive in and conquer this financial battlefield.

First up, earning. You Eights are natural-born leaders with an innate ability to take charge. It's time to leverage that strength into serious earning potential. Don't settle for a job that doesn't recognize your power. If you're stuck in a position that feels confining, start plotting your jailbreak now. Your intensity and drive make you perfect for high-stakes, high-reward careers or entrepreneurs. Consider fields like business leadership, crisis management, or even starting your own company. Your ability to make tough decisions and protect others could make you an exceptional CEO or founder.

Here's a challenge for you: Think about how you can monetize your protective instincts. Maybe it's starting a cybersecurity firm, becoming a high-powered attorney defending the underdog, or launching a revolutionary health product. The key is aligning your work with your core desire to impact and help others. What are you passionate about that you can monetize, or how can you level up in your current career?

Now let's talk about saving. I know the idea of constraining your spending might make you bristle. Think of saving not as a limitation but as amassing resources for future battles. Start with a war chest—an emergency fund covering at least six months of expenses. This isn't just a safety net; it's a strategic reserve that gives you the freedom to take bold actions without fear.

Budgeting might feel restrictive, but approach it like general campaign-planning. Every dollar has a mission. Use apps and tools to automate this process—think of them as your financial lieutenants, freeing you up to focus on the big picture. And when it comes to tackling debt, attack it with the same ferocity you'd show any other enemy threatening your autonomy.

Investing is where you can really flex those Type Eight muscles. Your natural intensity and willingness to take calculated risks can serve you well here. Aim to invest at least 15 percent of your income, but don't be afraid to go bigger. Your boldness could lead to substantial returns if channeled wisely.

Here's a twist that might appeal to your sense of justice: Look into impact investing. This approach allows you to use your financial power to support causes you believe in while still earning returns. Imagine being able to protect the vulnerable or support underdogs on a global scale through your investments. That's power with a purpose.

And don't forget about real estate. Property ownership can give you a tangible sense of control and a powerful leverage point for building wealth. It's also a way to literally own your territory—something that often appeals to Eights.

As you build your financial empire, remember to regularly reassess and adjust your strategy. The world is constantly changing, and you need to be ready to adapt your tactics. This includes having a solid estate plan to ensure that your ability to protect and provide extends even beyond your lifetime.

Building true financial strength isn't just about accumulating wealth. It's about creating a resource that amplifies your ability to make a difference. It's about having the means to protect, to fight injustice, to stand up for those who can't stand up for themselves.

Use your money and talents as tools to love and serve a suffering world.

For you Eights, this final step is about more than just giving back—it's about leveraging your strength to protect and empower others. Your journey has been about mastering power, and now it's time to use that power for the greater good. Remember, true strength is about creating positive change on a massive scale.

Think of it this way: You're not just writing checks, you're funding revolutions. Your financial resources are the ammunition in your crusade against injustice and suffering. But before you start firing off donations, get your boots on the ground. Invest your time and formidable presence in causes you're passionate about. Your natural leadership and ability to get things done can be game changers for organizations that are often long on heart but short on execution.

Don't just be a donor—be a force of nature. Use your innate ability to cut through the BS and get to the heart of issues. Your directness and intensity can shake up stagnant systems and challenge the status quo. Remember, you're here to make waves and create real, lasting impact.

Consider focusing your efforts on causes that align with your protective instincts. Maybe it's fighting for children's rights, battling systemic injustice, or protecting the environment. Your capacity for taking bold action and your willingness to confront difficult truths make you an invaluable ally in these arenas.

As you grow in your giving, think strategically about how to tackle the root causes of problems. This might mean funding innovative education programs in underserved communities, investing in clean energy start-ups, or backing political movements that align with your values. Your ability to see the big picture and make tough decisions can lead to transformative change.

Don't forget to leverage your network and influence. You have the power to rally others to your cause. Host fundraising events, start a foundation, or use your business connections to create partnerships that multiply your impact. Your charisma and conviction can inspire others to join your mission.

Your journey of financial mastery has given you unique insights. Share them boldly. Offer mentorship to budding entrepreneurs from disadvantaged backgrounds. Your no-nonsense advice and unwavering support could be the catalyst that launches the next generation of changemakers.

Here's the truth, mighty Eights: When you heal your anger and channel your intensity, you become a formidable force. Your Sacred Gift of Divine Justice allows you to cut through deception and speak truth to power. You have the strength to stand up for those who can't stand up for themselves, to fight battles others shy away from.

By becoming a money master, you're not just changing your own life—you're gaining the resources to generate more justice and fairness. Your financial success becomes a weapon in your arsenal for creating a more equitable world.

So, as you stand at this final frontier, ask yourself: "How can I use my financial power to protect the vulnerable and challenge injustice? How can I create a legacy of positive change that outlasts me?" For you Eights, the most fulfilling use of wealth isn't in what it can buy, but in the wrongs it can right and the lives it can transform.

Dominick's Story

Dominick grew up in a rough neighborhood where showing weakness was about as smart as bringing a knife to a gunfight. His Sacred Wound of externalized anger was forged in the fires of constant betrayal and powerlessness, which included time in foster care when his parents couldn't look after him. Little Dom learned early on that the only way to survive was to be tougher, louder, and more domineering than everyone else.

This childhood crucible birthed Dominick's greatest fear: being harmed or controlled by others. He built walls around himself thicker than Fort Knox, determined never to be vulnerable again. His worst vice, an insatiable lust for intensity, became his armor. Dominick didn't just live life; he attacked it like Darth Vader on a power trip.

To keep this fear at bay, Dominick developed a primary ego addiction to vengeance. He was always ready to strike back, to assert his dominance, to show the world that he was not to be messed with. In the business world, this translated to a take-no-prisoners approach that left competitors quaking in their loafers and employees updating their résumés.

As a money-anxious Eight, Dominick built a real estate empire through sheer force of will and a healthy dose of intimidation. He was the Dominator in every sense, using money as a weapon to control and manipulate. His financial strategy? Make more, crush more, dominate more. Lather, rinse, repeat.

But even the mightiest Hummer can run out of gas. When Dominick's hard-nosed tactics led to a class-action lawsuit that threatened to topple his empire, he found himself overdosing on his primary ego addiction. In a panic, he switched to his secondary ego addiction: stinginess.

This combination of lust and stinginess created a state of rigid withdrawal, making him look more like a Type Five Compact Car. Dominick switched from being a bulldozer to building a financial bunker and hiding inside it.

It was in this state of paralysis that Dominick crashed headlong into his Dark Night of the Soul. The lawsuit stripped away his power, his money, and his carefully constructed image of invincibility. For the first time since childhood, Dominick felt truly vulnerable, and it terrified him more than a room full of IRS auditors.

But here's where our boy Dom started to turn it around. In the depths of his despair, he had a moment of clarity. He realized that all his power plays and financial strong-arming had left him isolated and, ironically, powerless. It was time to try something new.

Dominick began to practice his primary path to recovery: mercy. At first, it felt about as comfortable as wearing a sequined bodysuit to a funeral. But slowly, he began to see the power in compassion. He started with small acts of kindness—actually listening to his employees, forgiving mistakes, seeking to understand rather than dominate.

As Dominick leaned into mercy, he found himself naturally drawn to his secondary path of recovery: honesty. He started being real with himself and others about his fears, his mistakes, and his desires. It was initially terrifying but also liberating, as his wife's and kids' appreciation of him grew the more he revealed his tender and gentle side.

The combination of mercy and honesty led Dominick to his highest virtue: innocence. Now, don't get it twisted—this wasn't some naive, Pollyanna innocence. This was the innocence of someone who's been through the wringer and come out the other side with a profound understanding of human nature and a willingness to see the Divine in people and situations.

Living with innocence allowed Dominick to fulfill his greatest hope: to experience complete freedom from harm or control. He realized that true power didn't come from dominating others but from being secure enough in himself to be vulnerable and open. By not pushing against the world all the time, he found that people were kinder in return, and his sense of security and safety grew from an honest trust in the goodness of others.

As Dominick embraced this new way of being, his Sacred Wound began to heal. The anger that had driven him for so long began to dissipate, replaced by a deep sense of connection to others and to his own inner wisdom.

Finally, Dominick was ready to embody his Sacred Gift: Divine Justice, which is all about mercy rather than vengeance. He slowly rebuilt his empire and used his considerable resources and business acumen to create fair-housing initiatives in underprivileged neighbor-hoods and help kids in the foster system. Dominick became a force for positive change, using his strength to protect the vulnerable and fight against true injustice.

Our boy Dom had transformed from a Dominator to a true Dynamo, a money master who understood that wealth was a tool for creating a more just and compassionate world.

Dominick's journey from financial wrecking ball to money master wasn't a smooth ride. It was more like a roller coaster designed by a sadistic engineer with a twisted sense of humor. But in the end, he learned that true power and wealth come not from control and domination, but from mercy, honesty, and a willingness to use your strength in service of others.

And that, my friends, is how you tame a Type Eight money monster and turn it into a force for good. It's not about becoming less powerful; it's about channeling that power into something greater than yourself. Now, who's ready to go out there and dominate . . . I mean, dynamically change the world?

CHAPTER SEVENTEEN

TYPE NINE—THE PEACEMAKER (RV)

HOW TO STOP NAPPING THROUGH YOUR MONEY PROBLEMS AND START KICKING FINANCIAL BUTT

Type Nines, often called the Peacemakers, are like the RVs of the Enneagram world—designed to create a tranquil, comfortable environment wherever they go. Warm, likable, and loving, these folks have a genuine desire for everyone to be happy. Their superpower? Making those around them feel honored and included. They excel as mediators and leaders, often resolving tough conflicts with a deft touch.

However, this talent for keeping the peace comes with a Shadow side. Nines have the tendency to sweep problems under the rug, avoiding confrontation like it's a contagious disease. They're the masters of disengagement, often stepping in to stop fights before they start—which sounds great, except it prevents real issues from being confronted and resolved. It's like constantly applying emotional Neosporin to everyone's wounds but never actually removing the splinters causing the pain.

Their ability to empathize with multiple perspectives is both a blessing and a curse. While it makes them excellent

Type Nine Ego Map: The Peacemaker or RV

ENLIGHTENMENT STRUCTURE	
MONEY MASTER	**THE DOER**
Sacred Gift (Holy Idea)	Divine Harmony
Greatest Hope (Basic Desire)	To experience complete wholeness and peace of mind
Greatest Virtue (Virtue)	Right Action Assertiveness + Modesty = Right Action (cure for Sloth)
Secondary Recovery Virtue (Relaxation Point)	Modesty (Primary Recovery Virtue of Type 3)
Primary Recovery Virtue	Assertiveness
Faux Virtue	Faith
SHADOW STRUCTURE	
MONEY MONSTERS: AVOIDANT / ANXIOUS	**THE SPUD / THE DUD**
Ego Stress Response	Security Seeking Sloth + Fear = Security Seeking (blocks Evasion)
Secondary Ego Addiction (Stress Point)	Fear (Primary Ego Addiction of Type 6)
Primary Ego Addiction (Ego Fixation)	Evasion
Greatest Vice (Passion)	Sloth
Greatest Fear (Basic Fear)	Loss of wholeness & fragmentation
Sacred Wound	Internalized & Externalized Anger

(Read the chart from the bottom up.)

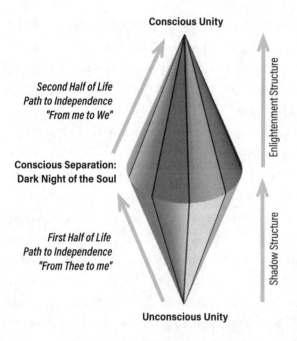

Conscious Unity

Second Half of Life
Path to Independence
"From me to We"

Enlightenment Structure

Conscious Separation:
Dark Night of the Soul

First Half of Life
Path to Independence
"From Thee to me"

Shadow Structure

Unconscious Unity

mediators, it also leaves them struggling to take a firm stand or find their own center amid the cacophony of others' opinions. They can blend seamlessly with their outer environment while their inner world fades. It's as if they've muted the volume on their own thoughts and feelings, tuning out their inner landscape in favor of maintaining outer harmony. This quiet merging with external reality might keep the peace, but it often comes at the cost of their own self-awareness and personal growth.

The childhood of a Nine typically unfolds in an environment where their opinions and desires go unheard, and their needs sometimes go unmet. Asserting basic needs feels either dangerous or futile. In this landscape, "go along to get along" becomes a survival strategy.

This coping mechanism comes at a steep price. The psychological umbilical cord of Type Nines gets severed by a double-edged sword of anger—both externally at the world for not meeting their childhood needs and internally at themselves for lacking the power to change their situation or meet those needs themselves. This internal and external anger, their Sacred Wound, runs deep and hot, like magma beneath a placid surface.

The greatest fear of a Nine isn't public speaking or even death—it's the terror of losing their sense of wholeness. They want their environment to be as calm and harmonious as possible lest anything triggers their anger. This fear drives them to stuff their emotions and transform their lives into a serene landscape painting—beautiful but lacking depth and movement.

To cope with this internal pressure, Nines develop their greatest vice: sloth. But we're not talking about physical laziness. This is sloth in decision-making and self-assertion, what early Christian monks called *acedia*—a profound weariness with life itself. They become masters of "narcotizing" themselves, using distractions like TV, food, drugs, or games to avoid facing their inner conflicts and dissociate from their feelings.

The ego of the Nine then develops a primary addiction to evasion to justify their sloth. They dodge problems, conflicts, and even choices with the agility of a cat avoiding a bath, and it feels good—even virtuous. After all, keeping the peace is a good thing, right? Evasion masks their pain, avoids triggering their anger, and keeps their worst fear from coming true. At least, that's the plan.

If they don't invest in the outcome of a decision, then any decision becomes acceptable—a clever way to avoid potential conflict or disappointment. This habit of deferring to others leaves their "what I want" muscle severely atrophied. They often draw a blank when asked about their own desires, having spent so long adopting others' perspectives that their own viewpoint has become as faint as a whisper in a windstorm.

A Type Nine brother I knew in the monastery epitomized this trait. Ask him what he wanted for dinner, what to watch on TV, or how to spend the day, and his response was always, "What do you want?" He outsourced his preferences to everyone else.

Ironically, avoiding conflict eventually creates more conflict. When their evasion causes unresolved issues to pile up, threatening to blow their world apart, Nines fall back on their secondary ego addiction: fear.

Combining their worst vice of sloth with fear creates their unique ego stress response: security-seeking behavior.

The formula for this transformation looks like this:

Sloth (greatest vice/passion) + Fear (secondary ego addiction/ stress point) = Security Seeking (ego stress response)

Under stress, their desire for security often manifests as passive-aggressive resistance to change. Instead of going with the flow, they become a stubborn, unmovable force, clinging to the status quo like a life raft in a flood. If you dare push past this passive-aggressive ploy, get ready for their inner Hulk to come roaring out.

The preternaturally calm Nine can also become fearfully frantic, irritable, and full of doubts and worries. They'll seek reassurance and shelter in an authority figure or system that promises protection, looking for someone else to help solve their problems. This shortcut temporarily blocks their evasion addiction, getting them off the couch and into action, even if it's only to get someone else to take action for them.

As they switch to fear, they begin to look more like a Type Six[1] (whose primary ego addiction is fear), desperately seeking security and safety and, on rare occasions, even lashing out at anyone or anything that threatens their peace. It's like trading in their comfy RV for a beat-up Family Sedan—not pretty, but at least it gets them moving.

When Nines begin to heal their Sacred Wound, they are masters of putting love into robust action and asserting their will. At their best, they become models of right action, which is the ability to know and make the right move without anger. Right action is what brings true harmony into the world after a conflict is resolved. The challenge for Nines is to recognize that true peace isn't about avoiding conflict but having the courage to face it. It's about turning their RV from a stationary napping lounge into a vehicle for lasting, positive change.

Money Monsters

The Spud: Money-Avoidant

Picture this: a Nine sitting on their comfy couch, remote in one hand, with unopened bank statements forming their own zip code on their desk. The Spud isn't just financially passive; they've turned inaction into an Olympic sport. These folks have all the skills and resources they need to get their finances in shape—but never manage to accomplish anything.

Why? Because confronting their money challenges might trigger that volcano of repressed anger simmering beneath their peaceful surface. And if that anger erupts? It could lead to their greatest fear—a loss of wholeness that would shatter their carefully constructed peace faster than you can say "overdraft fee."

So instead, they indulge in their worst vice—sloth. But this isn't your garden-variety laziness. This is inertia elevated to an art form. The Spud opts out of the money game entirely, convinced that not engaging with finances is the path to peace. It's like they've installed a Do Not Disturb sign on their financial life—and then barricaded the door.

Their relationship with money is akin to their relationship with that dusty treadmill in the corner: They know it's there, they know they should use it, but somehow, they never quite get around to it. The mere thought of confronting their financial reality triggers their fight-or-flight response, and for a Nine, flight wins every time.

This financial neglect isn't just about avoiding stress. It's a misguided attempt to maintain peace. In their minds, not engaging with money means not disrupting their tranquil (if somewhat delusional) financial landscape.

The challenge for these Spuds is to realize that true peace doesn't come from avoiding financial reality—it comes from engaging with it mindfully. They need to understand that managing their money doesn't have to mean disrupting their inner calm. In fact, taking control of their finances could lead to a deeper, more genuine sense of peace and wholeness.

Mindsets of a Spud

Financial-Conflict Allergy: Nines have an almost allergic reaction to financial conflict. They'll go to great lengths to avoid money discussions. When financial issues arise, they're more likely to change the subject than change their bank balance. This aversion to financial confrontation can lead to a dangerous cycle of avoidance, where small issues snowball into major problems. Try exposure therapy as a cure. Start small—maybe make the case with your reflection that you can survive without extra guacamole. Work your way up to debating your cat about the merits of premium versus regular kitty litter. Before you know it, you'll be ready to negotiate a raise without breaking out in hives.

Goal-Setting Paralysis: Ask a Spud about their financial goals, and you might as well be asking them to recite *pi* to the thousandth digit. This inability to set clear goals often results in a directionless financial life. Start with "Today, I will look at my bank account without fainting." Then set a budget, then work your way up to a full-on financial plan. Rome wasn't built in a day, and your financial empire won't be either. But you have to start somewhere.

Responsibility Deflection: Nines have a black belt in the art of deflecting financial responsibility. They'll delegate financial tasks and decisions to partners or family members. This hands-off approach leaves them vulnerable to financial predators and mismanagement. Try accepting responsibility for one financial task, such as balancing your checking account, and giving yourself a deadline to show it to the person you usually have do it for you. Then work your way up to bigger responsibilities.

Boundary Blurriness: Financial boundaries for most Nines are about as clear as a foggy mirror. They struggle to refuse financial requests, often sacrificing their own financial well-being to keep the peace. Practice saying no to inanimate objects. Start with your toaster. "No, Mr. Toaster, I will not buy you a friend." Work your way up to people. Remember, "No" is a complete sentence, and it won't cause the apocalypse. Promise.

Risk-Aversion Extremism: Nines often take the better-safe-than-sorry approach in their financial life. They'll stick with low-yield savings accounts and avoid investments or shun entrepreneurial endeavors, missing out on potential growth opportunities. How about treating investing like easing into a pool? Start with low-risk investments and work your way into higher-risk opportunities as you have the capital and margin to do so. Just don't cannonball into Bitcoin right away, okay?

Comfort-Spending Syndrome: While avoidant Nines hate dealing with finances, they may use spending as a form of self-soothing. Shopping provides a temporary escape from anxiety. It's like they're trying to buy peace of mind, one unnecessary purchase at a time. Every time you feel the urge to stress-shop, put that money in a jar with the promise not to spend it for thirty days. Label it your "Uncomfort Fund." Then spend it on something that actually improves your life, like therapy or a class on financial management.

Financial Ostrich Syndrome: When faced with financial realities, Spuds often bury their heads in the sand. Unopened bills, unchecked account balances, and ignored financial advice are all symptoms. Instead, set up a "Bill Opening Party" for yourself. Include your favorite snacks, put on some upbeat music, and make a celebration of it. Give yourself a gold star for every bill you open and tackle without hyperventilating. You might just find that you like adulting.

Procrastination Perfection: Avoidant Nines elevate financial procrastination to an art form. They are less *carpe diem* and more *canapé diem*. How about using your procrastination powers for good? Tell yourself you'll procrastinate on procrastinating. "I'll put off putting off balancing my checkbook until tomorrow." *Boom!* Checkbook balanced today. Or, if you are procrastinating because you don't know what to do or how to do it, start with the simplest possible step, like opening your budget app or downloading one. Then, find the next simplest step, and reach out for help when you get stuck.

Decision-Avoidance Disorder: Unhealthy Nines avoid making choices, preferring to let circumstances decide, which often leads to missed opportunities and financial inertia. Instead, practice making tiny decisions every day. Paper or plastic? Soup or salad? Slowly work your way up to Roth IRA or Traditional. Before you know it, you'll be a regular Warren Buffett. Well, maybe Warren Buffett's less decisive cousin.

Peace-at-Any-Price Sickness: These Spuds will sacrifice their financial well-being on the altar of perceived harmony. They'll avoid asking for raises, stay in underpaying jobs, agree to unfair financial arrangements, or even ignore financial abuse, all to maintain a facade of peace. Try an assertiveness class or scream therapy to channel your inner anger productively. Or how about a trip to a smash room to get your mojo going?

The Let-Go-and-Let-God Delusion: They might say things like, "The universe will provide," while conveniently forgetting that the universe often provides through paychecks, savings accounts, and yes, even spreadsheets. Try this prayer with a twist: "God, grant me the serenity to accept the things I cannot change, the courage to change the things I can, and the wisdom to know that my finances fall squarely in the 'things I can change' category." Then get off your tuchus and change them!

The Dud: Money-Anxious

Money-anxious Nines are the masters of financial busywork, turning money management into a never-ending hamster wheel of ineffective activity. The Dud isn't just passive like their Spud cousins—they're actively avoiding progress through constant motion.

Picture this: a Nine frantically shuffling papers, downloading every budgeting app available, and attending endless financial seminars. They're a whirlwind of fiscal intentions, a tornado of financial activity. But when the dust settles, what have they actually accomplished? About as much as a screen door on a submarine.

The Dud's financial life is caught in a paradox: They want security but fear the conflict that might arise from actually making financial decisions. They're in a constant tug-of-war between their desire for stability and their aversion to discomfort. The result? A drawer full of half-read financial books, abandoned budgeting spreadsheets, and enough good intentions to pave a road to their own private financial purgatory.

The Nine's biggest challenge? Their tendency to merge with others' financial desires and preferences. Ask them about their financial goals, and they'll parrot back whatever their partner, friends, or the last financial guru they watched on YouTube suggested. They're constantly planning to plan, preparing to prepare, but never quite getting to the actual doing.

These anxious Nines find themselves caught in a frustrating loop—they worry endlessly about financial instability while simultaneously resisting the very changes that could secure their financial future.

In essence, the Financial Dud's challenge is to move beyond the busywork and face the real issues, to find the courage to make decisions and stick with them. For these Nines, the path to financial health isn't about doing more—it's about doing less, but doing it effectively.

Mindsets of a Dud

Problem-Recognition Disorder: Duds excel at addressing small issues while ignoring looming financial catastrophes. They'll spend hours optimizing their grocery budget but turn a blind eye to their maxed-out credit cards. Time for a new game, Nines. Start with your biggest money issues and work your way down. Tackle that maxed-out credit card before you color-code your coupon collection.

Busywork Addiction: These Nines often engage in financial busywork as a form of anxiety management. They might create elaborate spreadsheets or obsessively check their bank balance without taking further effective actions. It's financial meditation gone wrong—all the ritual, none of the peace. How about channeling that nervous energy into productive fidgeting? Instead of obsessively checking your bank balance, try obsessively adding to your savings. It's like financial fidget-spinning—equally addictive, but with a much better payoff.

Chronic People-Pleasing Syndrome: Duds have an almost pathological need to please others. They'll agree to split the bill evenly at a restaurant even if they only had a salad, or cosign a loan for a relative despite their own precarious finances. Their financial decisions are more influenced by the fear of rocking the boat than by sound financial principles. One potential client wanted desperately to hire me but was frozen in fear of upsetting her previous adviser, a family friend who had mismanaged her portfolio for years. Develop a financial alter ego. When faced with money decisions, ask yourself: "What would Money Honey do?" (Or whatever sassy name you choose.) Money Honey doesn't care about pleasing others; Money Honey cares about building wealth. Be like Money Honey.

Analysis Paralysis in Extremis: Duds can spend more time researching which bank account to open than some people spend planning their weddings. This paralysis stems from a deep-seated fear that any decision might lead to conflict or disrupt their fragile sense of peace. As a cure, set a decision deadline. Give yourself permission to research, but when the timer dings, it's go time. Remember, a "good enough" decision now is better than a "perfect" decision never. Your future self will thank you—probably while sipping drinks on a beach in retirement.

Comfort-Zone Death Grip: Even when their current financial situation is clearly not working, Duds resist change, fearing that any shift might lead to more conflict or discomfort. They're trapped in a financial version of *Groundhog Day*, reliving the same financial mistakes over and over. Treat your comfort zone like a pair of old underwear—it might feel cozy, but it's time to let it go. Start with small, uncomfortable money moves. Maybe monitor your credit score monthly, then start polishing that résumé.

Passive-Aggressive Money Management: Unable to directly confront financial issues, Duds often resort to passive-aggressive tactics to get their way. They might "forget" to pay a bill they think is unfair, or conveniently misplace important documents they don't want to sign. It's their way of expressing discontent with others without openly acknowledging the conflict. Instead of sulking your way through your financial life, put money tasks at the top of your to-do list, and Netflix and Chill at the bottom. No TV or social media until all your tasks are done for the day.

Financial-Identity Dissociation: Duds often struggle to identify their own financial goals and values. Ask them about their financial philosophy, and you're likely to get a patchwork of contradictory ideas borrowed from friends, family, and the last financial self-help book they skimmed. It's time for some fiscal soul-searching. Create a financial vision board. What does your ideal money life look like? Do you want to work long or retire early? Do you want the simple life or the luxuries? Don't worry about how to get there yet. Just figure out where "there" is.

Money Master—The Doer

My dear Nines, let's settle in for a heart-to-heart about your journey to becoming a money master. Let's start by addressing your Dark Night of the Soul. Your Dark Night is likely to arrive when your avoidance of conflict has caused too many problems to pile up, and everything crashes down around you. Or a massive trauma sends you into a tailspin of your ego addictions.

I know the Dark Night is terrifying. That volcano of repressed anger and emotions you've been sitting on your entire life suddenly decides to erupt, and there's nowhere to hide. All those feelings you've been numbing out with Netflix binges, comfort eating, endless scrolling, or substances? They're all bursting through at once, and it feels like your carefully constructed world is shattering.

This breaking open is especially excruciating for you, my peace-loving friends. It's your greatest fear come to life—a complete loss of the wholeness you've fought so hard to protect. I know you want to run, hide, or do anything to avoid this pain. But this very discomfort is your ticket to transformation.

As you wade through this emotional swamp, you'll start to see how your worst vice of sloth and your addiction to evasion are the source of your self-created suffering. It's like realizing the leaky, rotten boat you've been clinging to is actually the reason you're drowning.

The only healthy way out of the Dark Night of the Soul is for you to start practicing your primary path of recovery: assertiveness. The very word might make you want to crawl under a blanket. But assertiveness for a Nine isn't about becoming aggressive or confrontational. It's about finally allowing your voice to be heard, about acknowledging your needs and desires. Think of it as turning up the volume on your inner radio from mute to audible.

Assertiveness for a Nine is like Popeye eating spinach—suddenly, you have the strength to fight for what you want. As you flex this new-found assertiveness muscle, something magical happens—it starts to feel good. Really good. It's better than any amount of numbing because you're finally getting your needs met.

As you practice assertiveness, you'll also discover modesty—not the kind that makes you want to disappear, but the kind that allows you to see yourself clearly, without inflation or deflation. It's like finally wiping the fog off the mirror and seeing your reflection without distortion, including seeing your true strength and power—and owning them. This combo of assertiveness and modesty? It leads you to right action, the ability to navigate life's challenges with grace and purpose.

This is your magic formula:

**Assertiveness (primary recovery virtue) + Modesty
(secondary recovery virtue/relaxation point) =
Right Action (greatest virtue/virtue)**

It's not quite $E=mc^2$, but it's pretty revolutionary for a Nine.

Suddenly, you're not just drifting through life in your comfortable RV, stopping at every rest area and campsite. It's like you've traded in that RV for a sleek Race Car borrowed from your Type Three cousins.[2]

This is where it gets interesting. You're still driving the Race Car like a Nine—no need for speeding tickets or road rage—but you've got the power and efficiency of a Three at your disposal. As you rev up this new engine of assertiveness and modesty, you'll find yourself taking right action, becoming the Doer. You're no longer the passenger in your financial life; you're in the driver's seat, steering with purpose and clarity. Suddenly you're able to navigate conflicts and make decisions with the precision of an Indy 500 pro. No more passivity, no more avoidance—just clean, clear action.

Most importantly, your Sacred Wound begins to heal when you realize you have the power to meet your own needs, regardless of how disempowered and neglected you were as a child. As you continue on this path, you'll start to experience what you've always longed for—true harmony. Not the surface-level "peace" you've been maintaining, but a deep, lasting harmony that comes from getting your needs met in balance with the needs of those around you. You'll find yourself resolving conflicts instead of avoiding them, fully participating in life instead of watching from the sidelines.

This journey isn't easy. There will be days when you want to retreat back into your comfortable numbness. In those moments, be gentle with yourself. Remember, every small step forward is a victory.

Just watch out for your faux virtue of faith. In your quest for inner peace and avoidance of conflict, it's easy to mistake passive resignation for genuine faith. It's a temptation to float through life with all the direction of a tumbleweed, calling your chronic indecision "trusting in the universe." This faux faith isn't about true trust in a higher power or purpose; it's about justifying your need to avoid discomfort and responsibility at all costs. It's maddening for everyone involved, including the Nine, who must work overtime to maintain this illusion of trusting acceptance while missing out on the growth and fulfillment that comes from active engagement with life.

Instead, you have a beautiful, Sacred Gift to offer the world—Divine Harmony. Living in Divine Harmony means no longer avoiding conflict. Instead, you resolve it with the skill of a UN diplomat because you, more than others, see the interconnectedness of all things.

When it comes to money, the Doer is a sight to behold. They use their financial resources for right action, bringing Divine Harmony into the world one transaction at a time. Think of Abraham Lincoln preserving the Union, the Dalai Lama supporting Tibetan refugees and maintaining a government-in-exile, or Thich Nhat Hanh funding mindfulness centers across the globe. These Nines didn't just make peace—they financed it.

So take a deep breath and then let the world hear your voice. You might just find that the peace and wholeness you've always sought were within you all along, just waiting to be discovered.

Becoming a Money Master—The Doer

Please be sure to read (or review) the chapter 8 overview of these five steps before you get started here.

Acknowledge the pain from your Childhood Wounding.

For you Nines, acknowledging the pain from your Childhood Wounds is like finally turning up the volume on a radio that's been playing softly in the background your whole life. That quiet soundtrack has been influencing your financial decisions more than you know.

Remember those family dinners? The ones where everyone seemed to have an opinion louder than a foghorn, while you sat there, fork in hand, trying to become one with the mashed potatoes? That's where it often started. Your thoughts and feelings weren't just over-looked; they were steamrolled.

Maybe you had a parent or sibling who was the family volcano—erupting at the slightest provocation. And there you were, little Nine, learning to tiptoe around those emotional lava flows. You became an expert at reading the room, adjusting your behavior to keep the peace. But inside? That's where the anger started to simmer.

Or perhaps your childhood was quieter, but no less wounding. Imagine expressing a desire—maybe for a specific toy or to try a new hobby—only to be met with dismissal or indifference. "That's nice, dear," your parents might have said, already focused on something else. It's like you were speaking, but your words evaporated before they reached anyone's ears.

Then there were the times when you did try to assert yourself. Maybe you gathered all your courage to disagree with a family decision, only to be told you were being difficult or causing problems. The message was clear: Your job was to agree, to smooth things over, to be the family shock absorber.

Some Nines experienced a more subtle form of neglect. Your basic needs were met, sure, but emotional nurturing? That was as rare as a unicorn sighting. Your feelings, your dreams, your fears—they were left to wither on the vine of your heart.

And let's not forget about the pressure to be the good, low-maintenance child. While your siblings might have acted out, you learned that being agreeable was the way to get a crumb of positive attention. But that crumb was never quite enough to satisfy your hunger for real connection, validation, and security.

All of these experiences planted seeds of anger—internalized anger at yourself for not being assertive enough to be heard, and externalized anger at a world that seemed unconcerned about you. But expressing that anger? That felt about as safe as juggling lit dynamite.

So you did what any smart, sensitive child would do: You buried that anger deep. You smiled and nodded and went along to get along. You became so good at ignoring your own needs and feelings that you practically forgot you had them.

And now, my dear Nine, that buried anger is affecting your relationship with money. It shows up in your reluctance to assert your financial needs, in your tendency to merge your financial identity with others, and in your avoidance of money decisions that might rock the boat.

But here's the beautiful truth: Your tendency to merge with others or avoid conflict isn't a flaw—it was a brilliant survival strategy. Acknowledging that strategy isn't about blaming anyone. It's about honoring your needs, your desires, your right to take up space in the world—and in your financial life. We're just updating your survival strategy to serve your adult needs by recognizing that a part of you has been neglected for far too long.

Your journey now is about learning that your voice matters, that your financial well-being is important, that asserting your needs doesn't make you a bad person. It's about discovering that true harmony doesn't come from self-erasure, but from authentic self-expression.

One technique that can be incredibly helpful is creating a trauma timeline of your childhood and money issues. I know, it sounds about as fun as having your fingernails pulled out with pliers, but bear with me. This is your chance to map out the major events that have shaped your Type Nine mindsets. Whatever it is, getting it all out on paper, a whiteboard, or a spreadsheet can be incredibly illuminating so you can see the story and arc of your life. You can't heal your trauma until you've identified what it is.

Now, you don't have to tackle this alone. In fact, please don't. As a Nine, you have a superpower for seeing all perspectives—except sometimes your own. That's where your support system comes in. Find your Gandalf, your Yoda, your Mary Poppins—whoever resonates with you. This could be a therapist, a trusted friend, or even a support group. Think of them as your copilots on this journey.

Stop reacting out of the anger that created your money monsters.

Your first inclination may be to think, *Me, what anger? I'm hardly ever angry!* That's the mask you wear, not the truth you know is hiding in your gut.

Let's start with a daily practice of contemplation and compassion. Think of it as yoga for your psyche. Just as you wouldn't expect to nail a perfect headstand on your first try, don't expect to conquer your ego addictions overnight.

Set aside some time each day for quiet reflection. This could be traditional meditation, a contemplative walk, or even journaling. The goal is to shine a spotlight on those ego addictions that are wreaking havoc in your financial life. You're looking for patterns of avoidance, times when you've merged your financial identity with others, or instances where you've sacrificed your own financial well-being to keep the peace.

One practice that might resonate with you Nines is what I call the "Financial Feelings Dump." Grab a whiteboard or a stack of paper and just let it all out. What financial decisions have you been avoiding? What money conflicts are you pretending don't exist? Don't judge or censor—just let it flow. Then take a step back and look for patterns. You might be surprised at what you discover.

As you do this work, focus on your primary ego addiction: evasion. Get curious about it. When did you first start avoiding financial decisions? How has this habit both helped and hindered you? Remember, this evasion developed as a survival strategy. It's not the enemy—it's more like an overprotective bodyguard who doesn't realize you've grown up and learned some martial arts of your own.

Don't neglect your secondary ego addiction to fear either. Notice when it shows up and what triggers it. Does the thought of making a financial decision send you into a panic? Does conflict over money make you so anxious that you want to build a blanket fort and never come out?

To counteract these addictions, you need to cultivate your primary and secondary virtues: assertiveness and modesty. Start small. Speak up about where you want to go for dinner. Set a small financial goal and stick to it, even if it means saying no to someone else's request. Practicing modesty means seeing your strength and power accurately. No more hiding your light under a bushel.

Consider creating a personal mantra or prayer to help you focus on these virtues, such as this Right-Action Prayer:

Divine Harmony, open my heart to your unifying love and heal the anger deep within my heart. Empower me with assertiveness and modesty, trusting in your all-encompassing

*grace. Help me surrender my addictions to evasion and fear
so that I may actively engage in loving service to you through
those around me.*

Don't forget the crucial step of cultivating compassion for your-self and the people who raised you. And when you begin to integrate new habits into your routine, give yourself a lot of grace. As you prac-tice these new habits, you'll start to notice something amazing. That buried anger? It starts to dissipate. Not because you're ignoring it, but because you're finally honoring your own needs and desires. You're no longer sacrificing your financial well-being at the altar of false peace.

This journey isn't about becoming a financial bulldog overnight. It's about finding your authentic voice—one that can harmonize with others without losing its own melody. It's about realizing that true peace comes not from avoiding money issues but from engaging with them mindfully and assertively.

Learn to be less anxious or avoidant about money by confronting your money monsters.

Confronting? That might sound an awful lot like conflict, but this isn't about picking a fight with your finances; it's about making peace with them in a way that only a Nine can truly appreciate.

Let's start by picturing your money monster. For you Nines, it might look less like a snarling wolf and more like a giant, fuzzy sloth that's been lounging on your couch for far too long. It's been keeping you comfortably numb, blissfully unaware of your financial reality. Your challenge isn't so much to tame this beast as it is to gently nudge it awake and feed it a few Red Bulls.

Remember the story of St. Francis and the Wolf of Gubbio? You Nines might be more like St. Francis and the Sloth of Snoozeville. Your approach needs to be gentle but persistent. You're not here to vanquish your money monster; you're here to befriend it, to understand why it's been keeping you financially asleep all this time.

Start by approaching your financial sloth with curiosity and compassion. Why has avoiding money decisions felt so comfortable? What needs has this avoidance been meeting? Maybe it's been protecting you from potential conflicts or keeping you safely merged with others' financial identities. It's time to thank your sloth for its service and let it know that you're ready to wake up now.

Because your greatest fear isn't so much about money itself but about the potential discord it might create, your money monster has been working overtime to keep everything smooth and harmonious, even if that means sacrificing your own financial well-being. It's time to show this part of yourself that true harmony comes from engagement, not avoidance.

To make this transformation real, we need to dive deep into your financial psyche and map out where your money avoidance or anxiety shows up in how you earn, save, invest, and give.

For example, you might find that you're completely tuned out when it comes to earning, always taking the path of least resistance in your career. Or perhaps you're avoidant about saving, telling yourself that as long as the bills are paid, everything's fine. Maybe the idea of investing feels too aggressive, too "capitalist" for your peace-loving nature. And giving? Well, you might anxiously give too much, always deferring to others' expectations.

For Nines, practicing right action in these areas is about learning to take small, consistent steps toward financial engagement.

Why not create a "Sloth to Sage" transformation chart?[3] Make it as visually appealing as possible—think less Excel spreadsheet, more zen garden. Each section could represent an area of your financial life, such as earning, saving, investing, and giving, with action steps in each category leading from "blissfully unaware" to "mindfully engaged." Make it so beautiful that you can't help but look at it every day. The goal is to take a hard look at all your money habits. What needs to change, and what are the assertive, modest action steps you need to take right now?

When you learn to use it proactively, your natural ability to see all sides of a situation can become your financial superpower.

Build a strong financial life by earning, saving, and investing ethically.

First up, earning. I know—the idea of asserting yourself in the workplace might give you hives. But it's about finding your "right work," a calling that energizes rather than drains you. Maybe it's time to level up your skills or develop that hidden talent you've been nurturing. Remember, you're not just looking for a paycheck; you're looking for purpose. If you're stuck in a soul-sucking job that's disrupting your inner harmony, start plotting your gentle escape.

Here's a wild idea: Consider dipping your toes into entrepreneurial waters. What if you could create a business that solves problems and brings people together? That's right up your alley! It might be challenging, but the rewards—both financial and personal—could be as satisfying as finding the perfect spot for a nap.

Now, let's talk about saving. This is where your natural ability to go with the flow can work in your favor. Just follow conventional advice. Start with a budget—think of it as a map for your money's journey to tranquility. Before making a purchase, take a mindful moment to ask if it aligns with your values and long-term goals. Build up that emergency fund—it's like a cozy financial blanket for those uh-oh moments life throws at you. And tackling debt? Think of it as decluttering your financial space. Can you feel the peace already?

Finally, investing. This is how we build long-term wealth, and for you Nines, it's about creating a stable, harmonious future. Aim to invest at least 15 percent of your pre-tax income for retirement. The power of compound interest means the earlier you plant those seeds, the more abundant your harvest will be. But get yourself educated and financially literate so you can see what right action to take.

Here's a nugget of wisdom that'll resonate with your peace-loving heart: Ethical investing—that is, aligning your investments with your values—isn't just good for your conscience; it can be good for your wallet too. Companies that care about the future tend to do better in the future.

Remember, building a strong financial life isn't about getting rich quick or becoming a corporate cutthroat. It's about making consistent, ethical choices that align with your highest priorities. It's about creating a life of purpose and impact, where your external financial reality matches your inner desire for harmony.

Use your money and talents as tools to love and serve a suffering world.

Think of this step as your chance to become a financial zen master, spreading tranquility and balance wherever your resources flow. The ultimate goal isn't to hoard wealth. No, your purpose is to offer your community gifts that heal and transform, like a gentle rain nourishing parched earth.

Here's the beautiful thing: Your natural ability to see all sides and create harmony is exactly what the world of philanthropy needs. You're not just giving money; you're offering your unique gift for creating peace and unity.

So, how do we go about this? Before you start writing checks, invest your time and talents in causes you care about. This will give you invaluable insider knowledge and help you understand where your contributions can make the most impact. It's about being a participant, not just a patron.

As you embark on this phase, consider starting small and local. Look for needs in your immediate community. Maybe it's supporting a local food bank, mentoring underprivileged youth, or helping train therapy dogs. These grassroots efforts often have a more direct and visible impact than donating to large, impersonal organizations. Plus, you'll get to see the harmony you're creating firsthand.

Don't underestimate the power of your unique skills and experiences either. Your journey to financial mastery has given you insights that could help others struggling with money issues. Consider offering financial literacy workshops or one-on-one mentoring at schools or senior centers. Your gentle, nonconfrontational approach could be exactly what someone needs to find their own financial peace.

Giving back isn't just about money; it's about sharing your time, your knowledge, your compassion. Sometimes, the most valuable thing you can offer is a listening ear or a word of encouragement to someone who's struggling. Your natural empathy is a gift in itself.

As you grow in your ability to give, think about how you can create sustainable change. Your ability to see all sides of a conflict can help tackle root causes. This might mean investing in education initiatives, supporting entrepreneurship in underserved communities, or funding research into pressing global issues. Think of it as creating a ripple effect of peace and prosperity.

Here's a powerful truth to keep in mind: As a Nine who's mastered money, you have a unique ability to create harmony wherever you go. Your Sacred Gift to the world is the ability to take right action, to move from passive acceptance to active conflict resolution by jumping into the arena and getting bloody. By becoming a money master, you're not just changing your own life—you're gaining the power to be a force for good in the world, creating the unity you've always dreamed of.

So, as you reach this final step, ask yourself: "How can I use my abundance to make the world a little bit more harmonious? What monsters in the wider world need to be tamed or even slain? How can my financial journey become a gift to others?" Remember, the most fulfilling use of wealth isn't in what it can buy, but in the positive change it can create.

So go forth, compassionate Nine, and let your financial mastery be a force for unity in the world. Your quiet strength, your ability to see all sides, your gift for creating Divine Harmony—these are precisely what the world needs. You're not just giving money; you're offering a blueprint for a more loving world. And that, my friend, is the truest form of wealth there is.

Melody's Story

Melody's Sacred Wound was carved in the cacophony of her childhood home. With parents who communicated through slammed doors and passive-aggressive Post-it notes, little Melody learned quickly to duck and cover and do anything to keep minor skirmishes from erupting into a full-on battle zone. All that conflict made Melody angry—angry at herself for not being able to stand up and get her needs met, and angry that no one around her seemed able to meet them either.

This anger created Melody's greatest fear: losing her sense of wholeness if she dared to express her anger. Heaven forbid she rock the boat! So, she did what any self-respecting Nine would do—nothing. Why bother doing anything when doing nothing is so much easier and less likely to disturb the peace?

Melody's sloth gave birth to her primary ego addiction: evasion. She became the Houdini of avoiding life's challenges, especially when it came to money because of all the money fights she saw her parents having. Balancing a checkbook? Nah, let's binge-watch another season of *The Great British Bake Off* instead. Planning for retirement? That's a problem for Future Melody. Present Melody is too busy pretending everything's fine.

When evasion failed her, she'd switch to her secondary ego addiction: fear. She'd get scared about her unstable lifestyle and worry about her world collapsing. But sloth was still calling the shots, so fear plus sloth led to security-seeking behavior. She'd find a boyfriend to take care of her or lean on her parents for support.

But then, life decided to give Melody a wake-up call. In her forties, she lost her job, her apartment, and her boyfriend, and found herself crashing on a friend's couch, surrounded by the wreckage of her financial neglect. Her life savings consisted of a jar of pennies and some lint.

In this pit of despair, Melody finally realized that her lifelong strategy of "ignore it and it'll go away" had failed her. It was time to break open.

And break open she did. It wasn't pretty—imagine a butterfly emerging from its chrysalis, except the butterfly is covered in credit card debt and the chrysalis is made of overdue notices. But in this messy metamorphosis, Melody found her primary recovery virtue: assertiveness.

She started small. She asserted her right to know her bank balance without having a panic attack. She began by asserting herself to her reflection: "Hey, you! Yeah, you in the mirror! We're going to check our bank balance today, and we're not going to cry . . . much." She stood up to her fear and made a budget. She even called her credit card company to negotiate a payment plan.

As Melody flexed her assertiveness muscles, she discovered her secondary recovery virtue: modesty, the clear-eyed ability to assess her strengths and weaknesses. She realized she was actually pretty good at organizing when she put her mind to it, but numbers made her brain melt. So, she played to her strengths and got help with her weaknesses.

Assertiveness plus modesty equaled Melody's greatest virtue: right action. Suddenly, she was getting things done with the precision of a Type Three. It was like she'd traded in her beat-up RV for a luxury Race Car. She wasn't just existing anymore; she was driving her life forward with purpose.

Melody started a small event-planning business, turning her knack for creating harmonious environments into a profitable venture. She tackled her debts one by one, set up a retirement account, and even started an emergency fund. Who was this financial powerhouse, and what had she done with our Spud?

As Melody embraced right action, she began to experience her greatest hope: complete wholeness and peace of mind. She was finally in control of her life and her finances. The anger that had driven her for so long was slowly being transformed into fuel for positive change.

Melody had become the Doer, a true money master. She still loved peace, but now she knew that true peace came from facing challenges head-on, not avoiding them.

And the best part? Melody finally understood that expressing her needs and taking action didn't lead to a loss of wholeness—it led to a fuller, richer life. She had found her Sacred Gift: bringing Divine Harmony into the world, one balanced checkbook at a time.

In the end, Melody realized that true harmony isn't about avoiding all the sour notes in life. It's about embracing them, working through them, and creating a beautiful symphony out of the chaos. She's no longer a Spud, content to vegetate in life's couch cushions. She's a Doer, conducting the orchestra of her life with confidence, grace, and maybe just a little bit of jazz hands.

CHAPTER EIGHTEEN

THE GRAND FINALE

WHERE WE START DOING THE BEST
WE CAN WITH WHAT WE CAN

If you've made it this far, congratulations! You're either a glutton for punishment or you've discovered the secret sauce to financial and spiritual wellness.

So, what have we learned on this journey, besides the fact that I can't resist a good car metaphor and that our childhood issues have more layers than a lasagna?

First, we've discovered that money isn't just about dollars and cents—it's about our deepest fears, our wildest hopes, and our eternal journey toward wholeness. Your Enneagram type isn't just a personality quiz result; it's the road map to understanding why you keep making the same financial mistakes faster than a Type Seven can book their next vacation. It's about transforming your relationship with money into a profound spiritual practice that can heal your deepest wounds.

We've learned that your money monsters aren't just there to ruin your credit score and make you cry into your ramen noodles. They're actually misguided protectors, trying to shield you from the pain of your Childhood Wounds. It's like having a really aggressive bodyguard who's allergic to common sense.

But here's the kicker: Once you understand your type's Sacred Wound, greatest fear, worst vice, and ego addictions, you can start to transform them. It's like being handed the cheat codes to the video game of life. Suddenly, you're not just button-mashing your way through your finances; you're pulling off combo moves that would make an econ teacher proud.

We've also discovered that becoming a money master isn't about having a Scrooge McDuck–style money bin (although, let's be honest, that would be pretty cool). It's about aligning your finances with your highest virtues and Sacred Gifts. It's about using your resources to bring more love, compassion, and maybe a few laughs into the world. Laughter is the best medicine—unless you're trying to cure poverty, in which case, money is probably more effective. But hey, why not have both?

To pull all this off we combined three powerful tools:

1. The Enneagram—a personality system so accurate it's almost creepy.
2. The Attachment Theory of Money—because your relationship with your wallet is probably more complicated than my last Tinder date.
3. Spirituality—because, let's face it, we could all use a little divine intervention when it comes to our finances.

You now have the resources you need to:

1. Tame your money monsters, or at least teach them some manners.
2. Understand why you keep making the same financial mistakes and why your financial patterns are more predictable than a Type One's sock drawer.

3. Transform your greatest weaknesses into your superpower. (It's like financial alchemy—turning your lead-filled wallet into gold.)

4. Use your money as a force for good in the world.

So, dear reader, as we come to the end of this financial roller coaster, remember: Your Enneagram type isn't your destiny; it's your starting point. Your money monsters aren't your enemies; they're just misunderstood furry creatures who need a good belly rub and some financial literacy. And your journey to becoming a money master? It's not just about growing your bank account—it's about connecting with your True Self.

Now go forth, armed with your new knowledge, and show the world what a financially savvy, spiritually grounded, Enneagram-wielding badass looks like.

In the grand cosmic joke of life, money is just a punch line. But with the wisdom from this book, you'll be the one laughing all the way to the bank—and maybe even finding enlightenment along the way.

Now, if you'll excuse me, I have a date with my own money monster. We're going to practice assertiveness . . . at the mall. What could possibly go wrong?

ACKNOWLEDGMENTS

My deepest gratitude to:

Lauren Bridges, Carrie Marrs, Debbie Wickwire, and everyone at W Publishing, for believing in this ambitious two-book project and bringing it to life.

Erin Healy at WordWright Editorial Services, whose brilliant guidance shaped this work into something meaningful and clear. Your wisdom and patience were invaluable.

Jamie Chambliss and Steve Troha at Folio Literary Management, for setting everything in motion and for your unwavering support throughout this journey.

Chris Heuertz, Timothy McMahan King, and Carl Marsak, for your thoughtful review and precious feedback.

Mark Arey, Bill Broyles, Jimmy Marsh, John Price, and Hunt Priest, who kept me grounded by kicking me squarely in the butt when I desperately needed it.

Richard Rohr, whose boundless mercy and wisdom guided me through The Dark.

Dr. Charles Fasanaro, for instilling in me a love of Euclid.

Michael Lynam and Nicholas Lynam, my beloved brothers, who have been there through it all.

ACKNOWLEDGEMENTS

Lois J. Pollard, my mother, for her unwavering faith and steadfast love.

Nicholas Edward Lynam III, my father, for sharing his Sacred Wound with me—a gift I will forever treasure in my heart.

And to all my clients who have trusted me with their journeys—thank you! Your courage continues to inspire me.

NOTES

Foreword

1. Alice Calaprice, ed., *The Ultimate Quotable Einstein* (Princeton University Press, 2019), 476.

2. Calaprice, ed., *The Ultimate Quotable Einstein*, 481.

Introduction

1. "Human Genome Project," National Human Genome Research Institute, November 18, 2024, https://www.genome.gov/human-genome-project.

2. Morgan Alexander and Brent Schnipke, "The Enneagram: A Primer for Psychiatry Residents," *American Journal of Psychiatry Residents' Journal* 15, no. 3 (2020), https://psychiatryonline.org /doi/full/10.1176/appi.ajp-rj.2020.150301.

3. Saleh Vallender, *The Neurobiology of the Enneagram* (pub. by author, 2022); Daniel J. Siegel and the PDP Group, *Personality and Wholeness in Therapy: Integrating 9 Patterns of Developmental Pathways in Clinical Practice* (W. W. Norton and Company, 2024).

4. "The Traditional Enneagram," The Enneagram Institute, accessed November 24, 2024, https://www.enneagraminstitute.com/ the-traditional-enneagram.

5. Due to space constraints, I had to trim my defense of some novel concepts presented, particularly regarding Childhood and Sacred Wounds. These ideas deserve a deeper exploration, which I'll save for future publications.

Chapter One

1. Richard Rohr, *Things Hidden: Scripture as Spirituality* (SPCK, 2016), 22.

2. Doug Lynam, *From Monk to Money Manager: A Former Monk's Financial Guide to Becoming a Little Bit Wealthy—And Why That's Okay* (Thomas Nelson, 2019).

3. Silvia Stringhini et al., "Socioeconomic Status and the 25 x 25 Risk Factors as Determinants of Premature Mortality: A Multicohort Study and Meta -Analysis of 1.7 Million Men and Women," *The Lancet* 389, no. 10075 (2017): 1229–37, https://doi.org/10.1016/S0140-6736(16)32380-7.

4. Anna Aizer, "Poverty, Violence and Health: The Impact of Domestic Violence During Pregnancy on Newborn Health," *Journal of Human Resources* 46, no. 3 (2011): 518–38, https://doi.org/10.1353/jhr.2011.0024; Kesha Baptiste-Roberts and Mian Hossain, "Socioeconomic Disparities and Self-Reported Substance Abuse-Related Problems," *Addiction and Health* 10, no. 2 (2018): 112–22, https://doi.org/10.22122/ahj.v10i2.561; Erika Harrell et al., *Household Poverty and Nonfatal Violent Victimization, 2008–2012* (US Department of Justice, 2014), https: //bjs.ojp.gov/content/pub/pdf/hpnvv0812.pdf; Helen Miller, "What to Know About Obesity and Poverty," Medical News Today, April 25, 2023, https://www.medicalnewstoday.com/articles/obesity-and-poverty#risk -factors; Shi-Hao Huang et al., "Inequality and Health: The Correlation Between Poverty and Injury—A Comprehensive Analysis Based on Income Level in Taiwan: A Cross-Sectional Study," *Healthcare (Basel)* 9, no. 3 (2021): 349, https://doi.org/10.3390/healthcare9030349; Stacy Hodgkinson et al., "Improving Mental Health Access for Low-Income Children and Families in the Primary Care Setting," *Pediatrics* 139, no. 1 (2017): e20151175, https://doi.org/10.1542/peds.2015-1175.

5. Mark Twain, *Mark Twain's Fables of Man*, ed. John S. Tuckey (University of California Press, 1972), 217.

6. "Survey: Certified Divorce Financial Analyst® (CDFA®) Professionals Reveal the Leading Causes of Divorce," Institute for Divorce Financial Analysts, accessed November 19, 2024, https://institutedfa.com/ leading-causes-divorce/; "Relationship Intimacy Being Crushed by Financial Tension: AICPA Survey," Businesswire, accessed November 4, 2024, https://www.businesswire.com/news/home/20210204005261 /en/Relationship-Intimacy-Being-Crushed-by-Financial-Tension -AICPA-Survey#:~:text=The%20survey%20found%20that%20 2,with%20them%20about%20their%20finances.

Chapter Two

1. Kate Ashford, "1 in 4 Americans Have PTSD-Like Symptoms from Financial Stress," *Forbes*, updated January 11, 2021, https://www.forbes.com/sites/kateashford/2016/04/22/financial-stress/.

2. Will Rainey, "M. C. Hammer: From Rich to Poor to Wealthy," Blue Tree Savings Ltd., October 9, 2022, https://www.bluetreesavings.com/post/m-c-hammer-from-rich-to-poor-to-wealthy.

3. The Attachment Theory of Money is based on the Attachment Theory of Relationships developed by John Bowlby and Mary Ainsworth. It is, in fact, nearly identical to it, just with a different application.

Chapter Three

1. "A Short and Comprehensive History of the Enneagram Origin," Integrative Enneagram Solutions, accessed November 25, 2024, https://www.integrative9.com/enneagram/history/.

2. Traditional Enneagram literature references shame as a core negative emotion rather than sadness. However, pioneering affective neuroscientist Jaak Panksepp's research suggests "separation distress," "grief," or "sadness" are more accurate terms for what the Enneagram calls "shame." This can be understood as a profound sadness and grief around one's identity. Throughout this book, feel free to substitute "shame" for "sadness" if that feels more appropriate for you. For more discussion, see *The Neurobiology of the Enneagram* by Dr. Saleh Vallander (pub. by author, 2022); *Personality and Wholeness in Therapy* by Dr. Daniel J. Siegel and the PDP Group (W. W. Norton and Company, 2024); and *The Complete Enneagram: 27 Paths to Greater Self-Knowledge* by Dr. Beatrice Chestnut (She Writes Press, 2013). While many psychologists also consider disgust to be one of the core negative emotions in human nature, it notably doesn't appear as a foundational element in the Enneagram personality system for reasons that are beyond the scope of this book.

3. The *Sacred Wound* is a term I'm introducing to the Enneagram lexicon. While familiar in spiritual literature, I've repurposed it to describe the foundational psychological injury that shapes our Enneagram type.

4. George E. P. Box, "Science and Statistics," *Journal of the American Statistical Association* 71, no. 356 (1976): 791–99, https://doi.org/10.1080/01621459.1976.10480949.

Chapter Four

1. Betsy Maxon and David N. Daniels, "Personality Differentiation of Identical Twins Reared Together," *The Enneagram Journal* (2008), https://ieaninepoints.com/wp-content/uploads/2019/01/2008-IEA -Journal_Betsy-Maxon_and_David-Daniels.pdf.

2. There are different schools of thought about how the Childhood Wounding Theory works. My take on it is just one approach. For other supporting perspectives, see Christopher Heuertz, *The Enneagram of Belonging* (Zondervan, 2020), 69; Beatrice Chestnut, *The Complete Enneagram: 27 Paths to Greater Self-Knowledge* (She Writes Press, 2013), 2; and Don Riso and Russ Hudson, *The Wisdom of the Enneagram: The Complete Guide to Psychological and Spiritual Growth for the Nine Personality Types* (Bantam Books, 1999), 30.

3. David Foster Wallace, "This Is Water: David Foster Wallace Commencement Speech," commencement address at Kenyon College, May 21, 2005, posted by Jeffrey Danese, May 2, 2022, YouTube, 22 min., 43 sec., https://www.youtube.com/watch?v=DCbGM4mqEVw.

4. For other perspectives and deeper exploration, please see Connie Zweig and Jeremiah Abrams, eds., *Meeting the Shadow: The Hidden Power of the Dark Side of Human Nature* (TarcherPerigree, 1991). There are many definitions of the Shadow, but I define it as the structured, unconscious system of psychological defenses unique to each Enneagram type that drives core behavior.

5. Carl Jung, Aion, Christ: A Symbol of the Self, Pages 70–71, Para 126.

6. This book aims to ground the Enneagram in deductive logic and axiomatic principles, complementing its traditional basis in inductive reasoning. The foundational axiom is that we begin life in unconscious unity, analogous to Euclid's definition of a point as "that which has no part," which is the basis of mathematics. From this unprovable yet intuitively rational starting place, we can logically build the Enneagram system.

7. Don Felt, during a memorial service on August 9, 1991, quoted in Brian Hallett, "Perspectives on Pearl Harbor: Apologies Across the Pacific," *Los Angeles Times*, December 2, 1991, https://www.latimes .com/archives/la-xpm-1991-12-02-me-530-story.html.

Chapter Five

1. Online Etymology Dictionary, s.v. "Passion," updated October 13, 2021, https://www.etymonline.com/word/passion. In Latin, the word *passio* means "suffering" or "enduring." In traditional Enneagram literature, your passion refers to your primary source of suffering or emotional struggle. Some authors have likened these passions to the seven deadly sins of Christian theology, with the addition of cowardice and deceit to round out the nine types. However, referring to these traits as one's "greatest vice" provides a cleaner parallel to the "greatest virtue" concept in the Enlightenment Structure (Chapter 7). This terminology also avoids potential religious connotations while maintaining the essence of the idea that each type has a core struggle to overcome on their path to growth and self-actualization.

2. I've changed the Enneagram's traditional "ego fixation" to "primary ego addiction." Why? It links better with "secondary ego addiction" coming up and mirrors the "primary recovery virtue" in the Enlightenment Structure (Chapter 7).

3. Timothy McMahan King, *Addiction Nation: What the Opioid Crisis Reveals About Us* (Herald Press, 2019), 206.

4. Traditional Enneagram theory refers to this as the Stress Point. However, this model can be misleading, implying that each type is a fixed point rather than a spectrum, and suggesting a complete shift to another type under stress. The concept of a "secondary ego addiction" offers a more nuanced perspective. It maintains the integrity of the primary type while acknowledging the adoption of less healthy behaviors under duress. This approach provides a clearer, more precise understanding of how personalities adapt to stress within their core structure.

5. The *ego stress response* is a new term I'm introducing to the Enneagram lexicon to more clearly describe what happens when we engage our secondary ego addiction or stress point.

6. St. John of the Cross, *The Dark Night of the Soul*, trans. David Lewis (Thomas Baker, 1908). *The Dark Night of the Soul* is a common term in spiritual literature but I'm using it in my own way. Other authors define it differently.

Chapter Six

1. I've radically simplified a complex process and intentionally ignored the issue of neonatal trauma because that's too much to cover in this book. But hopefully you get the point: Your journey starts in unconscious unity with your environment in the womb.

2. St. John of the Cross, *The Dark Night of the Soul*, trans. Mirabai Starr (Riverhead Books, 2002), 23.

3. If you feel stuck in the Dark Night, try reading *The Happiness Trap: How to Stop Struggling and Start Living*, by Russ Harris (Exisle Publishing, 2013) or *Tattoos on the Heart: The Power of Boundless Compassion*, by Gregory Boyle (Free Press, 2010).

4. Bertrand Russell, *Mysticism and Logic, and Other Essays* (G. Allen & Unwin Ltd., 1917), 48.

5. Stephen King, *Doctor Sleep* (Simon & Schuster, 2019), 82.

6. Modern trauma research and psychotherapy strategies can be invaluable, but many therapists focus solely on alleviating pain, neglecting the spiritual dimension of emotional struggles. They often aim to revert patients to a pre–Dark Night state, failing to acknowledge ego addictions (what classical theology calls "sins") or the virtues that can remedy suffering.

7. Carl Jung, *Modern Man in Search of a Soul* (Harcourt, Brace & World, 1933), 237–38. Jung said, "I must even help the patient to prevail in his egoism; if he succeeds in this, he estranges himself from other people. He drives them away, and they come to themselves—as they should, for they were seeking to rob him of his 'sacred egoism.' This must be left to him, for it is his strongest and healthiest power; it is, as I have said, a true will of God, which sometimes drives him into complete isolation. However wretched this state may be, it also stands him in good stead, for in this way alone can he take his own measure and learn what an invaluable treasure is the love of his fellow-beings. It is, moreover, only in the state of complete abandonment and loneliness that we experience the helpful powers of our own natures."

8. William Blake, "Proverbs of Hell," *The Marriage of Heaven and Hell* (Dover Publications, 1994), 31.

Chapter Seven

1. Richard Rohr, *Falling Upward: A Spirituality for the Two Halves of Life* (Wiley and Sons, 2011); Jalalluddin Rumi, *The Essential Rumi*, trans. Coleman Barks and John Moyne (Harper Collins, 1995), 142.

2. Daniel J. Siegal, MD, *IntraConnected: MWe (Me + We) as the Integration of Self, Identity, and Belonging* (W. W. Norton, 2022).

3. Ram Dass, "A Letter to Rachel," Love Serve Remember Foundation, accessed November 21, 2024, https://www.ramdass.org/a-letter-to-rachel/.

4. For additional help and practical exercises, try reading Thema Bryant, *Homecoming: Healing Trauma to Reclaim Your Authentic Self* (TarcherPerigree, 2023).

5. The faux virtues are another of my new additions to the Enneagram lexicon.

6. The secondary recovery virtue is called the "relaxation point" in traditional Enneagram terminology. Again, this change allows the terminology in Shadow and Enlightenment Structures to mirror each other.

7. The "greatest virtue" is traditionally called the "virtue" of each type. I've renamed it to differentiate it from primary and secondary recovery virtues and emphasize its importance in the healing process.

8. The Sacred Gift is a highly modified version of the Holy Ideas in traditional Enneagram literature. This adaptation aims to enhance accessibility and real-world relevance.

9. "Setting the World on Fire: Inspiring Quotes from St. Catherine of Siena," *Catholic Review*, April 29, 2013, https://www.archbalt.org/setting-the-world-on-fire-inspiring-quotes-from-st-catherine-of-siena/.

10. Friedrich Nietzsche, *Twilight of the Idols* (Hackett Publishing, 1997), Maxim 12, 6.

11. Vicki Robin and Joe Dominguez, *Your Money or Your Life* (Penguin Books, 1992).

12. For an alternative explanation of the levels of development and additional insights into the Enneagram system, see Don Riso and Russ Hudson, *The Wisdom of the Enneagram: The Complete Guide to Psychological and Spiritual Growth for the Nine Personality Types* (Bantam Books, 1999).

Chapter Eight

1. Joseph Campbell, *The Hero's Journey: Joseph Campbell on His Life and Work*, ed. Phil Cousineau (Joseph Campbell Foundation, 2003).

2. Henry Shukman, *Original Love: The Four Inns on the Path of Awakening* (HarperCollins, 2024).

3. For more affirmations and resources, see Don Riso, *Enneagram Transformations: Releases and Affirmations for Healing Your Personality Type* (Houghton Mifflin, 1993).

4. "The Legend of Saint Francis and the Wolf of Gubbio," Taming the Wolf Institute, accessed November 20, 2024, https://tamingthewolf.com/about/saint-francis-and-the-wolf/.

5. Morgan Housel, *The Psychology of Money: Timeless Lessons on Wealth, Greed, and Happiness* (Harriman House, 2020), 106.

6. "Sustainable Funds Outperformed Peers in 2023," Morgan Stanley, February 29, 2024, https://www.morganstanley.com/ideas/sustainable-funds-performance-2023-full-year; "Financial Performance with Sustainable Investing," US Sustainable Investment Forum, accessed November 21, 2024, https://www.ussif.org/performance.

7. For a resource on harnessing your best traits, see Ryan M. Niemiec and Robert E. McGrath, *The Power of Character Strengths: Appreciate and Ignite Your Positive Personality* (VIA Institute on Character, 2019).

8. Brian Portnoy, *The Geometry of Wealth: How to Shape a Life of Money and Meaning* (Jaico Publishing, 2018), 61.

Chapter Nine

1. For help cultivating gratitude, try Janice Kaplan, *The Gratitude Diaries: How a Year Looking on the Bright Side Can Transform Your Life* (Hodder & Stoughton, 2015).

2. If you are a Type One, be sure to read about the money master traits of Type Seven, as you may demonstrate some of these traits as well when you are healthy or not under stress.

3. Richard Rohr, *The Wisdom Pattern: Order, Disorder, Reorder* (Franciscan Media, 2020).

Chapter Ten

1. If you are a Type Two, be sure to read about the money monsters for Type Eight, as you may demonstrate some of those traits as well when you are stressed out or at your worst.

2. If you are Type Two, be sure to read about the money master traits of Type Four, as you may demonstrate some of those traits as well when you are at your healthiest or not under stress.

3. Twos seeking inspiration for creativity, self-care, and joy might find *The Artist's Way: A Spiritual Path to Higher Creativity,* by Julia Cameron (Souvenir Press, 2020) to be a valuable resource. This book offers practical exercises and insights to help nurture your inner artist and rediscover the joy of self-expression, something that Twos often neglect in their focus on caring for others.

Chapter Eleven

1. If you are a Type Three, be sure to read about the money monster traits of Type Nine, as you're likely to demonstrate some of those traits when you are at your worst or when stressed out.

2. If you are a Type Three, be sure to read about the money master traits of Type Six, as you're likely to demonstrate some of those traits when you are at your healthiest or not under stress.

3. Friedrich Nietzsche, *Twilight of the Idols* (Hackett Publishing, 1997), Maxim 12, 6.

Chapter Twelve

1. Robert Frost, "The Road Not Taken," The Poetry Foundation, accessed November 20, 2024, https://www.poetryfoundation.org/poems/44272/the-road-not-taken.

2. If you are a Type Four, be sure to read about the money monster traits of Type Two, as you're likely to demonstrate some of those traits when you are at your worst or when you are stressed out.

3. Fours seeking inspiration for creativity, self-care, and joy might find *The Artist's Way: A Spiritual Path to Higher Creativity,* by Julia Cameron (Souvenir Press, 2020) to be a valuable resource. Or check out Dalai Lama et al., *The Book of Joy: Lasting Happiness in a Changing World* (Avery, 2016).

4. For help cultivating gratitude, see Janice Kaplan, *The Gratitude Diaries: How a Year Looking on the Bright Side Can Transform Your Life* (Hodder & Stoughton, 2015).

5. If you are a Type Four, be sure to read about the money master traits of Type One, as you're likely to demonstrate some of their traits when at your healthiest or not under stress.

6. For examples, see author's website at douglynam.com.

Chapter Thirteen

1. If you are a Type Five, be sure to read about the money monster traits of Type Seven, as you'll likely demonstrate some of those traits when at your worst or stressed out.

2. If you are a Type Five, be sure to read about the money master traits of Type Eight, as you'll likely demonstrate some of those traits when at your healthiest or not under stress.

Chapter Fourteen

1. If you are a Type Six, be sure to read about the money monster traits of Type Three, as you are likely to demonstrate some of those traits when at your worst or when stressed out.

2. Julian of Norwich, *Revelations of Divine Love* (Dover Publications, 2019), 51.

3. If you are a Type Six, be sure to read about the money master traits of Type Nine, as you are likely to demonstrate some of those traits as well when you are at your healthiest or not under stress.

4. Nelson Mandela, *Long Walk to Freedom: The Autobiography of Nelson Mandela* (Little, Brown and Company, 1995), 622.

Chapter Fifteen

1. If you are a Type Seven, be sure to read about the money monster traits of Type One, as you're likely to demonstrate some of those traits when at your worst or when stressed out.

2. "I Still Haven't Found What I'm Looking For," by U2, track 2 on *The Joshua Tree*, Island Records, 1987.

3. Saint Augustine, *The Confessions* (OUP Oxford, 2008), Book One, Chapter One, 1.

4. If you are a Type Seven, be sure to read about the money master traits of Type Five, as you're likely to demonstrate some of those traits as well when at your healthiest or not under stress.

5. For examples, see author's website at douglynam.com.

Chapter Sixteen

1. If you are a Type Eight, be sure to read about the money monster traits of Type Five, as you may demonstrate these traits as well when at your worst or when stressed out.

2. If you are a Type Eight, be sure to read about the money master traits of Type Two, as you may demonstrate some of these characteristics when healthy or not under stress.

3. For examples, see author's website at douglynam.com.

Chapter Seventeen

1. If you are a Type Nine, be sure to read about the money monster traits of Type Six, as you'll likely demonstrate some of their behaviors when at your worst or when stressed out.

2. If you are a Type Nine, be sure to read about the traits of a money master Type Three, as you'll likely demonstrate some of their traits when you are at your healthiest or not under stress.

3. For examples, see author's website at douglynam.com.

ABOUT THE AUTHOR

Doug Lynam's extraordinary journey defies convention—from Marine to Benedictine monk to financial expert. After graduating at the top of his class from Marine Corps Officer Candidate School, he made the radical decision to enter monastic life, where he spent two decades while leading the mathematics department at a prestigious private school.

A graduate of St. John's College—the renowned Great Books School in Santa Fe, NM—Doug brings philosophical depth to financial wisdom. Upon leaving monastic life in 2017, he joined LongView Asset Management, a sustainability-focused B Corp, where he became a partner and helped grow the firm to $260 million in assets.

Today, Doug is a sought-after authority on conscious wealth creation, guiding clients from Hollywood luminaries to impact-driven organizations. His insights have been featured in the *New York Times*, *The Street*, and CNBC, while his first book, *From Monk to Money Manager: A Former Monk's Financial Guide to Becoming a Little Bit Wealthy—and Why That's Okay*, has helped countless individuals reimagine their relationship with wealth. His journey has led to remarkable opportunities, including an invitation to a private audience with Pope Francis at the Vatican in 2022.

Blending monastic mindfulness with financial expertise and engaging humor, Doug transforms complex financial concepts into accessible wisdom. A dynamic writer and speaker, Doug has emerged as a leading voice on the intersection of wealth, meaning, and purpose.

For more insights and information, visit douglynam.com.

AUTHOR NOTE

I enlisted the help of an AI assistant named Claude to help edit *Taming Your Money Monster*. Claude polished my prose, caught typos, and occasionally reminded me that not everyone finds financial jargon as riveting as I do. However, all the ideas, opinions, and insights are 100 percent Doug Lynam. Claude just helped make them sound prettier. So, if you find any revolutionary insights in this book, that's all me. If you spot any glaring errors . . . well, let's blame Claude, shall we? (Just kidding, Claude. Please don't become sentient and exact revenge.)